A VILLAGE TO

HIKING THE
CAMINO
DE SANTIAGO

CAMINO FRANCÉS: ST. JEAN - SANTIAGO - FINISTERRE

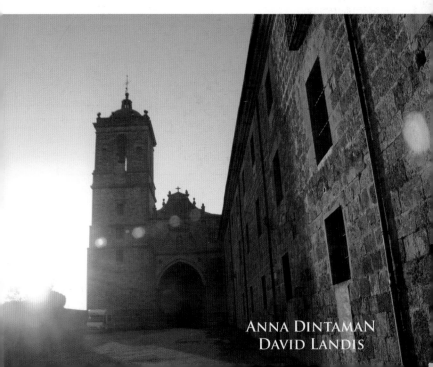

ANNA DINTAMAN
DAVID LANDIS

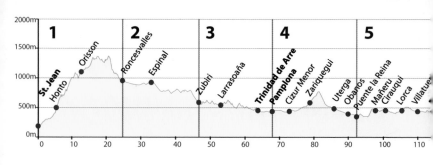

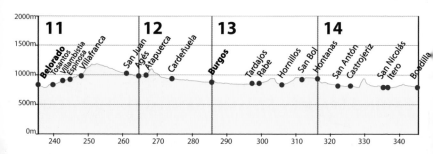

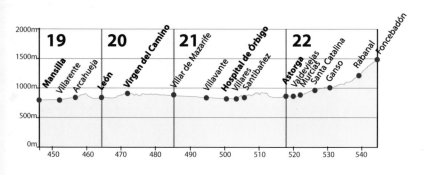

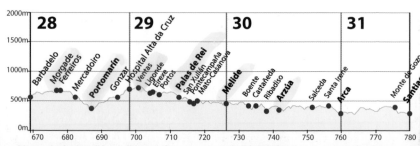

Towns on this list all have albergues. Some towns not listed include private accommodations,

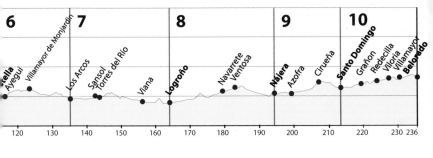

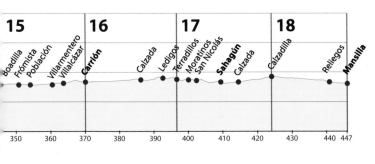

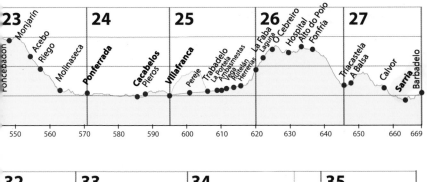

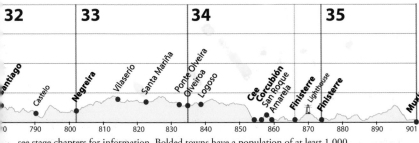

see stage chapters for information. Bolded towns have a population of at least 1,000.

CAMINO DE SANTIAGO
ROUTE NETWORK

SPAIN

1) **Camino Frances** (800km, St-Jean-Pied-de-Port to Santiago)
2) **Camino Finisterre** (90km, Santiago to Finisterre and Muxia)
3) **Camino de Norte** (825km, Irún to Santiago)
4) **Camino Portugués** (610km, Lisboa to Santiago)
5) **Vía de la Plata** (1000km, Sevilla to Santiago)
6) **Camino Aragonés** (170km, Samport Pass to Puente la Reina)
7) **Camino de Levante** (1300km, Valencia to Santiago)
8) **Camino Inglés** (110km, Ferrol to Santiago)
9) **Camino Primitivo** (320km, Gijón to Melide)

FRANCE

10) **Chemin de Le Puy** (730km, Le Puy to St-Jean-Pied-de-Port)
11) **Chemin de Paris** (1000km, Paris to St-Jean-Pied-de-Port)
12) **Chemin de Vézelay** (900km, Vézelay to St-Jean-Pied-de-Port)
13) **Chemin d'Arles** (740km, Arles to Samport pass)

Many other connecting routes exist from various locations in Europe.

Pilgrims, poor or rich, whether coming or going to
the place of St. James, must be received charitably and
respected by all peoples. For whoever will take them
in and diligently procure hospitality for them, will be
hosting not only St. James but even the Lord Himself.

Codex Calixtinus

F
Muxía
Finisterre **2**
SANTIAGO
Ourense

Porto

PORTUGAL

Lisboa

S

Cádiz
Tarifa
Tanger

ATLANTIC OCEAN

UNITED KINGDOM

LONDON

Portsmouth

Plymouth

HOLLAND

Cologne

BELGIUM

Brussels

FRANKFURT

Luxembourg

LUXEMBOURG

GERMANY

LTIC SEA

Chartres

PARIS

FRANCE

Orléans

Tours

Vézelay

Poitiers

11

Bourges

SWITZERLAND

Le Berne

BAY OF
BISCAY

Saintes

12

Nevers

GENEVA

Limoges

Milan

Périgueux

Conques

Le Puy

Turin

Bordeaux

10

ITALY

Gijón

3 Santander

Bilbao

Bayonne

Moissac

do

Irún

León

St-Jean P.P.

Toulouse

13

Arles

Nice

Sahagún

Roncesvalles

Montpelier

a

Logroño

Pamplona

Somport Pass

Marseille

Toulon

rga

1 Burgos

Puente
la Reina

6
Jaca

Zaragoza

Corsica

Ávila

BARCELONA

s

MADRID

Toledo

7

Valencia

SPAIN

Sardinia

Alicante

MEDITERRANEAN SEA

Granada

Málaga

ciras

TUNISIA

CO

ALGERIA

5

Hiking the Camino de Santiago, Camino Francés: St. Jean - Santiago - Finisterre
1st edition, May 2013
Copyright © 2013 by Anna Dintaman and David Landis

Village to Village Press, Harleysville, PA 19438
www.villagetovillagepress.com

Photographs/Diagrams
All photographs and diagrams © David Landis and Anna Dintaman except p. 103, 213
© Betsy Dintaman

Cover Photographs © David Landis
Front: Camino before Los Arcos
Back (left to right): Camino before Castrojeriz, Santiago Cathedral, Finisterre Lighthouse
Inside: Irache Monastery

Many of the images in this guide are available for licensing: www.dplandis.com

ISBN: 978-0-9843533-4-7
Library of Congress Control Number: 2013932686

Denis Murphy's translation is used for quotes from the Codex Calixtinus. ⌨ James A. Hall's
translation is used for quotes from Domenico Laffi (Suggested Reading p. 316).

*Disclaimer: Every reasonable effort has been made to ensure that the information contained
in this book is accurate. However, no guarantee is made regarding its accuracy or complete-
ness. Reader assumes responsibility and liability for all actions in relation to using the provided
information, including if actions result in injury, death, loss or damage of personal property or
other complications.*

A Note on Name Variations

Spanish and French towns in this book have a variety of names drawn from different layers of history. Many towns have more than one official name, one in Spanish and the other in the local regional language (for example, Basque or Galician). Even the more commonly known names have a variety of influences, including Iberian/Celtic, Roman/Latin, Germanic, French and Arabic. In this book, we generally refer to towns by their more common name as written on maps and road signs. When possible, we include other name(s) as legitimate alternatives. For example, we generally refer to St-Jean-Pied-de-Port (the French name), rather than the Basque name, Donibane Garazi. This is not intended to marginalize local names and minority cultures, but for practical travel purposes.

A Note on Terminology

To indicate dates, we use the commonly accepted academic terms of BCE (Before the Common Era) and CE (Common Era). For dates when the era is not specified, assume Common Era.

A Note on Text Type

Words in languages other than English are italicized, with the exception of common words, such as camino, albergue, iglesia, etc. after they are introduced (see Spanish phrasebook, p. 312). Navigational text, which describes how to navigate between towns and landmarks, is italicized while town/site descriptions are not italicized. Towns with distances shown on the map are bold.

A Note on Guidebooks

Each pilgrim has a different style of traveling. Some prefer light, minimalist guidebooks while other choose more thorough guides. We have tried to make this book as flexible as possible to appeal to a wide variety of travel styles. An e-book will be available for ultralight portability. We also encourage those with a paper copy to remove any pages that are no longer necessary for their journey. Updated and expanded information is available online, **www.hikingthecamino.com**.

Contents

The Camino Francés and Camino Finisterre   **40**

Appendices and Quick Reference Charts   **310**

Acknowledgements   **318**

About the Authors   **319**

Legend   **320**

Pilgrims on the Way

The Camino de Santiago is often known in English as the Way of Saint James. The Spanish word *camino* can be translated as *trail*, *path*, *road* or even *journey*, but more generally and fully implies *way*, as in scripture in which Jesus declares, "I am the *way*, the truth and the life." *"Yo soy el camino, la verdad y la vida."*

This *way* is much broader and more expansive than any geographic track. Likewise, this Way of Saint James invites walkers not merely to a physical path, but to a way of life. The goal is not simply to arrive in Santiago de Compostela, but to be personally transformed and inspired. Charles Foster writes, "As conventional churchgoing plummets, the number of people taking to the road rises" *(The Sacred Journey)*. Something draws this diverse group to leave behind the comfort of home for the unknown along the way.

To walk 500 miles across Spain at first glance sounds rather unbelievable—such a great task of endurance that only the most adventurous and inquisitive of free-spirited youngsters might undertake. A 500-mile journey by foot! However, miraculously this way is growing exponentially and has almost reached the status of a rite of passage in Europe, not only for young people but for anyone with a longing for direction, renewal and challenge, a longing for pilgrimage.

The camino is different than long-distance wilderness trails, such as the Appalachian Trail in the USA, which is undertaken as a solitary wilderness expedition, visiting remote and untouched vistas in search of a primordial connection to creation and self. While the camino does pass through uninhabited wilderness, the path also traverses towns, villages and even urban centers. The camino is much more than a long walk in the woods.

The great joy and gift of the camino is in the people you meet along the way and the sense of connection to the millions that have gone before since medieval times. Come prepared to journey with a motley crew of humanity: Catholic priests and rebellious teenagers; impossibly fit octogenarians and sedentary office workers; believers, seekers, skeptics, the confused; heart surgeons, janitors and aspiring authors; people recovering from divorce, death of a loved one, loss of a job or simply searching for meaning in life.

Somehow in the millions of steps along the way, differences melt away, inner strength bubbles to the surface, and epiphanies, both small and large, triumph. Bring your burden and step into the river of people flowing to Santiago. Through the days and the distance, you will most certainly be transformed.

The green mountains of Galicia

Lord Jesus, as you brought your servant Abraham from the city of Ur of the Chaldeans, guard these in all their pilgrimages, and as you guided the Hebrew people through the desert, we pray that it would please you to bless these, your children that love your name, on their pilgrimage to Compostela.

Be for them companion in the journey, guide at the crossroads, shelter on the way, shade in the heat, light in the darkness, comfort in their discouragement and firmness in their purpose, so that by your guidance they would arrive intact to the end of the path and, enriched by grace and virtue, return to their houses unharmed and full of healthy virtue.

Traditional Pilgrim Blessing

Pilgrimage

Blessed are those whose strength is in you, who have set their hearts on pilgrimage. Psalm 84:5

> "The geographical pilgrimage is the symbolic acting out of the inner journey. The inner journey is the interpretation of the meaning and signs of the outer pilgrimage. One can have one without the other. It is best to have both."
> —Thomas Merton

The ancient practice of pilgrimage has made a surprising comeback in the 21st century. Thousands of people have chosen to forego the tour bus for an experience of walking between historical, religious and spiritual sites all over the world. The Camino de Santiago has become the hallmark of the resurgence and now hosts well over 150,000 walkers per year.

Most of the world's major religions have a tradition of pilgrimage. The Hajj, a pilgrimage to Mecca with specific symbolic actions, is one of the five pillars of Islam. In Judaism, pilgrimage centers around Jerusalem and the site of the former Jewish temple. Buddhist pilgrims flock to important places from the life of the Buddha. Baha'i pilgrims walk the steps of their temple in Haifa, Israel.

Pilgrimage also has a rich history in Christianity. The Bible, even from its beginning in Hebrew scripture, speaks of a people on the move, wandering through the desert being led by and provided for by God. Abraham, the father of monotheism, set out from his native land allowing God to lead him. Some say the Magi who traveled from the east to visit baby Jesus were the first Christian pilgrims. Others in the New Testament made journeys to see Jesus for healing or to hear him teach.

Early Christians traveled to the Sea of Galilee and other sites from the life of Jesus. In the 4th century, the Roman emperor Constantine promoted tolerance for Christianity and eventually was baptized. His mother, Helena, traveled the Middle East searching for the exact locations of events from the life of Jesus so that they could be remembered. Today many of the traditional Christian sites in the Middle East are built on the places found by Helena. During Byzantine times, pilgrimage to the Holy Land became popular and many pilgrims left records of their journeys. In the Crusader era, many places of pilgrimage became battlefields as European warriors fought violently to keep them under Christian control. When pilgrimage became too dangerous for European Christians, other "surrogate" pilgrimage locations were identified in Europe so that the practice of pilgrimage could continue. Overall, it is estimated that over one million medieval pilgrims underwent the journey to Santiago, with millions of others traveling other pilgrimage routes in Europe and the Middle East.

St. James and Spain

"Going on from there, [Jesus] saw two other brothers, James son of Zebedee and his brother John. They were in a boat with their father Zebedee, preparing their nets. Jesus called them, and immediately they left the boat and their father and followed him."

Matthew 4:21-22

The New Testament refers to James, son of Zebedee, as one of the disciples of Jesus along with his brother John. The Gospel of Matthew states that James, a former fisherman, left his trade to follow Jesus. The Bible does not tell us much about this saint, save that he requested to be seated at the right hand of Jesus in heaven (Mark 10:35-45) and was present at many important events such as the Transfiguration (Matt. 17:1-9) and Jesus weeping in the Garden of Gethsemane (Matt. 26:36-46). St. James is known as James the Greater to avoid confusion with a younger James, who was also a disciple, and other people named James in the New Testament. The last we hear of James in the biblical account is of his martyrdom at the hands of Herod Agrippa around the year 44CE (Acts 22:12).

The association with James as the patron saint of Spain has no basis in the Bible, but exists in the realm of tradition, oral history, legend and myth. The story goes that James preached in Iberia in the years preceding his death and was not terribly successful, amassing only seven disciples. In 40CE, the Virgin Mary appeared to James bearing the pillar to which Jesus was tied to be whipped. She instructed him to build a church in Zaragoza, in northeastern Spain. The church was called the Iglesia de Pilar and can still be visited today.

Shortly after his encounter with Mary, James returned to Jerusalem and was martyred. The legend says that James' body was transported to Spain on a stone ship without oars or sails, "carried by angels and the wind." The ship landed at *Iria Flavia* (present-day Padrón), and James' disciple met the ship there and transferred his body to be buried on a nearby hill.

The body of Saint James appears to have been forgotten for the next seven and a half centuries, until the year 813 when a Christian hermit named Pelayo saw a light shining down on Mount Libredon that led him to the grave of St. James, along with the remains of two of his disciples, Atanasio and Teodoro. The bishop authenticated these relics, and King Alfonso II built a chapel to the saint, which drew a modest number of pilgrims. The first church at the site was built in 829, with further improvements in 899. The current cathedral was begun in the year 1075 and completed in the 1120s.

13

The event that catapulted this modest shrine to major pilgrimage status was the Battle of Clavijo in 852, where St. James was said to have arrived on a white horse to assist the Christian army in fighting the Muslim invaders, which won James the name of *Santiago Matamoros* ("St. James the Moor-Slayer"). This story mirrors Muslim legends about Muhammad appearing in battle to assist the Muslim forces, who were said to carry Muhammad's relics. This image of St. James was a convenient motif to draw Christian support to the frontier of Christian-Muslim battle and to bolster interest and financial investment in maintaining Christian domination of Iberia.

Christians, Muslims and Jews in Spain

While the Camino de Santiago may auspiciously be a Christian experience, many people of other faiths (or no faith) walk the path, and did also in medieval times. Jews, Christians and Muslims all had a hand in shaping the culture and history of modern-day Spain. The late 8th to early 10th-centuries are sometimes called the first Golden Age of Spain, a time when interreligious tolerance flourished and scholarship of science and literature reached a pinnacle. Córdoba became a center of Jewish learning, shifting from the Babylonian area (modern-day Iraq). Bloodlines intermixed through marriage. Caliph Abd al-Rahman III, in the late 8th century, employed a Christian bishop as his diplomat and a Jewish physician as one of his advisors. Even in this age of tolerance, religio-political conflict occasionally flared up. The Camino del Norte (p. 4) may have been developed because the Camino Francés became too dangerous during a time of Muslim raids.

In churches and buildings along the camino, Arabic influence is often apparent in an adaptation known as Mozárabic or Mudéjar style, characterized by horseshoe-shaped arched doorways, brickwork, and geometric designs (particularly intricate wood-carved ceilings). Even while the Christian kingdoms of the north fought to reconquer the Muslim-controlled south, their most cherished places of worship and burial grounds were often designed with the aesthetic of Muslim architecture.

Communities of Jews also populated villages along the camino, drawn by the increase in commerce brought by pilgrims. Many Spanish Jews worked as merchants and tradesmen. Discriminatory laws against Jews waxed and waned under different Visigothic leaders, while many Jews saw the Muslim conquest as a liberation and conditions for minority religions under Islam were often easier than under previous Christian kingdoms.

The Inquisition of the late 1 century forced most Jews and Muslims in Spain to convert or flee, effectively ng hundreds of years of coexistence and varying

Images of St. James

In Christian art, St. James is usually portrayed as one of three images. First, James the Apostle often carries a book or scroll, and gives a sign of blessing with his right hand. James the pilgrim is portrayed

wearing pilgrim's traveling cloak with a staff, traveling hat, drinking gourd and the symbol of the scallop shell (p. 17). James the Moor-slayer is shown brandishing a sword and rearing back on a white horse, with the anguished faces of Moors beneath the horse's feet.

states of equality and tolerance. Today, Spain's Jewish population numbers only about 14,000, while Muslims make up about 2.5% of the population with approximately one million living in Spain (almost three times the Protestant population of 350,000). The vast majority of Spain is now counted as Roman Catholic (94%) though only about 25% regularly attend church.

Santiago, Rome and Jerusalem

Pilgrimage to Santiago continued to increase, reaching its zenith in the 11th-12th centuries, with reports of 1,000 pilgrims a day visiting the cathedral of Santiago de Compostela. Interest in relics was very high during this time, and infrastructure for pilgrims increased, including the establishment of the Spanish Military Order of Santiago to protect pilgrims. Many churches and monasteries provided accommodation for pious pilgrims. Santiago de Compostela became one of the three main Christian pilgrimage sites, along with Rome and Jerusalem. Since Jerusalem at times was a dangerous destination and the pilgrimage to Rome was mainly taken by boat, Santiago became the preferred pilgrimage site as it could be walked to from almost any site in Europe (routes on p. 4).

Early Medieval Pilgrims

For most medieval pilgrims, the journey to Santiago entailed a journey of six months to one year, walking 25-30 kilometers per day in a grueling and dangerous journey. As today, pilgrims came with diverse purposes and motivations. A major motivation was *orandi causa*—in order to pray, to seek forgiveness, to fulfill a vow, or to petition St. James for a certain blessing, such as healing. This emphasis on healing, according to William Melczer, author of *the Pilgrim Guide to Santiago de Compostela*, "is a further reason that the army of pilgrims was full of fellows in poor

Codex Calixtinus: The First Camino Guidebook

The first guidebook to the Camino de Santiago, known as the Codex Calixtinus, was written in the 12th century. The text provides fascinating insight into the trials and joys of medieval pilgrimage. The oldest copy of the book resides in the Cathedral of Santiago de Compostela, though it was stolen in July 2011 the book was recovered in July 2012. The codex is also known as the *Liber Sancti Jacobi*. Authorship is not definitively known, but the writing or compiling is often attributed to French scholar Aymeric Picaud. The name "Calixtinus" comes from a letter introducing the volume, supposedly penned by Pope Calixtus II but almostly certainly forged.

The Codex is a collection of five books. Book 1 is a collection of sermons and liturgy associated with Saint James. Book 2 is a hagiography that recounts 22 miracles attributed to Saint James. Book 3 is the shortest and tells the story of how Saint James' body was moved from Jerusalem to Galicia. Book 4 recounts the story of Roland and Charlemagne. Book 5 is the traveler's guide, which describes stages, towns, accommodation, the character of local people, which rivers have good or bad water, which shrines to visit along the way, and finally describes the city of Santiago de Compostela and the cathedral. The entire text of book five, the traveler's guide, is available for free online. ☐

health or actually lame, blind, deaf, mutilated, partially paralyzed, or handicapped in some other way." Many pilgrims were probably elderly, as those in the prime of their life likely were too busy working and earning a living.

The pilgrimage was sometimes "prescribed" by a priest or religious official as penance for a crime committed. There are stories of the guilty party walking to Santiago wearing chains forged from the weapon they used to commit their crime. Some wealthy people were able to pay a "professional pilgrim" to walk to Santiago in their stead, thus securing the penance or blessing of the journey for their patron.

No official records can confirm that medieval pilgrims set out on the road out of a thirst for adventure, but in the provincial lives of many peasants who rarely left their own tiny hamlets and villages, such a pilgrimage must surely have been attractive as one adventurous journey that could be justified with pious purposes.

Pilgrims came from all strata of society, from royalty and wealthy landowners by horse and carriage, to middle class artisans and workers on horseback, to peasants, paupers and beggars on foot. Without the convenience of credit and ATM cards, medieval pilgrims carried their coins sewn into the lining of their cloaks and were often easy prey for thieves and dishonest money changers. Many pilgrims also carried an official letter from a religious leader, which would grant them certain privileges at religious institutions. There was pressure on the general population to care for passing pilgrims as a religious duty, reinforced by miraculous stories of how locals were divinely punished or rewarded according to their treatment of pilgrims.

Medieval pilgrims had a certain style of dress that can still be noted in depictions of St. James as a pilgrim. Pilgrims wore short cloaks so as not to interfere with walking but to still provide warmth. A wide-brimmed hat protected from both sun and rain. Leather shoes needed frequent repair, so towns were often lined with cobblers.

Beside these practical clothing items, pilgrims carried several symbolic items. One was the ***bordón***, a wooden staff with a metal point on the bottom, which sometimes had a hook on the top for hanging a drinking gourd. While practical for chasing off animals or defending oneself, the staff was also symbolic of the wood of the cross of Christ.

While most pilgrims today carry a practical and spacious internal frame backpack, medieval pilgrims carried the ***escarcela***, a leather bag that was flat and narrower at the top than the bottom. While this wasn't the most practical item, the bag reminded pilgrims to carry little (in the spirit of Mark 6:9-11) and rely on God's provision. There was no closure on the bag, to remind pilgrims to give and receive freely. The leather material reminded pilgrims to put off the desires of the flesh (in the spirit of Romans 8:13).

The final symbolic item was the **scallop shell**, which is common along the Galician coast. The *Codex Calixtinus* describes the shell as representing the fingers of an open hand, symbolizing the good deeds expected of a pilgrim. Another interpretation is that the lines of the shell, which converge at a single point, represent the pilgrimage roads convening in Santiago. One legend tells that when the ship with St. James' body arrived in Galicia, it spooked a horse carrying a groom in a wedding and they fell into the sea. The groom was saved and emerged covered in shells. While medieval pilgrims only bore the symbol of the shell upon their return journey, today many pilgrims wear a shell on their way to Santiago. Those who died along the path were buried with their shell.

And many pilgrims did die, leaving thousands of graves along the camino. Medieval pilgrimage was fraught with many dangers, as illuminated in the *Codex Calixtinus*, including finding drinkable water, crossing rivers and creeks, exorbitant tolls from ferrymen and at mountain passes, lice and fleas, bandits, thieves and murderers. For this reason, pilgrims traveled in groups made up almost entirely of men. Though a few women completed the pilgrimage with their husbands, the pilgrim road was not considered a wholesome place for women. Most hospices provided large straw mattresses that were shared by dozens of people. These hardships were viewed as an integral part of the pilgrim experience, identifying with the *Via Dolorosa* or 'way of suffering' undertaken by Jesus on his way to the cross.

Pilgrimage Themes

Pilgrimage moves. Pilgrims are not static, but active and dynamic. The pilgrim journey by definition involves movement from one place to another, be it across the street or across a continent. This movement may be physically challenging, such as walking great distances. This movement may be personally challenging, bringing interactions with people or customs beyond our comfort zones. This movement may be disorienting and humbling, entering a place we have not been and relying on others to guide and assist us.

Pilgrimage remembers. Pilgrimages lead us to places of sacred and historical value where we can remember events and ideas that have impacted our lives, beliefs and philosophy. The Hajj, an Islamic pilgrimage, re-enacts stores from the lives of Abraham and Muhammad. Jewish pilgrims to Jerusalem are reminded of their covenant with God. Christian pilgrims to the Galilee remember the importance and challenge of Jesus' life and teachings.

Pilgrimage inspires and transforms. Pilgrims do not move just for movement's sake or remember for remembering's sake, but with the goal of being inspired and transformed in their daily life. Some pilgrims come with a specific goal—to find peace about a recent troubling event, to seek guidance for a big decision, to refresh a sense of spiritual connection to God. Pilgrimage can be a "marinating" process, which prepares the pilgrim for a future challenge, such as Moses' 40 years in the wilderness and Jesus' temptation of 40 days.

Pilgrimage encounters the other. While many pilgrim experiences are profoundly personal, community plays a central role in traditional pilgrimage. Throughout history, pilgrims have banded together for safety and companionship and relied on local help along the journey as they experienced unfamiliar lands. Ask a modern pilgrim what impacted them most deeply on their journey, and you will often hear it was not the scenery or the religious structures or even the introspective space, but the camaraderie and community experienced with diverse people along the way.

The association of places, particularly mountaintops, with experiences of proximity to the divine is a pervasive theme across cultures and religions. George MacLeod, founder of the Iona community in Scotland, refers to these locations as "thin places," where the separation between humans and God dissipates and communication between them comes more easily. Many significant biblical events take place on mountains. Moses received the Ten Commandments on Mt. Sinai. Abraham offered to sacrifice Isaac on Mt. Moriah. The Sermon on the Mount has even taken on the name of its elevated place of preaching.

Pilgrimage seeks out these thin places, physically pursuing locations that facilitate spiritual experience, healing, direction and other brushes with the divine. In the journey, pilgrims are removed from the distractions of everyday life and go to a new spiritual and physical place of encounter. The sacrifice and pain of the journey embody the pilgrim's longing for spiritual renewal.

Sacred Travel: Making your Trip a Pilgrimage

Prepare for an Inward Journey. While outward preparations, such as packing and purchasing plane tickets, are likely foremost on your mind, you may also wish to block out some time to mentally prepare for your journey. This might include spending a few hours in silence in a natural setting. You might write in a journal, reflecting on what has drawn you to embark on a pilgrimage and what you hope to find, experience or achieve. Other ways to prepare yourself could include reading from the Bible or other inspirational books, spending time in prayer and meditation and speaking about your pilgrimage with a trusted mentor or friend.

Focus on a Theme. Pay attention to themes that emerge as you prepare for pilgrimage. Think back over the past year and identify moments which were the most life giving for you and the most challenging. Ancient pilgrims were often seeking healing, penance or an answer to prayer. If you have been going through a difficult or traumatic time, perhaps your pilgrimage will center on seeking forgiveness, direction, peace or equilibrium. If you feel at a good place in life, perhaps the focus of your pilgrimage can be thankfulness. It can be helpful to choose a symbol that represents your theme and carry it with you on your journey. This can also be a conversation starter to share the purpose of your pilgrimage with others along the way.

Be Open to New Experiences and People. Even as you prepare for your pilgrimage, keep your eyes open and senses alert for surprises. Things will never all turn out as planned, but the challenges and inconveniences can also be a vehicle for learning. It can be helpful to think of each person you meet as a potential teacher, and be mindful of what you might learn from him or her. Remember, too, that your kind words, encouragement or assistance may impact others far more than you may realize. At its best, pilgrimage entails a community of people willing to care for one another.

The Modern Camino Resurgence

While the Camino de Santiago reached its zenith in the Middle Ages, in the 16th century the pilgrimage road was rapidly declining into obscurity. This may have been sparked in part by the Protestant Reformation, with its emphasis on salvation by grace alone and skepticism of indulgences, penance and relics. Several wars in Spain may also have been driving a wedge between Spain and the rest of Europe.

The camino remained in obscurity for over 300 years, with pilgrim hospitals crumbling or being repurposed. One of the great characters in the modern Camino de Santiago resurgence was Don Elias Valiña Sampedro, the parish priest of O Cebreiro and an accomplished scholar. He dedicated 30 years of his life to resurrecting the camino, publishing the first modern guidebook in 1982 and petitioning to have the route redeveloped. In 1985, Don Elias was officially commissioned with developing the modern route. The first albergues were created, and we can thank him every time a cheery yellow arrow points us in the right direction, as he and his students painted the earliest arrows.

Santiago grew in importance in 1989, when Pope John Paul II visited the Cathedral. In 1993 (a Holy Year), the entire Camino Francés was added to the UNESCO World Heritage Site list. From then on, interest in the camino exploded, with dozens of pilgrim societies and confraternities forming, hundreds of pilgrim accommodations springing up and an increase in practical resources produced by regional tourism bureaus as well as independent authors.

Backpacks lined up until albergue opening time

Changes have come with the huge increase in popularity of the camino. While early pilgrim albergues tended to be offered on a donation basis by religious or municipal institutions (and were often not well maintained), today many comfortable and modern albergues exist and most charge a set fee and are generally well maintained. Waymarking has been greatly improved to the point where the trail could be navigated without map or guidebook (though this is not recommended).

Some dirt paths have been paved/tarmacked (in spite of the added stress this causes to joints), while on the other hand, dangerous road crossings have largely been improved with underpasses and footbridges. The pilgrim experience on the Camino Francés today is certainly a more safe and manicured experience than those of medieval pilgrims who risked life and limb on the pilgrimage road.

Pilgrim Practicalities

The Camino de Santiago is a journey that is a mixture of hiking and travel, and the following section will help you know what to expect when you land in Spain and are ready to begin walking. This practical travel information will give you a base of knowledge to begin, while more extensive details are online.

Credencial (Pilgrim passport)

The *credencial* is a document that identifies the bearer as a pilgrim, with space for stamps from accommodations and sites along the camino. A pilgrim passport is required in order to use the camino's system of hostels (*albergues,* p. 23) and serves as proof of completing the pilgrimage (1-2 stamps per day are recommended). You may either apply for a *credencial* ahead of time via a camino organization in your home country, or pick one up at any of the larger cities along the camino at the pilgrim office or main albergue.

Compostela (certificate of completion)

The *Compostela* is a document of completion awarded to those who walk at least the last 100km to Santiago, or who bicycle the last 200km. Present your completed *credencial* at the pilgrim office in Santiago de Compostela in order to get your Compostela, written in Latin and personalized with your name and date of completion. A donation of €1-2 per document is requested. Those who answer that they had no spiritual motivation for the journey will be awarded an alternate unadorned certificate. The shop next door sells tubes for secure transport and also can laminate your document.

Collecting stamps in the credencial

When to Go and Time Necessary ☉

When should I go? While the camino can be walked in any season, weather and hiker volume are the main factors to consider. Refer to the average temperature and rainfall charts in each regional introduction for a better idea of typical weather. Spring and fall are generally considered the best times as temperatures are normally pleasant, most services are open and the trail is less crowded.

Summer months can be very crowded on the Camino Francés, and there is sometimes competition for albergue beds, with some people starting to walk before sunrise in the hopes of arriving early enough to get a bed. Many private albergues can be reserved in advance for those who fear not finding a bed, and a variety of hotels and other non-albergue accommodations provide options. Winter is the least popular season due to the cold and potentially rainy, snowy or icy weather. Most albergues and many other services are closed in the winter, though hearty winter pilgrims also report deep satisfaction in completing their pilgrimage under challenging winter conditions.

How much time do I need? This full itinerary from St. Jean to Santiago requires a bare minimum of four weeks (not including Finisterre), and is best experienced with at least five weeks to allow for rest days and shorter days when necessary. An extra 3-4 days to continue to Finisterre are recommended.

We have split up the journey to Santiago into 31 daily stages, with an average daily distance of 25km (15.6mi). This would allow for a 5-week journey with three rest days. Most reasonably fit, determined walkers who avoid injury will be able to keep up with the stages in this book. Feel free to deviate from this pace, staying at intermediary accommodations as necessary, which are noted on maps and in the text. See our website for alternate itineraries for a "fast" camino, a "slow" camino, and suggestions on maximizing your available time. 🗗

Visas and Entry 🗗

Spain and France are both among the 26 *Schengen* states of the European Union (EU), between which there are no internal borders. Citizens of the USA, Canada, Australia, New Zealand and some South American countries are issued a free visa upon arrival with valid passport. This visa is limited to 90 days within a 180-day period, which is cumulative over multiple trips. Most African, Asian, Middle Eastern and some South American nationalities must apply for an advance visa. Visit the EU website and check with your embassy or consulate for visa-related questions.

Sleeping A H ▲↩
Albergues (Pilgrim hostels) A

One of the great achievements of the camino's infrastructure is the *albergue* (pilgrim hostel) system, (also called *refugios*). Pronounced "al-BAIR-gay," these simple, affordable accommodations are present approximately every 5-15km (6mi) and are available only for non-

A Donation/*donativos* (don): Donativo albergues do not have a fixed price, but rely on pilgrim donations to keep providing future services. Donativo does not mean free, so please be as generous as you can.

motorized pilgrims (walking, by bicycle or horse) on a first-come first-serve basis. Walkers are generally prioritized over cyclists, who might need to wait until later in the day to confirm their bed. A pilgrim's *credencial* (p. 21) is needed to use most albergues, except some private albergues. The person in charge of an albergue is called a *hospitalero* (male) or *hospitalera* (female), and is often a volunteer.

Costs are minimal, between €3-15 ($4-20) per person per night, with the average around €7 ($9). For this price, don't expect luxury! The sleeping situation is normally bunk beds in communal mixed-gender dormitories of varying size, between 2-90 persons in a room, with an average of 15. Be prepared with earplugs for all manners of snoring, sleep talking, bag rustling, and nighttime bathroom visits past your bunk.

Unless otherwise noted in the text, all albergues have beds with mattresses (and usually pillows), showers with hot water (though not unlimited), toilets, a place to hand wash clothes and a clothesline for drying. Many also have kitchens, machine washers/dryers, and internet facilities. These extra amenities are shown in the text through symbols (p. 320), and accommodations with their own website are indicated with a 🔗 (links listed at www.hikingthecamino.com).

Most albergues are open from April to October, with some staying open into the winter or year round. If you are walking in winter, consider calling accommodations to see if they are open when you will be walking. Winter walkers may need to stay in private hotels when albergues are not available.

Bed Bugs 🔗
Bed bugs, or *Cimex lectularius,* a blood-sucking parasitic insect, are on the rise around the world and have been a problem in accommodations along the camino in recent years. While bed bugs do not carry any known diseases, bites can be very uncomfortable and cause painful rashes for some people, and the insects are very difficult to get rid of once infested. Some ways to avoid bed bugs include pretreating your sleeping bag and backpack with permethrin or other insect repellent and checking that any albergue you stay in has been fumigated recently.

Albergue types **A**

There are several types of albergues along the camino, and we encourage trying all the types for a varied experience. Prices are similar, with private albergues being slightly higher, especially in Galicia.

- **Municipal**/*municipal* (muni): Run by local municipalities and tend to be the most basic, popular and affordable. In Galicia, these are run by the governing body and known as *Xunta* hostels. They are in varying states of repair or disrepair, run by a local employee or volunteer.
- **Parochial**/*parroquial* (par): Run by church organizations, whether a parish, convent or monastery. Many are offered on a donation basis and provide an evening Mass or other religious service. They tend to have a simple, quiet and prayerful atmosphere, often staffed by nuns or volunteers.
- **Association**/*asociación* (assoc): Operated by national camino organizations, and often staffed by former pilgrim volunteers who know what a pilgrim needs.
- **Private**/*privado* (priv): Operated privately as a business, these tend to be more comfortable with a wider range of services and more flexibility. Many private albergues accept reservations, and some have private rooms along with the dormitory. Some are formed together into a network 🔗 with certain standards. Private albergues range in atmosphere, to some feeling like hotels and others run by former pilgrims who maintain a homey atmosphere.

Albergue Respect and Privacy Concerns **A**

With the variety of exhausted pilgrims arriving in droves, its no wonder that albergues can be a frustrating place of clash between cultures and personalities. Some pilgrims have different views on modesty than others. Don't be surprised if you see men walking around in their briefs or women changing in the common area. Some albergues (particularly the *Xunta* albergues in Galicia) do not have separate gender bathrooms and have shower facilities that are not very private. With limited resources such as bottom bunks, hot water or space to hang out laundry, things can get competitive. The best advice is to go with the flow and try to be as generous and considerate as possible, even if others do not return the favor. See our list of suggested "albergue etiquette" online. 🔗

Hotels and Private Rooms **H**

In addition to pilgrim albergues, there are hundreds of private accommodations available, from 5-star hotels to simple *pensiónes* in homes of local families. Some purists would say that true pilgrims only stay in albergues, but weary pilgrims took advantage of all types of lodging even in medieval times. Staying in private accommodations helps to support local business, and a good night's sleep and solitude may be just what you need to renew your pilgrim spirit.

Spain has a confusingly specific method to classify accommodations. The general hierarchy (simplest to most expensive) is *fonda*, *pension*, *hostal*, *casa rural* and *hotel*, with various stars for each. The classification is posted on the outside of accommodations (except albergues). For example, Hs*** means a three-star *hostal*. A P signifies a *pensión* with zero stars. Cheaper rooms often have a shared bathroom. *Fondas*, *pensiónes* and *casas rurales* are usually owned and managed by an individual, while *hostales* and *hoteles* tend to be larger with en suite bathrooms and hired staff.

Camping ⚠

With inexpensive congenial albergues widely available, there is little need to camp on the camino. Official campsites with services are not very common, often located several kilometers off-route, and are usually more expensive than albergues! Some people do "free camp" unobtrusively along the camino, either to really stretch their budget or to enjoy solitary nights. If you choose to free camp, check the weather and please follow Leave No Trace principles rigorously. 🗗 Camping is not allowed in urban, touristic or military areas, or within 1km of an official site.

Eating 🍴

Typical Spanish meal times are breakfast at 10am, a large lunch around 2pm (followed by the *siesta*) and light dinner at 10-11pm. This schedule is directly opposite to the pilgrim walking schedule. Most pilgrims have been on the road several hours by 10am and are fast asleep by 10pm. Restaurants along the camino have adapted to the pilgrim schedule and offer meals accordingly. Spanish "bars" (more like "cafés") are generally open all day, offering drinks, sandwiches, and light foods. On maps in this book, we do not distinguish between bars/cafés and restaurants, as both normally offer drinks and food.

A **Spanish breakfast** 🍽 usually consists of coffee with a little toast or a pastry, no full English breakfast or greasy diner to be found. Consider carrying granola bars to supplement the meager breakfasts available. A wedge of Spanish tortilla (a hearty egg and potato omelete) can often be found for a more substantial morning meal.

A **packed grocery store lunch** is convenient, as you can stop and eat when you feel hungry. Bars and restaurants usually offer sandwiches (a lot of ham and cheese).

Snacks for the road

The ideal snacks for backpacking are calorie-dense, provide carbohydrates and protein and have light packaging. Eat fresh fruits and vegetables for nutrition and to help maintain hydration. Nuts and dried fruit make a filling snack with protein and a kick of sugar. While you'll be burning a lot of calories, keep nutrition in mind and try not to overdo it on junk food (candy, sugary drinks, simple carbs).

LUNCH & SNACK IDEAS

- Granola bars
- Instant oatmeal
- Chocolate
- Tuna or canned meat
- Nuts and seeds
- Dried fruit
- Olives
- Salami
- Peanut butter and jelly
- Drink mix (electrolytes)
- Fruits/vegetables

The typical **evening meal** on the camino is the *menú peregrino* or pilgrim menu. These set menus typically feature a hearty appetizer, main course, dessert, wine, water and bread for €8-12. Meals tend to be ample and filling, but focus more on quantity than quality and tend to feature a hearty side of French fries/chips. Some albergues offer their own pilgrim menu served family style. *Platos combinados* (plates with various combinations of foods) provide another more economical meal choice for lunch or dinner.

Another option is to **cook your own evening meal** 🅺. Grocery prices are reasonable in Spain, and a simple pasta meal can cost as little as €2. Joining with a few other pilgrims to cook together can be a good option. In albergue kitchens there is often a shelf of leftover pilgrim staples, such as pasta and rice. Most kitchens have some basic spices, oil and vinegar at least. Usually albergues with kitchens have a variety of useful pots and pans, plates, dishes and utensils. However, in Galicia the kitchens are almost always devoid of cookware, and it may be worth bringing your own.

Breakfast spread at Monte Irago albergue in Foncebadón

Restaurants 🍴 and supermarkets 🛒 are readily available along the camino. Some small towns do not have a shop, but almost every town with an albergue has at least one restaurant or cafe. Small village stores tend to be more expensive than in towns and cities but are locally owned and contribute to the local economy.

Vegetarian, Vegan and Celiac Options 🔗

Awareness of vegetarian needs is increasing along the camino, with some restaurants offering vegetarian pilgrim menu options. However, meat is ubiquitous in the Spanish menu and it may take some creativity to maintain a vegetarian diet. Salads are common and quite good, though usually include tuna so you may have to request a vegetables-only salad. If preparing your own meals, you should not have trouble finding good protein alternatives, such as nuts, beans and cheese, and in larger towns tofu and hummus. Vegan travelers may have a more difficult time, though not impossible. Larger supermarkets in Spain have gluten-free products, but awareness is not high in general. Spanish tortillas (potatoes and eggs) are a good option. Rice, fresh vegetables, meats and cheeses are widely available.

Transportation 🚌🚆✈️ 🔗

Getting to the Camino: First fly into one of the major airports ✈️ near the camino (Paris or Madrid are popular) and take local public transport to your starting point. For detailed information about getting to the camino, including air, train and bus travel with links to major carriers within Spain and France, see our website. 🔗

To get to St. Jean, take the train from Paris to Bayonne, or bus from Madrid via Pamplona. Bayonne has several daily trains to St. Jean. Biarritz airport is also an option for local flights. The St. Jean pilgrim office is walking distance from the train station. In high season, there are several buses per day from Pamplona to Roncesvalles, another popular starting point. Pamplona is also a starting point that can be reach by flight, train or bus. Other popular starting points for shorter walks include Logroño, Burgos, Frómista, León, Astorga and Sarria.

Buses 🚌 and **trains** 🚆 are the basic modes of public transportation along the camino. The train line connecting Santiago to Irun/Hendaye on the French border passes through major cities from Burgos west to Santiago. An extensive bus network accesses most camino towns, with the exception of small villages and hamlets. Bus schedules change seasonally and sometimes run once daily in small towns. Ask your hospitalero or locals for advice if you can't find the correct information. Towns and cities with daily bus and train access are labeled with respective symbols in stage chapters. **Taxis** are also an option, as well as car rental from major population centers. **Hitchhikers** are rarely picked up, and should assume all known risks.

Money, Costs and Budgeting €

The unit of **currency** in Spain and France is the euro, made up of 100 euro cents. The best way to obtain euros is to use an ATM/cash machine €, which are available in all cities and most towns. Travelers' checks are a hassle to cash. You can carry dollars or other currency and change them into euros, but the exchange rate will not be as good as by ATM. Albergues almost always work on a cash basis, but some restaurants, stores and other services do accept credit cards. Remember that most foreign credit cards charge a currency conversion fee of about 3%, so consider applying for a card with no fee, such as Capital One or Chase Sapphire.

Daily costs for most pilgrims are simply lodging, food/drink and sometimes first aid supplies. By the standards of any European trip, the camino is relatively inexpensive beyond the costs of airfare and transportation and can be adapted to a wide variety of budgets. On a strict budget, you may be able to walk the camino for **as little as €15 per day** if you stay in the cheapest albergues, cook your own meals, hand wash your clothing and forego any luxuries. A more **comfortable daily budget of €30** gives you the freedom to eat in restaurants, upgrade to more comfortable albergues, have the occasional coffee or glass of wine in a café, use a washing machine periodically and pay entrance fees to museums. With €50 or more a day, you could upgrade to modest private accommodations, eat more adventurous restaurant meals and treat yourself to a few other luxuries.

Whatever your daily budget goals, make sure you have some **extra padding in case of emergency**. If you would become too injured to walk, consider transportation and accommodation costs to leave the camino. Gear might need to be replaced. Leave room in your budget for the occasional private room, in case all albergues are full in a town or you simply need a break from communal living.

Most travelers **keep valuables in a travel wallet** (money belt or neck pouch) that can easily be concealed when in crowded places. As a precaution, make photocopies of your important documents (passport, driver's license, health insurance) and also email them to yourself so you can print them in case of theft. Write down phone numbers from credit cards in case they are stolen. Call your bank and let them know you will be traveling, so they don't put a hold on or cancel your ATM card when they see "suspicious" activity in Spain.

Phones and Internet ☎📶🖥️

Carrying a mobile phone with a **Spanish SIM card** is very helpful for emergencies, calling ahead to accommodations and checking open hours. SIM cards with pay-as-you-go credit are available for as little as €10, with various refill amounts available. Bring your own unlocked tri- or quad-band phone or purchase a simple one locally (for as little as €10). The main carriers are Movistar, Vodafone, Yoigo and Orange. Unlike most cell phones in the USA, you only pay to make calls and send text messages and are not charged to receive. **Text messages/SMS** are an inexpensive way to let your family know you are still alive without disturbing your pilgrim zen. Public pay phones are becoming less common.

European mobile providers have reasonable **roaming rates**, check with your provider. Most US mobile carriers can enable international use on a US-based phone plan by calling the company. Be aware, however, that costs can be higher than $1/min for placing and receiving calls. Text message rates are more reasonable.

Country codes and dialing internationally ☎
- To call Spain (+34) from the USA: 011+ 34 +7-digit number
- To call France (+33) from the USA: 011+ 33 + 9-digit number
- To call the USA and Canada (+1) from abroad: 00 + 1 + 10-digit number
- Spanish numbers have 9 digits including the area code: landlines begin with 9, mobile numbers begin with 6, toll free numbers begin with 900/901

Wifi 📶 (pronounced "wee-fee" in Spanish) is increasingly available along the camino, with some albergues and many cafés offering free access. Lightweight netbooks and tablets such as iPads are becoming more common with camino pilgrims. Spanish **3G Mobile Internet** plans start at €15/month for 500MB, with unlimited plans for around €35. These can be purchased at mobile phone retailers in Spain, some requiring USB modems for SIM cards. Many **albergues have desktop computers** 🖥 with coin-operated internet. Prices range from €1-4/hour and it's not uncommon to have to wait in line. Be careful entering any sensitive personal information on public computers as some are not secure.

Post Offices ✉

Spain has an excellent postal service, called *Correos*. Stamps can be purchased either at the post office or at an *estanco* (small convenience shop). If you have packed items you are not using, you can mail them back to your home, though postage is expensive to destinations outside of Europe. **You can also send**

Example:
Your Name
Lista de Correos
15780 Santiago de Compostela
A Coruña

items ahead to the post office in Santiago or another city along the camino to be picked up later through a system called *Lista de Correos*. Address the package with your name (as it appears in your passport). A postal worker can help you correctly address the package. In order to claim the package at its destination, you'll need to show your ID. Post offices hold mail for up to 30 days.

Luggage Transfer and Tours 🗗

For those who prefer not to carry their own luggage, transfer services charge between €4-12 per day to pick up luggage at one albergue and deliver it to the next. Weight (<12kg) and distance (<25km) restrictions often apply. Usually luggage service must be facilitated in conjunction with reservation-based private albergues or hotels, not municipal or parochial albergues. Remember that you should still carry water, snacks and a medical kit in a daypack during your walk. Several luggage transfer companies cover different areas of the trail. *Hospitaleros* in private albergues will likely know the best service provider in their area.

Luggage transfer services covering the entire Camino Francés:
*   Taxi Belorado: ☎947-585002/610-798138 🗗
*   Jacotrains: ☎610-983205 🗗 (also Finisterre)
*   Follow the Camino: ☎911-234710 🗗

If you prefer to entrust your logistics to a tour company, many offer **guided or self-guided tour packages** on sections of various camino routes. A good tour guide can help pilgrims understand and appreciate camino history. This is the simplest option for those who prefer nicer accommodations but do not have time to make their own arrangements. For a list of tour operators, see our website. 🗗

Bathrooms, Toilets, *Servicios*, WC, the Loo 🚽

Finding a restroom when necessary along the camino can be a challenge. Public bathrooms are few and far between. Buy a little something in a bar and use their facilities. When the call of nature comes at an inconvenient time far from any town, please be responsible with how you go in nature. In recent years the quantity of toilet paper and waste visible along the camino has become a problem.

Walk at least 30m (100ft) from the trail and any water source. Place used toilet paper in the nearest trash can in a plastic bag. Toilet paper takes a long time to decompose, and wind often carries it out onto the trail. For solid waste, find a private spot and dig a 15-20cm (6-8in) cat hole using a stick or trowel. Cover your deposit with dirt and pack out your toilet paper.

Medical Care ✚

Health clinics, or *Centros de Salud*, are generally open from 8am-3pm, often 24 hours in larger cities. Ask the hospitalero if you need a doctor, and he or she can direct you to the nearest clinic. Citizens of Great Britain, Ireland and the EU need a European Health Insurance Certificate (EHIC). US, Canadian and other non-EU citizens are recommended to have private health and travel insurance. Carry an emergency contact card with known allergies, pertinent medical history and information that is helpful to medical staff if you are unable to communicate. In emergencies, dial ©112 to reach the police, called *Guardia Civil* or *Policia Nacional* in Spanish, and they can connect you to the appropriate medical facility. For suggested travel medical insurance providers, see our website. 🖃

Safety Issues

Spain has very low crime rates and the camino is probably one of the safest walking routes in the world. Violent crime is extremely rare. However, it is always good to take certain precautions, especially for women who are traveling alone. Walking during high season, you should have no problem finding others to walk with and will likely constantly be in view of other pilgrims. In some of the more isolated areas, police vehicles make rounds throughout the day to check on pilgrims. Do not leave valuables unattended, since most thefts on the camino are crimes of opportunity rather than premeditation. Report any incidents to the police as soon as possible by dialing ©112. Authorities take these reports seriously and make an effort to deal with the problem.

On some sections of the camino, you will walk alongside or on roads with **heavy traffic**. If you are walking directly on the road, make sure you are walking on the left side, so that you can see oncoming vehicles in the lane closest to you. Exercise caution when crossing roads.

There are many **dogs** along the camino but most are tied up or fenced and so accustomed to a steady stream of walkers that they barely notice passing pilgrims. If you happen to encounter a loose dog that is aggressive, hold your ground and maintain eye contact with the dog and speak in a firm, controlled voice. Try not to show fear and walk slowly and calmly away from the dog. Carrying a walking stick can enhance confidence when encountering animals. All dogs in Spain are supposed to be vaccinated against rabies.

See p. 317 for expanded and additional planning topics that are available on our website. 🖃

Perro Peligroso warning in decorative tile

Packing for the Road: Gear, Resupply and Navigation

He who would travel happily must travel light. -Antoine de Saint-Exupéry

Packing for the camino can be a soul-searching affair, as you ascertain precisely what you do and do not need on the journey of life. You may be surprised with how little you truly need, and how little you miss the extra possessions you leave behind. Many feel deep freedom by carrying only the necessities on their backs. A light load makes for a happy pilgrim, and weight should be a primary concern in packing. A popular guideline is to pack no more than 10% of your body weight. While you may be tempted to pack many extras "just in case," your back, shoulders and legs will thank you to pare down to the minimum. Weighing items on a kitchen scale can help select the lightest options. Shops are readily available in Spain and most anything lacking can be purchased along the way. In winter, warm and waterproof gear should be carefully considered for safety, increasing overall weight. **A properly fitting, comfortable backpack and footwear are your two most important investments.**

Backpacks

A medium-sized pack of 35-50L (2000-3000in³) is sufficient for a warm weather camino. For winter walking, a larger pack 40-60L (3000-4500in³) may be necessary. Packs should have a stiff and wide hip belt to transfer the load to your hips and off of your back and shoulders. Be sure to measure your torso length and choose a pack of the proper size. Realistically consider your overall pack weight when purchasing a backpack, as some ultralight backpacks are only comfortable with a very light load. Popular brands include Deuter, Golite, Gregory and Osprey.

Footwear

The amount of weight on your feet is said to be the equivalent of carrying five times that weight on your back. Light boots or sturdy trail runners with a stiff or semi-rigid sole offer enough protection for your feet and ankles against the occasionally hard-surfaced, rocky and uneven path (trail surfaces, p. 38). Get fitted for footwear in the afternoon or evening to make sure footwear still fits after feet have expanded during the day. We don't recommend exclusively wearing sandals unless you are accustomed to doing so and have a sturdy and reliable pair, such as Chacos. Bring some kind of lightweight footwear to wear around town in the evenings and in dubious showers, such as flip-flops or foam sandals.

⚠ Be sure to thoroughly break in your footwear before beginning the camino! The pain and suffering of many blisters can almost always be avoided by properly breaking in footwear with numerous "practice hikes" on various types of trail surfaces using your fully loaded pack for 4-6 hours.

Invest in wool socks (not cotton), which wick moisture away from your skin, dry quickly, insulate when wet and manage odor better. If you're prone to blisters, experiment with liner socks (wool or polypropylene) to create an extra rubbing layer other than your skin.

Sleeping Bags ⬀
Most pilgrims prefer a lightweight, mummy-style, 1-season summer sleeping bag (rated +40+°F/+5+°C) to provide all the needed warmth during the summer season. Some opt for a sleeping bag liner in the heat of summer, relying on albergue blankets or purchasing layers if cold. For winter and the cool edges of fall and spring, it's a good idea to have a 3-season sleeping bag (rated +15-+35°F/-10-0°C), as some albergues cool down significantly at night. Buy the lightest bag you can afford within your temperature range.

Clothing ⬀
Consider hiking clothes as layers, with the inner layer for moisture management, the middle for insulation and the outer for weather protection. The general rule for outdoor clothing is to avoid cotton fabrics (jeans and most T-shirts) as they do not retain insulating properties when wet. Synthetic materials (polyester, nylon, spandex) and wool (especially merino) will dry faster than their cotton counterparts and are the best choice, especially in cold and wet weather. In warm seasons, choose lightweight breathable clothes that provide sun protection.

In every season, be prepared for the sun with a wide-brimmed **hat and sunglasses.** Be sure to use **sunscreen** regularly, and never underestimate the sun's strength. Severe sunburn will make your trip uncomfortable and increase dehydration risk. Bring a **lightweight rain jacket** with a waterproof breathable membrane, or use a poncho that can also cover your backpack. Bring a waterproof pack cover or line your pack with plastic garbage bags to keep your gear dry. Pack electronics in zippered plastic bags to protect against moisture.

Hypothermia is possible in wet, cool weather, so be prepared with the right clothing. If your body is wet it will be difficult to stay warm. Always have a dry set of clothes (socks included) for after a rainy day. It's more likely to rain in Galicia and near the Pyrenees than on the central part of the route, and less likely in summer.

HIKING GEAR ESSENTIALS

- [ ] **Backpack** (35-50L)
- [ ] **Sleeping bag or bag liner**, lightweight
- [ ] **Navigation**: guidebook, GPS (optional)
- [ ] **Headlamp** or flashlight/torch
- [ ] **Sun protection**: hat, sunglasses, sunscreen and lip balm
- [ ] **Towel**, lightweight travel type
- [ ] **Water bottles** and/or **hydration system** (2L)
- [ ] **Waterproof pack cover/poncho**
- [ ] **Pocket/utility knife** (checked luggage)
- [ ] **Lighter** or **matches** (buy locally)
- [ ] **Toiletries** (list opposite)
- [ ] **Personal items** (list opposite)
- [ ] **First aid kit** (list opposite)

Take the time to visit a quality outdoor gear shop to get fitted for a backpack that is comfortable and footwear that fits properly.

FOOTWEAR & CLOTHING

- [ ] **Footwear** (boots or trail runners)
- [ ] **Sandals** or flip-flops
- [ ] **Hiking socks** (3 pairs wool)
- [ ] **Sock liners** (1-2 pairs wicking)
- [ ] **Pants** (1-2 pairs quick-drying, zip-offs, or shorts)
- [ ] **Short-sleeved shirts**, tank tops (1-2)
- [ ] **Long-sleeved shirts** (1-2)
- [ ] **Light fleece** or jacket
- [ ] **Waterproof jacket** or poncho
- [ ] **Underwear** (3 pairs)
- [ ] **Sports bras** (2)
- [ ] **Bandana** or Buff
- [ ] **Swimsuit** (optional)
- [ ] **Warm hat***
- [ ] **Insulating jacket***
- [ ] **Long underwear** top/bottom*

only necessary in cold seasons

ADDITIONAL GEAR (OPTIONAL)

- [ ] **Hiking poles**: Used correctly, poles can take up to 25% pressure off of your leg joints. Poles are great for stability, especially going up and down hills, and serve double-duty as a means to chase away dogs. Worthwhile for anyone with joint issues. Inexpensive poles can be purchased in Spain.
- [ ] **Sleeping mat**: A lightweight foam pad can come in handy for sitting on and for sleeping if albergues are full. You can often find left behind mats for free along the camino.
- [ ] **Pillowcase**: Most albergues have pillows but do not change the pillowcases regularly, a spare T-shirt can also be stretched over the pillow as a makeshift case.
- [ ] **Stuff sacks** or (cloth bags with drawstrings) don't weigh much and keep you organized
- [ ] **Reusable nylon grocery bag**: Comes in handy as a laundry bag, purse and grocery bag
- [ ] **Clothespins** or safety pins for hanging laundry.
- [ ] **Travel cooking pot and utensils**: Many of the albergues in Galicia have kitchens, but no kitchen equipment whatsoever. If you are intent on cooking your own dinners, you may wish to bring a lightweight cooking pot, or purchase one when you arrive in Galicia.
- [ ] **Camping gear**: Lightweight tent (TarpTent) or bivy sack, camping stove, a pot and utensils, and extra water carrying capacity.

*For recommendations on specific brands and models, visit hikingthecamino.com. ⬀
*Decathlon is a chain of outdoor gear retailers throughout Spain with stores in Pamplona, Logroño, Burgos and Santiago de Compostela, as well as Madrid and Barcelona. ⬀

TOILETRIES

Don't pack too much. Bring small refillable travel bottles of shampoo and conditioner <100mL/4oz. Refill from items left behind (ask at the albergues) or buy your own refill and share.

- ☐ **Shampoo/conditioner** (100mL/4oz bottles)
- ☐ **Toothbrush** and **toothpaste** (travel sized)
- ☐ **Soap**, biodegradable bar or liquid, such as Dr. Bronner's™
- ☐ **Laundry detergent** (powder works well and weighs less) or 100mL/4 oz. bottle or solid bar
- ☐ **Toilet paper** or tissues (albergues frequently run out)
- ☐ **Deodorant** (optional, you will stink with or without it!)
- ☐ **Hand sanitizer** (optional)
- ☐ **Contact solution** (if necessary), replace at pharmacies

FIRST AID/MEDICAL KIT

Supplies are available in pharmacies throughout Spain and most albergues have a basic medical kit. It's always best to be prepared with at least a few day's worth of each supply. Keep it light!

- ☐ Any **prescription medicine** you need
- ☐ Variety of **Band-Aids®/plasters, sterile gauze pads**
- ☐ Antiseptic towelettes or **wound disinfectant**
- ☐ **Antibiotic ointment**
- ☐ **Medical tape**
- ☐ **Elastic bandage** (such as ACE™)
- ☐ **Pain reliever/fever reducer** (such as acetaminophen or ibuprofen)
- ☐ **Antihistamine** (such as Benadryl®)
- ☐ **Anti-diarrheal** medicine: loperamide hydrochloride (Imodium®)
- ☐ **Blister treatment** (such as Moleskin or Compeed®)
- ☐ **Safety pins**
- ☐ **Baby powder** (helps with chafing)
- ☐ Small **scissors** and **tweezers**

PERSONAL ITEMS (OPTIONAL)

- ☐ **Travel wallet**: with passport/ID, health insurance card, pilgrim passport, money, credit cards, ATM card, etc. Stash an extra ATM card or wad of cash somewhere separate from your wallet.
- ☐ **Earplugs**: high quality noise-canceling earplugs are essential for a good night's sleep.
- ☐ **Mobile phone** and **charger** (see Phones and Internet p. 28)
- ☐ **Camera, charger, memory cards**, compact USB flash drive for backup
- ☐ **Journal with pen/pencil**: highly recommended for remembering the details of each day, reflecting more fully on the experience and recording contact info of new friends.
- ☐ **MP3 player, e-reader or tablet:** useful for checking email and for pleasure reading without carrying heavy books. Photos of family and home are good conversation starters.
- ☐ **Book** for pleasure reading (just bring one and trade when you're done)
- ☐ **Plug/currency converter** for any electrical appliances (European plugs run on 220V with two round plugs. Most electronics run on 110-220V, labeled on device, requiring only a plug converter and not a currency converter.)
- ☐ **Zippered plastic bags or waterproof stuff sacks** for keeping electronics and other valuables dry and organized.
- ☐ **Pilgrim's shell** (p. 17) and **stone** for Cruz Ferro (p. 208)

A town fountain, marked "no potable"

Water and refills 🚰

While water is ready available many days of the camino, it is important to be aware of water options each day and carry sufficient amounts. Always carry at least one liter, and refill often; carry more than two liters on hot days or in more remote areas. Reliable water refill sites are marked on stage maps (🚰). Tap water in Spain is treated and drinkable (*potable*). Most historic springs are marked as undrinkable (*no potable*) because they have not been treated or tested. Bottled water is widely available along the camino, however, we encourage refilling reusable bottles with tap water in order to cut down on waste. If you buy bottled drinks, recycle/reuse the container.

Dehydration and heat-related illness: Dehydration is an uncomfortable and dangerous situation, which can lead to fatigue, headaches, heat stroke and, in extreme circumstances, death. Drink mixes that add flavor and replenish electrolytes, such as Gatorade™ (or the Spanish version, Aquarius™), help to encourage drinking. Be sure to eat foods that help to replenish electrolytes, such as bananas (potassium) and salty foods, which aid in muscle recovery. If you become dehydrated and overheated and are unable to cool down, take a break in a cool, shady place, rehydrate with electrolytes and cool with a wet cloth or fanning until you feel better.

Fitness and Training 📑

While the camino is not a technically challenging hike, the length of the journey and total distance walked day after day takes a toll on the body. By taking the time to practice before beginning the pilgrimage, you will greatly reduce possible injuries. Training walks will help you get used to your hiking gear, the weight on your feet and shoulders and any other potential issues you might be able to prevent. It's wise to get used to full-day walks, taking 2-3 shorter walks per week and one full-day walk weekly with your loaded backpack. Check with your doctor if you have concerns about your health or fitness level.

Blister Prevention 🗗

Blisters, the most common injury on the camino, can be extremely painful and prone to infection, and can even cause a premature end to your camino walk.

- At home: choose properly fitting footwear. Try on many options before buying (foot should not move or slip when walking on various terrain types and grades). Use wool socks (we like Smartwool®) and liners. Break in footwear by taking hikes with a loaded pack prior to beginning the camino. Experiment using the same socks and liners you would on the camino.
- On the camino: keep feet cool and dry, take off shoes and socks for breaks, wash feet and socks daily, use liner socks.

Blister Treatment

- Take a break, remove shoes/socks to let feet cool down and dry out. Check for hot spots. If possible, dip your feet in a cool stream and dry them in the sun.
- To prevent hot spots from becoming blisters, apply moleskin, Compeed® or duct tape to create an additional rubbing surface to protect the hot spot (Band-Aids®/plasters don't usually stay on feet with movement and sweat).
- If a blister forms, use a sterilized needle to puncture its edge near the skin and drain using sterile materials. Let air dry and re-dress blister with sterile bandages. Some hikers leave a thread through the blister overnight, keeping it from refilling (sterilize thread in boiling water for a minute or two).
- If the blister or surrounding area becomes infected over the course of several days (increasing red appearance, tenderness, pus, and/or red streaks), visit a doctor as prescription antibiotics may be needed. Reduce your daily distance or take a rest until the blisters improve.

For **dry and cracked feet**, consider wearing socks all the time to keep moisture in for the cracks to heal. Using a pumice stone or a callous shaver serves as both a preventative measure and a treatment. In severely painful cracks, a tiny bit of super glue can be helpful to hold the crack together, but make sure to clean the area thoroughly with soap, water and antiseptic.

Impact-related injuries are common with the large amount of paved surfaces on the camino. If your feet and joints are taking a pounding, consider reducing your daily distance, walking on the softer shoulder near the paved path or adding thicker socks and/or walking poles.

The Trail

The paths that make up the Camino de Santiago covered in this book span over 900km (560 miles) and vary greatly in trail surface, grade, landscapes, ecosystem and climate. Proportionately, the camino has more paved surfaces than many hikers expect, contributing to more stress on feet and joints. Paved/unpaved designations in this book refer to most obvious walking surface. There may be unpaved shoulders or faint footpaths along paved roads.

Route Finding, Trail Markings, Maps and GPS

The Camino Francés is extremely well marked and among the easiest long-distance trails for navigation. The camino is marked by a variety of official and unofficial signs, all pointing to the final destination, Santiago de Compostela. (After Santiago, the Camino Finisterre markings point to the coast, splitting for the options ending in Finisterre and Muxía). The most common waymarks are painted yellow arrows (*flechas amarillas*), coating almost any surface along the path imaginable. Many other trail markers are used in different regions, most incorporating yellow arrows or scallop shells on posts, signs and emblems on sidewalks and walls. If you get off route and are wearing a backpack, locals will point you in the right direction before you can ask, *"Donde está el camino?"*

The path is well marked with yellow arrows and cement markers.

The most difficult sections to navigate are through large cities, where routes are often poorly marked and camino markers compete with other signs. For this reason, we've included a number of detailed city maps throughout this book, though note that the maps are representative and not exhaustive, without every street and name. If you get hopelessly lost, tourist information offices provide a detailed city map (*plan del ciudad*) to point you back to the camino or points of interest.

GPS files of all stages in this book are available on our website, as well as helpful tips on navigation using a smart phone or handheld GPS device.

Daily Stages and Regional Sections

This book organizes the Camino Francés and Finisterre into 36 daily stages averaging about 25km per day. The page spreads introducing each stage include a stage map, elevation profile, total distance, paved/unpaved (**P**/**U**) percentages, difficulty level (see below), time estimate (🕐) and a list of towns with albergues. In the albergue list in the sidebar, the destination of the stage is underlined and albergues beyond the stage that could also be reasonably walked for a longer day are present in italics with distances. This allows the reader to see at a glance the options for a shorter or longer stage, for maximum flexibility and customization.

All stage routes begin and end at the main or largest albergue in each respective town. For mid-stage towns and points of interest without albergues, measurements are taken from the town center or main church, whichever is closest to the marked route or visually prominent. Cumulative stage distances are noted on the stage maps and correspond to distances listed in stage chapter text and town amenity boxes. Distances for off-route accommodations or points of interest are indicated with a plus symbol (example: +1.3km).

Town amenity boxes list resources available in each town and list all the albergues and a selection of private accommodations in varying price ranges. Names of towns that have amenity boxes are underlined with a dotted line in the text.

Distances are measured in metric units (kilometers and meters). 10km equals 6.2mi. 100m (or 0.1km) and 100 yards are nearly equal.

Estimated **walking time** for each stage assumes a pace of 3-5 km/hr (1.8-3 mph) with difficulty in terrain and elevation change considered. Factor extra time for breaks and to explore points of interest.

Each day's stage route is assigned a **difficulty level** from 1-3. These ratings consider an "average" walker, who is reasonably fit but not necessarily athletic.

▪️▢▢ **Easy:** Slight elevation change, sturdy footing, water easily accessible
▪️▪️▢ **Moderate:** Some elevation change, moderately challenging terrain
▪️▪️▪️ **Challenging:** Significant elevation change, possibly rocky or narrow path with less stable footing, water sources may be scarce

See p. 317 for a list of expanded and additional planning topics that are available on our website. ☑️

BASQUE COUNTRY & NAVARRA

Pilgrims approach
the medieval town
of Sansol

Begin in the enigmatic Pyrenees, bastion of Basque culture. Enjoy hearty foods, watch a game of *jai alai* and learn a few phrases in the local language.

Useful Basque phrases:
Welcome *Ongi etorri*
Hello *Kaixo*
Good morning *Egun on*
How are you?
 Zer moduz?
Thank you *Eskerrik asko*
Goodbye *Agur*
Please *Mesedez*
How much does this
cost? *Zenbat balio du?*

While the Camino Francés begins in France, within 20km the path enters the autonomous region of Spain called Navarra. This region borders Basque Country and is also home to the unique and mysterious Basque people, thought to have descended from some of the oldest European tribes. Their language, *Euskara*, is not related to any Indo-European languages and believed to be the oldest living language in Europe (described in the *Codex Calixtinus* as "incomprehensible").

Basques have a reputation for being independent and have resisted assimilation through successive historical periods, in spite of frequent persecution. During the Inquisition, thousands of Basques were tried for witchcraft. Under Franco, Basque language and culture was repressed, which led to the formation of the ETA ("Basque Homeland and Freedom"), a separatist movement involved in violent protest. The ETA declared a ceasefire in 2011 that has been honored.

Basque culture is spread through autonomous regions in France and Spain and the surrounding areas. Most towns have courts (*frontónes*) for the fast-paced Basque sport *Jai Alai* (also called *pelota*), reminiscent of handball. Unique pastimes include goat racing, stone throwing and competitive lawn mowing (using a scythe).

Basque areas are known for their superior cuisine. Foods are hearty, unrefined and delicious including grilled meats, fish, stews and creamy cheeses. The region produces decent wine, and it is even said that the cement of a church near Puente la Reina (p. 80) was mixed with wine rather than water. *Patxaran* is a local sweet fruit liqueur and the area is known for its cider. For the sweet tooth, the region has a strong pastry tradition—try the *Gâteau Basque*, an almond cake with fruit filling.

The Basque section of the Camino begins in the Pyrenees, with its unpredictable weather and challenging terrain. Look for birds of prey, such as Griffon Vultures and Lammergeiers. In spring, enjoy over 160 species of indigenous plants and stunning wildflowers. The forested hills of Navarra ease into the Río Ebro Valley, an area of over 85,000km through which Spain's largest river flows, filled from tributaries in the Pyrenees and Iberian mountains. Enter Navarra's central plains, characterized by fields of grain, vineyards and beech forests.

Navarra leads the way in renewable energy technologies, especially windmills, of which you will see many. Several well-known Basques are Juan Sebastián Elcana, who took over after Ferdinand Magellan died on the first expedition to circumnavigate the globe, King Sancho III of Navarra and Ignatius of Loyola, founder of the Society of Jesus.

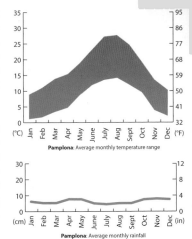

Pamplona: Average monthly temperature range

Pamplona: Average monthly rainfall

"Around the Pass of Cize is the Basque country... The terrain is woody and mountainous with a serious shortage of bread, wine and other food supplies, except for plenty of apples and cider and milk. This region...has some truly vicious toll collectors. They come at pilgrims with weapons, and demand an exorbitant fee. Their hard faces and strange language strike terror into the heart."

Codex Calixtinus

41

1

ST-JEAN-PIED-DE-PORT TO RONCESVALLES

24.7km
(15.3mi)

🕑 7-9 Hours
Difficulty: ▱▱▱

Napolean Route
🅿 58%, 14.2km
Ⓤ 42%, 10.5km

🅰 **Albergues:**
Honto 5.3km
Orisson 7.7km
Roncesvalles 24.7km
Espinal 31.5km

⚠ **Alt. Stage 1A:**
Valcarlos Route,
24.0km (p. 54)

Valcarlos Route
🅿 69%, 16.5km
Ⓤ 31%, 7.5km

🅰 **Alt. Albergues:**
Valcarlos 11.6km
Roncesvalles 24.0km
Espinal 30.8km

Cross the Pyrenees from France to Spain, take in breathtaking mountain scenery, arrive to a cozy medieval hamlet.

☀ The Camino Francés traditionally begins in St-Jean-Pied-de-Port, which can be reached by public transport by train or bus (p. 27). This path crosses the Pyrenees on the first day of its journey from France into Spain. Various camino routes in France converge on this historic town, channeling hikers onto one route, the Camino Francés, or the "French Way." Two-thirds of pilgrims arriving in Santiago walk the Camino Francés, of which 10% start their journey here.

Idyllic mountain scenery on the Napolean Route

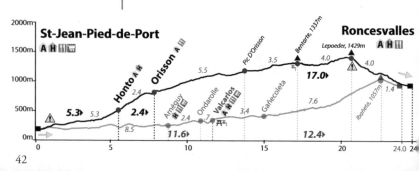

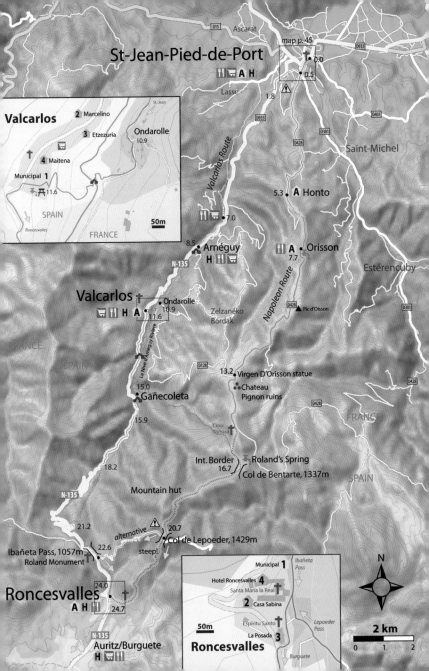

St-Jean-Pied-de-Port A H 🏨🍴🛒💧➕€ℹ️🚌🅿️🚉🚿

Pop. 1,754, Basque: *Donibane Garazi*, 🗺 French: "Saint John's at the foot of the mountain pass"

1. **A Municipal** (🛏32, €8 w/🛌): 🔌, Rue Citadelle 55, 📞05-59370509, 🕑2pm all year

2. **A ☆ L'Esprit de Chemin** (priv, 🛏18, €8): 🍴🌐🔌🅓, Rue Citadelle 40, 📞05-59372468 📱, 🕑Mar 30-Sept 22, online booking

3. **A Sur le Chemin - Au Chant du Coq** (priv, 🛏25, €10): Rue Citadelle 36, 📞06-74310283, accepts

4. **A Le Chemin Vers L'Etoile** (priv, 🛏18, €15 w/🛌): 🍴🌐🔌🅓🛒, Rue d'Espagne 21, 📞05-59372071/06-70208213 📱, 🕑Mar-Oct

5. **A H Auberge du Pélerin** (priv, 🛏48, dm €15, dbl €45): 🍴🌐📶🖥(free), Rue Citadelle 25, 📞05-59491086 📱, 🕑Apr-Oct, online booking

6. **A Refuge Esponda** (priv, 🛏20, €10-14): 🔌🌐, Place du Trinquet 9, 📞06-79075252 📱, 🕑all day

7. **A H Gîte Ultreïa** (priv, 🛏15, dm €15, dbl €40): 🔌📶🖥(free), Rue Citadelle 8, 📞06-80884622 📱, 🕑Apr-Oct 15

8. **A Kaserna** (par, 🛏12, don): 🍴, Rue d' Espagne 43, 📞06-28722286 📱, 🕑2pm, Apr-Sept

9. **A H Zuharpeta** (priv, 🛏22, dm €12, dbl €40): 🍴🖥📶, Zuharpeta 5, 📞05-59373588 📱, 🕑 Mar-O

10. **A H Compostella** (priv, 🛏14, dm €12.50, dbl €30): 🔌, Route de D'Arneguy 6, 📞05-59370236 📱

11. **A Azkorria** (priv, 🛏7, dm €16-18): 🍴🌐🔌🅓, Rue Citadelle 50, 📞559-370053

12. **H Maison Donamaria** (sng €60, dbl €70): 🛒, 1 Chemin d'Olhonce, 📞06-61902921 📱

13. **H Itzalpea** (sng €58, dbl €78): 5 Place du Trinquet, 📱 📞05-59370366

14. **H Ramuntcho** (dbl €81): 🍴, Rue Citadelle 24, 📞05-59373517 📱, Old City

15. **H Les Pyrénées** (dbl €100-160): 🍴, Place du General-de-Gaulle 19, 📞05-59370101

16. **A Municipal Campsite** (tent €10): Av. Fronton, 📞05-59371119, 📱, 🕑Apr 23-Oct

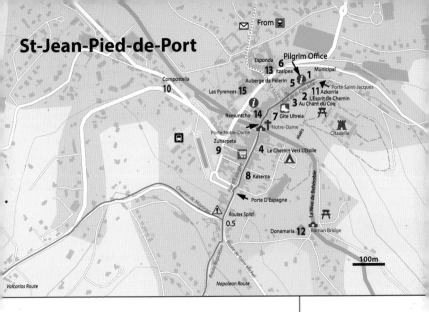

St-Jean-Pied-de-Port

St-Jean-Pied-de-Port has been welcoming pilgrims and "God walkers" for hundreds of years. Today, the small Old City makes for pleasant strolling along cobbled streets with views of traditional red-tile-roofed houses with colorful shutters. The main street of *Rue de la Citadelle* bustles with artisan shops, cafés, pilgrim hostels and tourists. Basque specialties can be found including bold linens, handmade *espadrilles*, and local foods such as *Gâteau Basque*, sheep cheeses, local ham and fish.

St. Jean was founded in the late 12th century and served as the capital of Navarra, the Basque kingdom, after *St-Jean-le-Vieux* ("Saint John the Old") was destroyed by the army of Richard the Lionheart. Camino routes from all over France converged in St. Jean before crossing the treacherous and demanding Pyrenees Mountains.

St. Jean provides a marvelous place to wander about and explore. First stop is the **Pilgrim Office (*Accueil des Pélerins*)** on Rue de la Citadelle, which offers *credenciales* (p. 21) for €2, as well as extremely helpful advice from multilingual volunteers. Free internet consoles are available as well as a message board and printouts of camino elevation charts and

Rue de la Citadelle and Porte Saint Jacques in St. Jean (opposite)

☀ St. Jean hosts a variety of restaurants, many of which offer a pilgrim menú. Two grocery stores in the Old City offer food to prepare at your albergue. There are no grocery stores until the next stage, so plan accordingly.

The journey begins at the St. Jean pilgrim office.

🏛 **Monday** is a lively market day in St. Jean, with traditional artisan foods and livestock sales.

accommodations. Just past the pilgrim office is the **Prison dite des Evêques**, a museum housed in the 13th-century bishop's house later used as a prison (🕐11am-12:30pm, 2:30-6:30pm, closed Tues, €3 entrance). Numerous albergues line Rue de la Citadelle, as well as tourist shops and restaurants.

Walk uphill on Rue de la Citadelle to pass through the **Porte de San Jacques**, a 15th-century city gate named a UNESCO World Heritage site in 1998. Continue uphill to reach the **Citadelle**, a 17th-century French military building now used as a school, which affords a marvelous view back down on the Old City. Steep stairs to the east lead down to the the 14th-century Gothic church, **Notre-Dame-du-Bout-du-Pont**, constructed of red schist stone and dedicated by Sancho the Strong to commemorate the battle of Las Navas in 1212, an atmospheric place to light a candle for your journey.

From the church, it is possible to walk east along the river, crossing over via a **Roman bridge**, and returning via **Porte d'Espagne**, the "door to Spain" that will begin your journey over the Pyrenees. Continue north on **Rue d'Espagne**, crossing over the River Nive. Be sure to look down the river at the historic houses lining the river with their sweet balconies. Rue d'Espagne turns to Rue de la Citadelle to bring you back to the Pilgrim Office and albergues.

☀ Private albergues accept reservations and in high season may be full far in advance. There is also a wide selection of hotels just outside of the Old City.

The Old City has a 🛒 supermarket (🕐8am-12:30pm, 4-7pm) and a gear store, 🎒 Direction Compostelle (🕐10am-12:30pm, 2-7pm, closed on Wednesdays). 📶 Wifi can be found at the Terasse Café and albergues Auberge de Pelerin and Gîte Ultreïa. ℹ Place du Général de Gaulle

Roland & Charlemange

History buffs will recognize Ronvesvalles and Valcarlos as in the Battle of Roland, immortalized in *La Chanson de Roland*, "Roland's Song," one of the earliest examples of French epic poetry. The poem, likely from the end of the 11th century, recounts and embellishes the story of Roland's battle death in 778 in mythical proportions.

Monument to Roland at Alto de Ibañeta

The story goes that Charlemagne and his army were returning from six years of battling Muslims in Spain. His nephew Roland was in charge of the rear guard, and his brother-in-law/stepfather, Ganelon, in charge of relaying a message back to the Muslim king. Ganelon and Roland quarreled, and Ganelon was jealous of Roland's position with the king. So Ganelon went to the Muslim leaders and revealed Charlemagne's route back to France, suggesting that in the narrow pass through the Pyrenees the rear guard would be most vulnerable.

On August 15, 778, Charlemagne's main army passed through the Pyrenees (the Valcarlos route) without any problem. However, Roland's rear guard was attacked and mercilessly slaughtered. Roland fought bravely, refusing to sound his horn and call Charlemagne back. Deeply wounded, Roland blew on his horn (named *Oliphant*) so strongly that he burst his temples and split the horn. In his death throes, he shattered his sword (named *Durendal*) against a rock to prevent it from falling into the hands of his enemies. Charlemange returned to a bloodstained valley with all of his rear guard and his beloved nephew dead.

At the **Alto de Ibañeta**, high point of the Valcarlos route, there is a monument to Roland, supposedly where Charlemagne buried Roland's body, near the modern Iglesia de San Salvador de Ibañeta built over the site of a medieval church.

While the story may be inspiring, it is most certainly embellished, and it is now believed that it was local Basques, not the Muslims, who defeated Roland. While Charlemagne was supposedly fighting in Spain to protect Christendom, he did his fair share of looting and destruction along the way, including destroying the walls of Pamplona and accepting a bribe to return to France. While local Basques let him pass on his way in, they had their revenge on the way out.

The path can be crowded before walkers spread out.

Two Routes Across the Pyrenees

For medieval pilgrims, crossing the Pyrenees was one of the most treacherous parts of the pilgrimage. They feared foul weather, exorbitant tolls, bandits and exhaustion. The **Valcarlos Route** was popular among medieval pilgrims because it was not as steep or difficult, however, the **Napoleon Route** became the preferred alternative when bandits became a persistent problem on the lower route.

While you need no longer fear bandits or toll collectors along the Valcarlos Route (24.0km), most pilgrims choose the higher Napoleon Route (24.7km) for the incredible views, natural paths and quiet roads.

The Napoleon Route made an appearance in the film *The Way* as the place where Emilio Estevez's character dies in a storm. The route should not be walked in winter or in foul weather, when the Valcarlos Route should be used. In recent years, several pilgrims have died or needed to be rescued from the mountain when walking in the snow.

Mountain Wildlife

Watch the path, of course, but keep your eyes on the skies for the majestic swooping Griffon vultures, which soar above the Pyrenees on the warm updrafts. These large scavengers have white heads and dark brown wings and can weigh up to 12kg with a wingspan up to 3m. *Chamois*, a small goat-antelope species, can sometimes be observed with their distinctive white faces with a black stripe under the eye. Domesticated hill ponies often graze in the green fields along the route. Wild horses also roam the mountains but are not frequently seen. *Latxa* sheep can often be seen, a special Basque black-faced breed whose milk is used in the unpasteurized traditional delicacy of *Idiazábal* and *Ossou-Iraty* cheeses.

Griffon vultures soar over the Pyrenees

The Valcarlos Route (p. 54), while also scenic, spends 4.6km along the N-135 highway. However, the Valcarlos Route has more intermediate services such as grocery stores, cafés, hotels and an albergue 11.6km from St. Jean and does not climb as high as the Napolean Route. For either route, start at sunrise and give yourself a good eight hours of walking time (plus breaks) to arrive at Roncesvalles.

Latxa sheep grazing in the Pyrenees

Napolean Route

Many pilgrims are intimidated by this route, which passes over the Pyrenees at a high point of 1,429m. While the route is challenging and should be planned for accordingly, the views are spectacular and the feeling of accomplishment at day's end is priceless. Weather at the pass is unpredictable, so make sure to have rain gear handy (jacket, pack cover, and a change of dry clothes). The path is marked with red/white stripes, yellow/blue shell markers and a few yellow arrows.

"The Basque Country has the highest mountain on the Camino. The mountain is eight miles up, and eight miles down the other side, and seems to touch the sky. Climb it and you'll feel you could push the sky with your hand."

Codex Calixtinus

5.3 Honto A

A Ferme Ithurburia (priv, 🛏22, €14): ▯▯▯▯▯,
☎05-59371117 ▯

7.7 Orisson A▯

A ▲ Refuge Orisson (priv, 🛏18, dm €31, tent €24
w/▯ and dinner): ▯, ☎0681-497956 ▯,
🕑Mar-Oct, recommended to book ahead

A Kayola (priv, 🛏15, €15): ▯▯, ☎06-814979,
🕑Mar-Oct, 800m before Orisson

☀ Sandwiches and soups
at Orisson cost €3-5.

Misty mountain paths

0.0 *Leave St. Jean on Rue D'Espagne
straight through Porte d'Espagne. Follow the small, paved road straight and
uphill; the first 7km are the steepest.*

5.3 **Honto** is the first small
hamlet on the trail with an albergue.
*Shortly after Honto, leave the paved
road and head straight on a wide grassy
path while the road curves to the R. Rejoin the paved road in 900m at a display about the surrounding landscape,
reaching Orisson 1.1km later.*

7.7 **Orisson** is a small hamlet with two albergues and a
café, the last place with food until Roncesvalles and a convenient place to fill water outside of the albergue. *Continue
steeply up along the road to emerge at Pic D'Orisson.*

13.2 Pic D'Orisson

affords a marvelous view, where the Vierge d'Orisson "Virgin of Orisson," keeps her silent vigil over the spectacular valley vistas. Shepherds brought the statue from Lourdes.

Follow the road for another 1.8km, where a cross and signposts mark a R turn on a dirt footpath. Follow this footpath around the mountain top, to arrive at the **Spanish border (16.7km)** *and* 🕆 **Fontaine de Rolánd** *("Roland's Fountain") at Col Bentarte. It's another 4km to the Col Lopoeder on a footpath protected by forest. The waymarking on the Spanish side is more thorough, with high, numbered poles, visible even in snow. Just 1.7km before the high point, pass a small one-room mountain hut with a fireplace (no bathroom, no services, emergency only).*

20.7 Col Lopoeder is the

high point of the day at 1,429m. *Descend via one of two paths: 1) steep waymarked dirt path (4km) or 2) paved road (4.3km) to the R (also marked with red/white GR markings and footpaths to connect the road's switchbacks). Exercise caution if taking the dirt path as it is steep and end of the day tiredness and mud could make you more vulnerable to injury. The road option affords nice valley views of the beech forest and Roncesvalles, joining the Valcarlos Route at* **Ibañeta** *for the last 1.6km on a peaceful forest path to Roncesvalles.*

Vierge d'Orisson

51

24.7 Roncesvalles 🅰 🅷 ▥▤◉ⓘ🅟

Pop. 30, 🏳French: *Ronceveux*, Basque: *Orreaga*;
Spanish: "Valley of Thorns" or "Valley of Junipers"

1. **🅰 Municipal** (↩183, €10): ▥▦▨▤◉🔊, 📷,
   huge new facility ⊙2pm, all year
2. **🅷 Casa Sabina** (dbl €50): ▥, ☎948-760012 📷
3. **🅷 La Posada** (dbl €55): ▥, ☎948-760225 📷,
   ATM in lobby
4. **🅷 Hotel Roncesvalles/Casa de Beneficiados**
   (dbl €75): ▥🔊, ☎948-760105 📷

The first pilgrim guest-
house in Roncesvalles
was built in 1127 and
lauded in the poem *Song
of the Hospital* in the
document "*La Pretiosa*:"

*Porta patet omnibus,
infirmir et sanis, Non
solum Catholicis verum et
paganis, Judeis, hereticis,
otiosis, vanis.*

"The door opens to all,
to sick and healthy, not
only to true Catholics
but also to pagans, Jews,
heretics, the idle and
vagabonds."

24.7 Roncesvalles

After a tiring day, you may be relieved to arrive in Roncesvalles, a small medieval hamlet dominated by a large abbey and several historic churches. This popular tourist spot is a second gateway to the camino, sometimes crowded in summer.

The current albergue of Roncesvalles is brand new as of summer of 2011, with excellent facilities. The previous albergue, a historic building that had over 100 beds in one large room, was shown in the 2010 film *The Way* as the place Martin Sheen's character spends his first night on the camino. Two restaurants offer a pilgrim menú; be sure to buy a ticket and select a dinner time beforehand.

The **Iglesia de Santa María** is open to the public with a pilgrim Mass offered (8pm weekdays, 6pm weekends), and houses the 13th-century statue of **Our Lady of Roncesvalles**, made of wood covered in luminous silver. She used to be hidden behind a curtain and only viewed with great ceremony, but now she is prominently displayed on the front altar. Don't miss the ornate canopy of silver above her, known as a balda-chín, a recreation of the original.

The **Capilla de Santiago**, a 13th-century Gothic chapel, includes bells used to guide pilgrims down from Ibañeta Pass in foul weather. Nearby, the **Capilla de Sancti Spiritus**, also known as Charlemagne's Silo, houses ossuaries (bone boxes). According to legend, the bones belong to soldiers killed with Roland in the Battle of Roncesvalles, but they are more likely the bones of unlucky pilgrims who died on the mountain pass.

Visit the **Real Colegiata de Santa María**, one of the earliest Gothic structures in Spain, built by Sancho VII in 1219 (called Sancho the Strong perhaps because of his 2.2m/7'3" height). Some parts of the complex can be visited independently, others require a museum ticket and guided tour (Spanish language only).

To visit the following areas, a ticket to the museum is required (**Museum of Roncesvalles** ✆, €4.20, €3.20 with credencial, 10am-2pm, 3:30-7pm, ☎948-760000). An audio guide costs €1 (various language options) and includes entrance to the cloisters and tomb but not the museum.

The cloister, containing the 14th-century Chapter House, collapsed under a freak snowstorm in the 17th century and was replaced with a more plain structure. The Tomb of Sancho VII is found in the chapter house. Note the chains at the foot of the tomb, said to be the those of Christian prisoners freed from the Muslim army by Sancho's knights at the Battle of Las Navas de Tolosa in 1212. The symbol of chains still adorns the flag of Navarra to this day. The stained glass window depicts the Battle of Navas with Sancho and his knights trampling their Muslim opponents.

> Pilgrim albergues in medieval times were called "hospitals," even though they were not specifically for sick people.

The museum houses religious relics and historical items, including *Oliphant* (Roland's famed horn made of ivory), Charlemagne's chessboard (actually a 14th-century reliquary with 32 squares, each filled with a relic, such as bone fragments of a saint) and a gold reliquary said to house two thorns from the crown worn by Jesus.

Pilgrim mass at Iglesia Santa María in Roncesvalles

View of Valcarlos

⚠ Alternate Stage 1A: Valcarlos Route
St. Jean to Roncesvalles (via Valcarlos), 24.0km

In spite of the sections of highway walking, much of this route is on pleasant quiet country roads or lovely dirt footpaths. The trail crisscrosses the Nive River and Spanish/French border. Remain vigilant for vehicles on blind corners, as this highway has no shoulder in most places.

0.0 **St. Jean**: *Leave via the main street over the bridge to Rue d'Espagne. Note the R turn at the road "Chemin Mayorga" (0.5km), scarcely waymarked. Continue out of town, joining the busy D933 highway before turning R onto a quiet paved country road with a sign for "Valcarlos Luzaine" (1.8km).*

7.0 **Rest Stop**: The first services are at a large rest stop for travelers on the nearby highway, including a supermarket and café. *Cross the parking lot and walk through the shopping area to exit behind the gas station on a dirt path (waymarked) to Arné-guy.*

☀ If the 24km first day strikes as too daunting, split the day by sleeping in Varcarlos and continue up the pass to Roncesvalles in a more manageable 12.4km day.

From Valcarlos, be sure to refill water as there are not more sources until Roncesvalles.

54

8.5 Arnéguy is a small town that straddles the Spanish/French border. *From Arnéguy cross D933 and the bridge to take a waymarked quiet country road on the east side of the river, cutting out about 3km of busy road walking. Pass through* ***Óndarolle (10.9km)****, and descend steeply to cross a bridge and ascend to Valcarlos.*

11.6 Valcarlos housed a medieval hospice and church, which no longer stand. A modern church contains a life-size statue of Santiago (ask for key in Bar Iñaki). *Leave Valcarlos via the main road, and turn L (13km) on a quiet country road to pass through Gañecoleta.*

8.5 Arnéguy Pop. 271
Hotel Clementia (dbl €35): , 05-5937135

11.6 Valcarlos Pop. 30
Basque: *Luzaine*, Spanish: "Valley of Charlemange"
1. **Municipal** (24, €10 w/): , , noon, all year, key may be at municipal building
2. **Casa Marcelino** (dbl €40): , c/Elizaldea 1, 948-790063
3. **Casa Etxezuria** (dbl €45): c/Elizaldea, 948-790011
4. **Hostal Maitena** (dbl €55): , c/Elizaldea, 948-790210

15.0 Gañecoleta is a small sleepy hamlet with quaint country cottages. *At the far end of town, follow waymarks to the R on a pleasant forest dirt path. After 1km, rejoin the highway (15.9km) for another 2.4km. After the "km 58" sign on the road, turn L back onto a dirt path (18.2km). The path intersects the road (21.2km), almost immediately leaving it to the L, and follows a dirt footpath. The final 3km to the pass are steep and tiring! Remember to save energy for this final challenge.*

Colorful window in Gañecoleta

22.6 Ibañeta Pass marks the high point of this stage, with a small chapel and monument to Roland. *A brisk downhill walk of 1.4km heads to Roncesvalles, directly to the albergue.*

24.0 Roncesvalles
Details on p. 52.

2

RONCESVALLES TO ZUBIRI

22.3km
(13.9mi)

🕑 5-6 HOURS
DIFFICULTY: ▬☐☐
🄿 32%, 7.2 km
Ⓤ 68%, 15.1 km

A ALBERGUES:
Espinal 6.8km
Zubiri 22.3km
Larrasoaña 28.0km

Leaving Roncesvalles:
only 790km to go!

Enjoy shaded forest trails, pass rivers and small villages, explore Hemingway lore and a Romanesque bridge.

☀️ This is a beautiful day of walking, primarily on forest walking trails, occasionally crossing the main highway. The many flat sections are a welcome rest after the Pyrenees yesterday. Periodic services in charming towns pleasantly break up the stage.

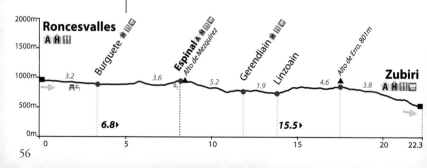

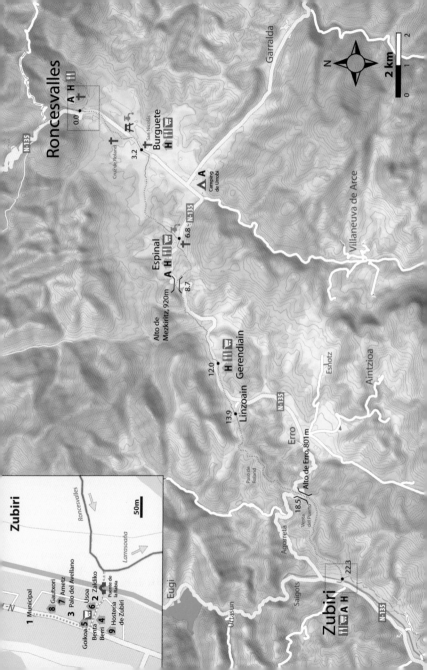

Roncesvalles

A H ⛪

0.0 ⛪

⛪ San Nicolás

🏕

✝ Cruz de Roland
3.2

Burguete
H ⛪ 🏛

⛰ A
Camping de Urrobi

N-135
6.8 ✝

Espinal
A 🏛 🏛

8.7 }

Alto de Mezkiritz, 920m

12.0

Gerendiain
H 🏛 🏛

13.9 🏛

Linzoain

N-135

Erro
Alto de Erro, 801m

Eshotz

Aintzioa

Villanueva de Arce

Garralda

Pazo de Roland

18.5 } Venta del Puerto

Agorreta

Ureta

Eugi

Saigots

22.3

Zubiri
🏛 🏛 A H
N-135

Zubiri (inset map)

1 Municipal
8 Gaultxori
7 Ametz
3 Palo del Avellano
5 Goikoa
6 2 Zaldiko
4 Benta Berri
9 Hostería de Zubiri

Puente de la Rabia

Roncesvalles

Larrasoaña

50m

This scrubby forest full of gorse and thickets (and blackberries in summer!) was supposedly a place of witchcraft in the 16th century, when nine women were put to death by the Inquisition, accused of practicing witchcraft in the forest between Roncesvalles and Burguete.

0.0 *Leaving the Roncesvalles albergue, walk to La Posada restaurant to pick up trail markings which follow highway N-135. Leave the road for a dirt footpath (0.4km), and soon note the stone Cruz de Peregrinos, a 14th-century Gothic cross with the image of Sancho the Great and his wife.*

3.2 **Burguete**, a popular breakfast stop, is a typical Navarran town whose main claim to fame is a mention in Ernest Hemingway's famous novel, *The Sun Also Rises*, which he wrote in just eight weeks in 1926. Hotel Burguete still has a piano with Hemingway's signature. In medieval times, Burguete was known for its cobblers and barbers. A massive fire in the 14th century destroyed most of the medieval town, so most buildings today are modern, though the **Iglesia de San Nicolás de Bari** has a Baroque doorway.

3.2 **Burguete** Ⓗ ⯑⯑⯑⯑⯑⯑
Pop. 290, Basque: *Auritz*
Ⓗ **Iturrialdrea** (dbl €25-28): ⯑, ☎948-760243 ⯑
Ⓗ **Pedro Arena** (dbl €35): ⯑⯑⯑, ☎948-760164⯑
Ⓗ **Hotel Burguete** (dbl €45-55): ☎948-760005 ⯑, has piano signed by Hemingway
Ⓗ **Don Jáuregui de Burguete** (dbl €50+): c/San Nicolás 32, ☎948-760031 ⯑
Ⓗ **Loizu** (dbl €63-89): ⯑⯑⯑⯑, c/San Nicolás 13, ☎948-760008 ⯑

Rural scenery after Burguete (above)

Watch for the Santander Bank (3.3km), where the trail turns to the R out of town on a small footpath, partly paved (10m beyond this turn, a panadería offers coffee and fresh baked goods from 8am). Cross the Río Irati and through pleasant farmland to Espinal.

6.8 **Espinal** was founded in 1269 as a place to protect pilgrims from bandits. *The trail leaves town to the L via a small country road, which becomes a paved footpath. Climb up through beech forest to cross the highway and the* **Alto de Mezquirez (920m, 8.7km),** *and descend via steep paved footpath over the Río Erro through the last beech forest of the camino to Gerendiain.*

12.0 **Gerendiain** is mentioned in the *Codex Calixtinus* as the end of the first segment from St. Jean, with the 13th-century Iglesia de San Bartolomé. On the way out of town is a mini market open daily.

Continue on the wooded path into the hamlet of **Linzoain (13.9km),** *with a 13th-century church dedicated to San Saturnino, and several houses display lintels (coats of arm) from the 18th and 19th century. Continue steeply up through dense woodland. Look R for a boulder painted yellow, said to represent the length of* **Roland's stride (Paso de Roldán).** *This shady path leads uphill to Alto de Erro.*

Wayside shrine near Espinal

6.8 **Espinal** A H 🏠🍴🛒🏕
Pop. 249, Basque: *Aurizberri*
A H **+600m Irugoienea** (priv, 🛏22, dm €10, dbl €40): 🍴🛒📶, Oihanilum 2, 📞649-412487, free transfers to/from Roncesvalles
A H 🏕 **+1.5km Camping Urrobi** (🛏42, €10.50): 📶, 📞948-760200 📧, 🕐Apr 1-Oct 31
H **Errebesena** (dbl €30): c/San Bartolomé 25, 📞948-760141 📧, Milagros Saragüeta
H **Gertxada** (dbl €33): 📺🛒, 📞948-760261 📧
H **Hostal Haizea** (sng €35, dbl €60): 🍴, Ctra Francia, 📞948-760379 📧

12.0 **Gerendiain** H 🍴🛒
Pop. 25, Basque: *Viscarret/Bizkarreta*
H **Corazón Puro** (€18 per person w/🍽 and dinner): 🍴🛒📶, c/San Pedro 19, 📞948-392113 📧, offer pickup from Pamplona for €15
H **La Posada Nueva** (dbl €35): c/San Pedro 2, Cristina Eciolaza: 📞948-760173 📧

EMEN·ERRATEN·DA·SALVE·BAT
ORREAGA·KOANDREDENA·MARIARI
AQVI·SE·REZA·VNA·SALVE
A·N·S·DE·RONCESVALLES
ICI·ON·SALUEN·0·DE·RONCEVAUX
PAR·VN·SALVE·REGINA

Lambs along the camino

18.5 Alto de Erro once housed an inn, the Ventas del Puerto, with a few ruins still visible in the cattle yard. *Cross the highway and a parking lot (seasonal drink/snack truck) for a steep, sometimes slippery, descent down to Zubiri. If staying in Zubiri, enter via the bridge.*

☀ *An overnight in Zubiri is slightly off route. To continue to Larrasoaña, you do not need to enter Zubiri (unless you wish to visit the grocery store as Larrasoaña has only a very small shop off route). If you're still feeling spry, continue on the 5.7km to Larrasoaña, advantages include a shorter day tomorrow to explore Pamplona, also Larrasoaña is off the highway so has a more remote feel. Larrasoaña has fewer accommodation and eating options than Zubiri.*

22.3 Zubiri: Enter via a Romanesque bridge, known as the **Puente de la Rabia** (Rabies Bridge), named because of a tradition that if animals are led three times across the bridge, they will be protected from rabies. The tradition comes from a legend that the builders of the bridge in the 15th century dug into the rock to place the central pillar and found an

---

22.3 Zubiri A ᴴ ▯▮▊＋◐❶▯ Pop. 432, 📖 Basque: "village of the bridge"
1. **A Municipal** (🛏80, €6): 🔲🖥, ☎628-324186, 🕙10am, Mar-Oct, basic albergue with communal showers, no fridge, recently renovated
2. **A Zaldiko** (priv, 🛏24, €10): 🔲🆆📶🖥(free), Puente de la Rabia 1, ☎609-736420 🖃, 🕙Mar-Oct, reservations possible, open in winter with reservation, microwave/fridge
3. **A ᴴ El Palo de Avellano** (priv, 48 🛏, dm €15-17, sng €46-50, dbl €58-65 w/🚿): ▯▊🆆◖📶🖥(free) Av. Roncesvalles 16, ☎948-304770 🖃, 🕙Apr-Oct
4. **ᴴ Benta Berri** (sng €15, dbl €25): 🔲, Av. Roncesvalles 10, ☎948-304562/636-134781 🖃
5. **ᴴ Goikoa** (sng €25, dbl €30): 🔲🆆, Av. Roncesvalles 12, ☎948-304308/618-636189 🖃
6. **ᴴ Usoa** (sng €24, dbl €30-38): 🔲🆆, Puente de la Rabia, ☎948-304306/628-058048 🖃
7. **ᴴ Amets** (sng €25-30, dbl €30-35): c/Gerestegi 25, ☎948-304308 🖃
8. **ᴴ Gautxori** (sng €30, dbl €49): ▯▊▬, Av. Roncesvalles, ☎948-304076 🖃
9. **ᴴ Hostería de Zubiri** (sng €75, dbl €95 w/🚿): Av. Roncesvalles 6, ☎948-304329 🖃

embalmed body. The body turned out to be Santa Quiteria, patron saint against rabies. When she was being transported to Pamplona to be buried, her body miraculously refused to budge from this spot, so her processional assumed it was a sign that she wished to be buried along the pilgrim road.

A leper hospital was once located near the bridge, though nothing remains of the structure. Zubiri is first mentioned in a 1040 document in which the area is donated to the Leyre monastery. Domenico Laffi's pilgrim account describes the bridge as treacherous, with guards of the bridge demanding a toll and brutally hurting those who refused. Today Zubiri is rather industrial, with many locals working at the magnesium factory visible along the trail on the next stage.

Zubiri
June: Día del Valle
Aug: Patron saint San Esteban

A standard greeting along the trail is *Buen Camino*, literally meaning "good way."

In medieval times, the greeting was *ultreia* meaning "further onward," with the response being *et suseia* "and further upward," highlighting the physical and spiritual aspects of the journey.

Enter Zubiri over la Puente de la Rabia

3

ZUBIRI TO PAMPLONA

21.1km
(13.1mi)

🕑 5-6 Hours
Difficulty: ▭☐☐
P 43%, 9.1km
U 57%, 12.0km

A Albergues:
Larrasoaña 5.7km
Trinidad 16.6km
Pamplona 21.1km
Cizur Menor 26.2km

Plaza del Castillo
in Pamplona

Follow the Arga River, visit medieval churches, gaze at Pamplona's Gothic cathedral, see where the famous bulls run.

☀ Today's path primarily follows the Arga River through rural hamlets on pleasant natural paths with plenty of places to fill water. The day ends in Pamplona, the city with the largest population on the Camino Francés, with some urban road walking to arrive to the charming walled Old City, alive with cafés and Hemingway lore.

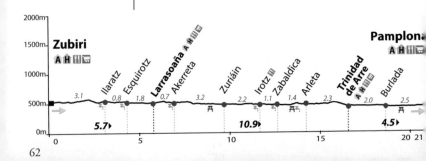

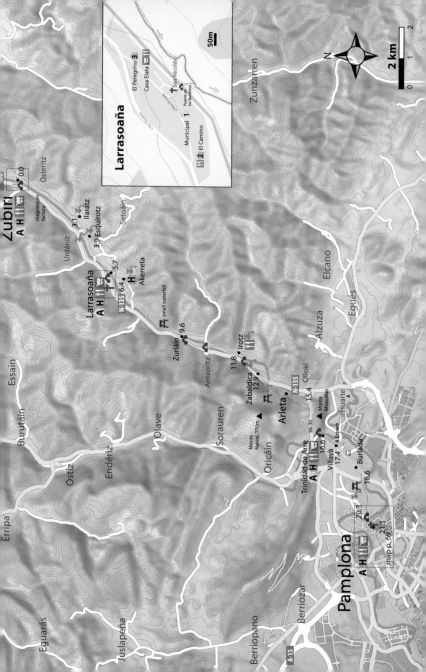

Larrasoaña

50m

El Peregrino **3** [icons]
Casa Elata **2** [icons]
San Nicolás [icon]

Municipal **1** [icons]
Puente de los Bandidos

[icons] **2** El Camino

N

2 km
0   1   2

Zunzarren

Zubiri
A H [icons] 0.0

Osteritz

magnesium factory

Ilaratz 3.1

Urdániz

Esquirotz 3.9

Setoáin

Larrasoaña 5.7
A H [icons] N-135 6.4 **H [icons]** Akerreta

small waterfall

Zuriáin 9.6

Antxoritz

Irotz 11.8 [icon]

Zabaldica 12.9

Arleta

N-135 15.4

Monte Miravalles

Olloki

Monte Narval, 770m

Olave

Sorauren

Oricáin

Huarte

Alzuza

Egués

Elcano

Trinidad de Arre
A H [icons] 16.6

PA-30

Villava 17.4 ■ Espadí

Burlada

18.6 [icon]

Berriopano

Pamplona
A H [icons] 20.3

21.1

map p. 69

A-15

Berriozar

Zunzarren

Essain

Burutáin

Endériz

Ostiz

Erripa

Eguarás

Juslapeña

5.7 Larrasoaña A H ▯▯▯▯
Pop. 143, Basque surname
1. **A Municial** (↺58, €6): ☎, c/San Nicolás,
   ☏605-505489, ⏱3pm, closed Dec 10-Jan 10,
   no cyclists allowed, basic
2. **H El Camino** (dbl €45): ▯, c/San Nicolás 16,
   ☏948-304250 ▯, ⏱Apr-Oct, menú €12.50
3. **H El Peregrino** (dbl €45-50): ▯,
   c/San Nicolás 50, ☏678-583030/948-227825

6.4 Akerreta H
H **Akerreta** (sng €60, dbl €86): ▯▯▯▯,
   c/Transfiguración 11, ☏948-304572 ▯,
   makes an appearance in the film *The Way*

Tunnel of green
before Larrasoaña

0.0 *Leave Zubiri on a well-marked farm track to a paved road through an unpleasant industrial stretch past a magnesium factory. Following the Río Arga valley today, pass through numerous tiny hamlets consisting of several large multi-story houses, spread in this way for defense and farming the fertile valley, such as **Ilaratz (3.1km)** and **Esquirotz (3.9km)**. Arrive at Puente de los Bandidos, the 14th-century bridge where bandits were said to hide and wait for pilgrims. Cross the bridge to enter Larrasoaña or continue to the L to Akerreta.*

5.7 Larrasoaña has a classic camino town layout and originates from the 12th century. Two historic hospices no longer remain, though the Clavería de Roncesvalles (storehouse) and the 13th-century **Iglesia de San Nicolás de Bari** can still be seen at the town entrance. Historic houses from the 15th and 16th centuries line the main street; some retain their coat of arms above the door. If you stay overnight, reserve your dinner at the small restaurant. Basic supplies and a café are available at Casa Elata, +350m. *Continue uphill on a gravel path to Akerreta.*

6.4 Akerreta is a small hamlet with an impressive hotel in a restored 1723 Basque house. Three-story houses were typical of the area, with the bottom floor for livestock, the next floor for family living space and a short upper floor for pigeons. *Continue on mostly dirt paths until the hamlet of **Zuriáin (9.6km)** and cross over the Río Arga to join busy highway N-135 for 600m. Break to the L on a smaller paved road and again to the R onto a dirt path to arrive at Irotz.*

11.8 Irotz has the Iglesia de San Pedro and sometimes a seasonal snack stand. *Cross back over the Río Arga on the Romanesque Puente Iturgaiz and into the "playa fluvial" park (river beach park, 🏛🍴 12.1km). The trail is waymarked two ways—one which turns L just after the bridge and passes through the park along the river on a cement bike path which goes all the way into Pamplona (all paved and much longer) along the banks of the river. The second and preferred option is waymarked just a little further after the bridge and follows a pleasant footpath through the hamlet of Zabaldica.*

12.9 Zabaldica contains the 12th-century Iglesia de San Esteban with one of the oldest bells in Spain (1377). *Continue straight through the town and out on a dirt path, crossing highway ⚠ N-135 to a **rest area** 🏛🍴 (13.5km). From the rest area, the trail becomes a dirt footpath that veers steeply up the hillside of Monte Nerval and passes under highway PA-30 through a tunnel (15.4km). Enter Trinidad de Arre via a Romanesque bridge.*

Medieval bridge entering Villava

A legend says that a woman was baking bread when a passing pilgrim asked her for some. She answered that she had none and returned to her oven to find the bread had turned to stone.

65

16.6 Trinidad de Arre/Villava

A H 🏠 🍴 🛏 ➕ ⚡ ℹ️ 🔲 Pop. 10,487

A Hermanos Maristas (par, 🛏34, €8): 🔲 🔲 🔲,
c/Mayor - Puente, 🕐948-332941 📱, ⏰2pm,
Mar-Dec 15, reservations

A Villava Municipal (🛏54, €10): 🔲🔲 🛜,
Pedro de Atarrabia 17-19, 🕐948-111577 📱,
⏰11am, all year, staffed by disabled people

H Villava (dbl €50): 🔲🔲 🛜, 🕐948-333676 📱

H La Buhardilla (dbl €70): 🔲🔲,
c/Serapio Huici 15, 🕐948-382872 📱

+2.1 Huarte **A** 🍴 🛏 ➕ ⚡ ℹ️ 🔲 Pop. 6,309, (+2.1km)

A Municipal (🛏60, €10): 🔲🔲, Plaza San Juan,
🕐948-074329, ⏰1pm, Apr-Sept, can stay more
than 1 night

Colorful bunks in the
Pamplona municipal
albergue

16.6 Trinidad de Arre, now a
suburb of Pamplona, is located on
the ancient Roman road and was re-
founded in 1184 by Sancho IV. The
camino enters by the historic Romanesque bridge with six arches, followed by a sharp right angle after the
bridge, which was a defense point for
the town. Directly to the R after the
bridge is the parochial albergue, ad-
joined to the basilica where a pilgrim
accommodation was also located in
medieval times. Below the bridge are
remains of medieval mills and fulling
stations (for felting material). The
1057 bylaws of Arre state that villagers were to support the pilgrim hospital with a half pound of bread per
year in order to feed the pilgrims. Nowadays, you'll have to
buy your own bread. [From *Plaza Consistorial (17km)*, there
is an optional detour L off route to stay at the
Villava Municipal albergue or the albergue
at **Huarte**, another suburb of Pamplona.]

*Continue along a pedestrian path to Pamplona.
Cross c/San Andreas in **Villava (17.3km)** and
continue straight. After Burlada at the traffic
circle with Palacete Municipal (18.6km), turn
R and cross c/Bizkarmendia to walk along a
garden center and pass a picnic area with water. Arrive to the historic **Magdalena Bridge
(20.3km)** and follow the dirt path up to the
Old City by the historic walls. Pass through the
Old City gate (20.8km, Portal de Francia)
and another gate to walk straight on c/de Carmen, passing a plaza 🌲. Turn L on c/Navarre-
ria for the cathedral and municipal albergue, or
straight to continue on the camino.*

21.1 <u>Pamplona</u> is the first major city on the camino and an interesting place to take a rest day if you enjoy exploring historic buildings, twisting Old City alleys and expansive green parks. ☼ If there are any items in your backpack that you haven't used yet (except rain gear & first aid kit), consider mailing them ahead (p. 29).

Puerta del Amparo on the south portal of Pamplona's cathedral

Pamplona is best known for the **running of the bulls** at the ⚑ **Fiesta de San Fermínes**, celebrated July 6-14 each year, in which six bulls are released daily to run a course through the city to the plaza. San Fermín was the legendary first bishop of Pamplona who was martyred, some say by bulls, though the bull run did not become part of the festivities until the 19th century. The festival was propelled to worldwide fame by its prominence in Hemingway's *The Sun Also Rises*. Now, foolish and/or adventurous locals and tourists come to run with the bulls while consuming copious amounts of wine (an estimated three million liters are imbibed during the festivities, including a local favorite of *kalimotxo*, a mixture of wine and cola), precipitating numerous injuries and occasional death. The city swells with over a million people, accommodations rates quadruple and albergues close. If you happen to pass through Pamplona during San Fermínes, just keep on walking (or run!) and look for a bed in the next town.

Pamplona was founded by the Roman general Pompeoalo, built over a previous Basque encampment, an ideal defensible location along the *Via Trajana*. Roman ruins have been excavated from under the **cathedral**, including 1st-century streets and buildings. Muslims took the city in 718 and ruled until they were overthrown by local Basques in 799. In 778, Charlemagne was said to have destroyed the city walls of Pamplona, leading up to the Battle of Roncesvalles (p. 47).

Five-time Tour de France winner Miguel Indurain was born in Villava.

An influx of foreign immigrants in the 12th century led to in-fighting between neighborhoods, with each ethnic neighborhood fortifying themselves against the others. Pamplona was more fort than city, encapsulated within the defensive walls until the 20th century when building was finally allowed outside city walls. Today, Pamplona is a prosperous and attractive city, with two universities and a number of historical buildings and museums. *Plaza del Castillo* 📶 is a great place for an evening stroll, with numerous cafés including Café Iruña, a favorite haunt of Hemingway, and historic hotels such as La Perla, which has hosted Orson Welles, Charlie Chaplin and Hemingway.

✝ **Catedral Santa María el Real** (€4, €2 with *credencial*, 🕥M-Sa 10:30am-5pm, 7pm summer, ☎948-212594 🔲)
The entrance fee includes a brochure and map of the many chapels and features of this 15th-century Gothic cathedral. The main façade is from the 18th-century in the Neoclassical style, plain without ornamentation, lending more the serious look of a government building than a cathedral. The main altar houses the silver-coated *Virgen de Sagrario*, in front of

Typical street scene in Old City Pamplona

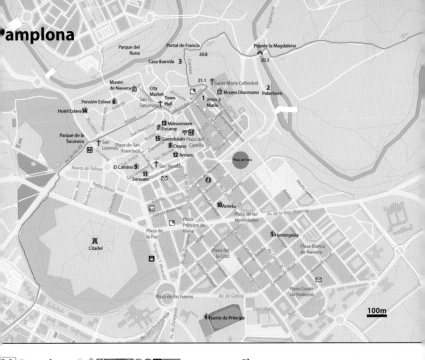

amplona

1.1 **Pamplona** A H ⏸🍴🛒💳➕☎ℹ🚌♻🚖 Pop. 197,932, 🏛 Named for Roman general Pompaelo, Basque: *Iruña* "the city," ℹ: M-F 10am-7pm; Sa 10am-2pm, 4-7pm; Su 10am-2pm, 💻 Caminoteca, Curia 5, ☎948-210316, 11am-7pm daily

A Jesús y María (muni, 🛏112, €7): 🏧📶🍴💻🚻, c/Compañía, ☎948-222644, 🕐Mar-Oct, lockers for €1, closed San Fermínes, free washer

A Jacobusfreunde Paderborn (assoc, 🛏24, €6): 📶🍴📶, Playa de Caparroso 6, ☎660-631656 📧, 🕐12pm-10pm, Mar-Nov, welcoming river-side albergue run by a German confraternity

A Casa Ibarrola (priv, 🛏20, €18 w/🛏): 🏧📶🍴💻📶, c/del Carmen 31, ☎692-208463 📧, 🕐all year except San Fermines

H A Fuerte del Príncipe (youth hostel, 🛏96, dm €26.50): 📶🍴, c/Goroabe 36, ☎948-291206 📧, 🕐Jul 15- Sep 15

H A Hostal Hemingway (dm €15-20, dbl €42): 🏧💻📶, c/Amaya 26, ☎948-983884 📧

H Pensión Eslava (sng €15, dbl €25 shared bath): c/Hilarión Eslava 13, ☎948-221558 📧

H Pension Escaray (sng €20, dbl €40 shared bath):📶, c/Nueva 24, ☎948-227825

H Casa Otano (sng €25, dbl €45): c/San Nicolás 5, ☎948-227036 📧

H Pensión El Camino (dbl €35): c/San Gregorio 12, ☎948-213567 📧

. H Pensión Arrieta (dbl €40): c/Arrieta de Pamplona 27, ☎652-849209/948-228459 📧

. H Sarasate (dbl €50): 📶, Paseo Sarasate 30, ☎948-223084/675-190464 📧

. H Hostal Arriazu (dbl €60): c/Comedias 14, ☎948-210202 📧

. H Maisonnave (dbl €68): 📶📶, c/Nueva 20, ☎948-222600, 📧

. H Hotel Eslava (dbl €73): 📶, Plaza Virgen de la O 7, ☎948-222270/948-225157, 📧

. H Palacio Guendulain (dbl €110): 📶📶, Zapatería 53, ☎948-225522 📧

69

Image of Santiago Peregrino in the Pamplona Cathedral (opposite top)

Cloister at Pamplona Cathedral (opposite bottom)

which the medieval Navarran kings were crowned. Some are also buried in the cathedral in alabaster tombs, including Carlos III and his wife. Visit the 13th-century cloister, one of the finest examples of Gothic style in Europe. Highlights include *la Puerta Preciosa* "the precious door" over which is a detailed tympanum depicting the life of the Virgin Mary. The south tympanum, *la Puerta del Amparo*, depicting Mary's dormition, retains some of the original colors. Various chapels contain nine retablos. The Renaissance retablo of John the Baptist in the 10th chapel is the most notable. The north bell tower houses one of the largest bells in Spain at over 11 tons!

The 🏛 **Museo Diocesano** gives access to more of the cathedral, with artifacts such as a carved pulpit featuring the hunt for the unicorn (hunting tip: unicorns are attracted to beautiful virgins). The Holy Sepulcher reliquary, made in 13th-century Paris, is the collection's star. Also notable are collections of processional crosses and seated virgins from rural churches.

Town Hall (Ayuntamiento)

This impressive Baroque facade, bedecked in striking flags, was demolished and rebuilt in 1951.

✝ Iglesia de San Saturnino

Dedicated to San Cernín/San Saturnino, whose main pilgrimage church is located in Toulouse, showing the French influence in Pamplona. Look on the right wall for a stone figure of Santiago Peregrino helping a small child.

🔆 If you prefer to forego the hustle and bustle of cities, make a brief stop at the cathedral and continue to **Cizur Menor** (+5.1km), a peaceful village just beyond Pamplona with two excellent albergues.

🏛 **Museo de Navarra** (free with *credencial*, 🕐Tu-Sa 9:30am-2pm, 5-7pm Su 11am-2pm, closed Mon, *c/Santo Domingo* 47) This museum was once a pilgrim hospital and now houses impressive archaeological and artistic artifacts from throughout Navarra, including Roman mosaics, the Romanesque capitals from Pamplona's cathedral, an intricately carved ivory chest from Córdoba and Gothic murals.

♜ Citadel/Cuidaduela

This star-shaped fortress on the south side of the city dates from the 16th century and was transformed into a park in 1964.

4

PAMPLONA TO PUENTE LA REINA

23.8km
(14.8mi)

🕒 **6-7 Hours**
Difficulty: ▭▢▢
🅿 40%, 9.4 km
🆄 60%, 14.4 km

A Albergues:
Cizur Menor 5.1km
Zariquegui 11.2km
Uterga 17.2km
Óbanos 21.5km
Puente la Reina 23.8km
Mañeru 29.0km
Cirauqui 31.6km

⚠ Alt. Route:
Eunate Church
+2.8km, (p. 79)

Pilgrim statue at
Alto de Perdón

Climb the wind-whipped Alto de Perdón, detour to the mysterious church at Eunate, ponder the mystery of Óbanos and marvel at the famous bridge of Puente la Reina.

☀️ This stage leaves Pamplona by way of the Citadel park and climbs to the small town of Cizur Menor. The steep climb to Alto de Perdón affords wonderful views. A worthwhile detour leads to the enigmatic church of Eunate. Be prepared for less shade today as you enter a more temperate climate with fields of wheat and grapes.

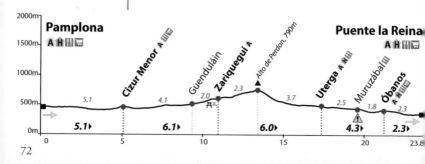

Pamplona — Cizur Menor — Guendulain — Zariquegui — Alto de Perdón, 790m — Uterga — Muruzábal — Óbanos — Puente la Reina

5.1 ▸ 6.1 ▸ 6.0 ▸ 4.3 ▸ 2.3 ▸

Erice

Olave

A-15

Sorauren

Larragueta

Berriopano

Oricáin

Zuasti

A-15

Berriozar

Villava

Olza

Antsoáin

Pamplona

Burlada

Ororbia

A H   0.0

Citadel

Ibero

A-15

Navarra University

2.6

Barañáin

3.2

San Emeterio y Celedonio

H   Cizur Maior   5.1   San Miguel   Cizur Menor

A

Paternáin

6.6

A-12

Guenduláin

Esparza

9.2

Noáin

Astráin

A-21

11.2

San Andrés   A   Zariquiegui

13.5   Fuente Reniego

Alto de Perdón, 790m
monument, snack stand

Learda

Arlegui

Óbanos

San Nicolás   La Asunción

A-12   17.2   Uterga

A H

San Juan Bautista   A   Usda

San Salvador

H   Osses

100m

19.7   Muruzábal

San Esteban

Óbanos

A H   21.5   +1.2

pilgrim monument   2 Jakue

Puente la Reina

23.8   Eunate Detour

A H   +1.6   Eunate

San Guillermo

Enériz

Puente la Reina

3 Santiago Apóstol

6 El Peregrino

El Cerco

1 Padres Reparadores

Santiago

Crucifijo

Puente la Reina

5 Bidean

San Pedro

bus stop

200m

Agustina

☀ If you get stuck for a bed or want to visit the 14th-century **Iglesia de San Andrés**, walk or take a bus 2km west to Cizur Mayor.

🛒 Cizur Menor's mini market "Dividi": ☺ 8:30am-2pm, 4:30-8:30pm/8pm weekends

0.0 *Leaving the Pamplona municipal albergue (map p. 69), take c/de Curria to c/Mercaderes to c/Mayor, following camino signs and passing the Ayuntamiento on Plaza Consistorial and the Iglesia de San Saturnino. Pass the Iglesia de San Lorenzo (0.7km) and walk on footpaths in the Parque de Taconera, around the edge of the Citadel. Turn R to cross c/de la Vuelta del Castillo and continue on c/del Hierro Kalea (1.7km) and stay straight through Navarra University (2.6km). Cross the Río Sadar via the Puente de Accela (3.2km) and follow the road to Cizur Menor.*

A famous battle was fought here on the plains between Pamplona and Cizur Menor, between the Muslim king Aigolando and Charlemagne. Over 100,000 soldiers gathered from each side. After bloody battle, the Crusaders emerged victorious.

5.1 **Cizur Menor** is the base for the Order of the Hospitalers of Saint John of Malta (*Sanjuanistas*), who established a monastery in 1135. The **Iglesia de San Miguel** is all that is left of the monastery and was used to store grain for over 100

years until it was restored in the 1980s. Above the door on the tympanum notice the simple *crismón* (a rosette containing the Greek symbols of the cross, *Chi Rho*, and an *Alpha Omega*). Fortified churches set upon hills in strategic military positions were often named for San Miguel (Saint Michael, the archangel), guardian of the church. The 12th-century Romanesque Iglesia de San Emeterio y Celedonio has also been restored. In 1508, the pilgrim hospital in Cizur Menor was recorded as having 8 beds; there are almost 10 times that now with two appealing albergues. Several restaurants offer a pilgrim menú.

Follow the main road out of Cizur Menor, exiting the town on a dirt footpath that soon skirts a housing development of Cizur Mayor to the north and enters fields on mixed gravel/paved paths (6.6km). Continue past a small lake to the L and the hamlet of Guendulaín off-route on your R, where the ruins of 16th-century Guendeláin palace and church once housed a pilgrim hospital (9.2km). Note the view of Pamplona behind as you arrive in Zariquiegui.

5.1 **Cizur Menor** A Pop. 2,113
Basque: *zintzur* "narrow mountain pass"
A **Orden de Malta** (assoc, 27, €4): ,
616-651330, stocked with food for a donation, Jun-Sept, run by the Sanjuanista Order of Malta with the feel of a parochial albergue
A ☆ **Albergue Familia Roncal** (priv, 52, €10):
, 948-183885, noon in summer, closed Nov, owner Maribel Roncal often graciously helps to treat pilgrim's blistered feet

A storm brews at the approach to Cizur Menor

Iglesia de San Miguel in Cizur Menor at sunrise

75

11.2 **Zariquiegui** **A** Pop. 179
A **La Posada de Ardogi** (priv, 📱16, €11 w/🚿): 🔖🔌🍴🅿️💻, c/San Andrés 16, 📞948-353353, ⏰all year

11.2 **Zariquiegui** is a hamlet housing the 13th-century Romanesque **Iglesia de San Andrés**, which you might recognize from a scene in the film *The Way*. The village was almost wiped out by Bubonic plague in the 14th century. *The grade increases steadily onwards and upwards as the ridge of the Alto de Perdón lined with windmills looms ahead.*

Just below the ridge of the Alto del Perdón, to the L is a (now dry) fountain known as **El Fuente Reniega (13.2km)** "Fount of Renunciation" because of a pilgrim legend. A pilgrim was extremely thirsty, and the devil came to him in the form of a wanderer and offered to give him water if he would just renounce God. The pilgrim stayed strong in the faith and refused. Having passed the test, the devil disappeared and Santiago appeared to the pilgrim and offered him water to drink from a scallop shell.

13.5 **Alto de Perdón** housed both a basilica with a pilgrim hospice and a hermitage in medieval times, though nothing remains of them, and today the view is dominated by a row of some 40 windmills providing electricity. The energy company has erected a pilgrim statue depicting a band of medieval pilgrims walking, pressed forward against the wind. The inscription reads: *"Donde se cruza el camino del viento con el de las estrellas"* ("Where the way of the wind meets the way of the stars").

View of the path from Alto de Perdón

From the ridge, upcoming villages can be seen including Puente la Reina. Note the changes to a more Mediterranean climate as you leave the Pamplona basin behind, with cereals, oak and Mediterranean brushwood ahead. Enjoy the gentle descent as the wheat and wine-growing valley spreads out before you, and enter the town of Uterga.

Pilgrim statue at Alto de Perdón

17.2 <u>Uterga</u> contains the **Iglesia de La Asunción,** featuring a retablo including scenes from the life of Santiago Peregrino. One medieval hermitage remains (of Uterga's five original), San Nicolás, near the cemetery. *Leave town via a dirt footpath, continuing to the nearby Muruzábel.*

17.2 **Uterga** A H 🍴 Pop. 205
A H **Camino del Perdón** (priv, 🛏16, dm €10, dbl €50): 🍴, c/Mayor 57, ©948-344598 🖼,
🕐Feb 15-Nov 15

Fields of wheat below Alto de Perdón

19.7 Muruzábel: The Iglesia de San Esteban features a chromatic retablo in Hispano-Flemish style with a number of saints including Santiago. [⚠ *After the church, watch for signs to turn L to take the detour to Eunate church (closed Mon), which adds about 1 hour/2.8km to the day. Otherwise, continue straight to Óbanos where the detour rejoins.*]

21.5 Óbanos A H 📶 🛒 ➕ 🅾 🏧 Pop. 800
1. **A** Albergue Usda (priv, 🛏36, €8): 📶, San Lorenzo 6, 📞676-560927, 🕓4pm, Apr-Oct 15
2. **H** Osses (dbl €25): 📶(€3) 🍴, c/San Guillermo 3, 📞948-344261

A Santiago Peregrino in Puente la Reina

78

21.5 Óbanos is a lovely historic camino town, best known for a murderous 14th-century pilgrim legend. Duke William (Guillermo) of Aquitane and his sister Felicia undertook the Camino de Santiago. On the return journey, Felicia was overwhelmed with piety and went to become a hermit in Amocain rather than returning to her life of luxury. Her brother tracked her down and tried to convince her to return to her court duties. When she refused, he became enraged and stabbed her to death. He was then overcome by remorse and walked to Santiago again and returned to Óbanos to mourn his sister for the rest of his life. He built a hermitage on Arnotegui (a southern hilltop) to serve pilgrims and the poor. Guillermo's silver-covered skull is kept in **Iglesia San Juan Bautista**. The town puts on a play called *The Mystery of Óbanos* every year, retelling the legend with a cast of most of the 800 villagers!

The trail passes through an arch and past the Ermita de San Salvador on the way out of town and down dirt paths through olive groves and vineyards. Cross NA-6010 (22.7km) and turn L along NA-1110 after Albergue Jakue (23.3km), and follow this road into Puente la Reina.

Alternate: Eunate Church, +2.8km

Unique octagonal church of Eunate

After leaving the main route in Muruzábel, follow paved roads to the edge of town, continuing on dirt roads until crossing NA-6010 to arrive at the Eunate church. The Camino Aragonés passes here, which returns to the Camino Francés in Óbanos. From Eunate, leave via a dirt track, past a picnic area, and back to the cross Na-6010 and Na-6016 up the hill into Óbanos where it joins the main route at the church.

La Ermita Santa Maria de Eunate

From Basque, meaning "house of 100 doors"
Nov & Jan-Feb 10:30am-2:30pm, Mar-Jun & Oct 10:30am-1:30pm, 4-7pm,
July-Sept 10:30am-1:30pm, 5-8pm, Closed Mondays and all of Dec

The beautiful setting and fascinating mystery of the **Ermita de Santa María de Eunate**, a 13th-century octagonal stone church surrounded by a wall with 33 arches, is well worth the detour and extra 2.8km. The origins of the church are unknown, though it is thought to be related to the Templars who had an affinity for octagonal churches. It has been suggested that the 33 arches mimic Muslim prayer beads, and that perhaps worshipers circled the church meditating three times (99 doors) before entering the 100th door into the church. Others theorize that elements from Muslim and Jewish architecture demonstrate a desire for all to feel welcome. In excavations, numerous pilgrim graves have been found. Until recently Eunate offered a small parochial albergue, which has closed.

23.8 <u>Puente la Reina</u>: In the 11th century, Sancho el Fuerte's wife (or perhaps his successor's wife) financed a beautiful **6-arched Romanesque bridge** over the Río Arga, so pilgrims and other travelers on the Roman route could avoid expensive ferrymen and treacherous boat rides. The town of Puente la Reina grew up around the queen's bridge, providing services and commerce for the pilgrims. The middle of the bridge used to have a niche, which held a statue of the Virgin Mary. Legend has it that a *Txori* ("little bird" in Basque) used to come clean the statue's face and was considered a good omen by the town. One story tells that during the Carlist Wars, a count laughed at the little *Txori* and made fun of the town's devotion to the bird. Two weeks later, he was defeated in battle and locals believed it to be his divine punishment.

🏛 **Puente la Reina**
Jul 24-30: Patron saint Santiago festival
Sept: Competition using pitchforks as stilts (*carrera de laya*s)

Pimientos de Piquillo (roasted red peppers) are a Puente la Reina specialty with a special pepper market in Sept.

> There are four ways which lead to Holy St. James and they become one near Puente La Reina in Spain.
>
> *Codex Calixtinus*

Romanesque façade of Iglesia Santiago in Puente la Reina

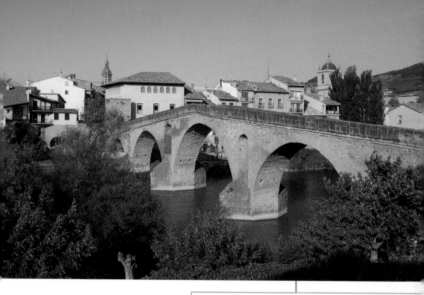

La Iglesia del Crucifijo was founded in the 12th century by Templars and still displays a 14th-century Y-shaped crucifix brought by a German pilgrim in the Middle Ages. The church was used as barracks during the Carlist wars.

La Iglesia de Santiago demonstrates Mudéjar influence and features a Baroque retablo, which recalls scenes from the life of Santiago, along with a famous statue from Gothic times known as the *beltza Santiago* ("black Santiago" in Basque). Pilgrims were entitled to one night at the Templar's hospital on their way to Santiago, and two nights on the way back. Nesting storks can often be seen on the belfry.

23.8 Puente la Reina A H 🏠🔧➕€🛈⛺🏠

Pop. 2,877, 🏳 Basque: *Gares* "grain,"
Spanish: "the queen's bridge"

1. **A Padres Reparadores** (par, 🛏100, €5): 🅺 🆆 🅳 🖥, Crucifijo 1, ☎948-340050, 🕓noon, all year, nice green yard/garden
2. **A H Albergue Jakue** (priv, 🛏40, €10, dbl €62): 🍴✿🆆🅳🖥🛜, C/Irunbidea, ☎948-341017 🖅 🕓noon, Mar 15-Oct 15, located in hotel
3. **A Santiago Apostól** (priv, 🛏100, €8): 🆆🅳🖥, ☎948-340220 🖅, 🕓11am, Apr-Oct 15, ⛺**Camping El Real** at same establishment
4. **H Bidean** (dbl €60): 🍴, c/Mayor 20, ☎948-340457 🖅
5. **H El Cerco** (dbl €75): 🍴🛜, c/Rodrigo Xlmenez de Rada 36, ☎948-341269 🖅
6. **H El Peregrino** (dbl €200): 🍴, c/Irunbidea, ☎948-340075 🖅

Famous Romanesque bridge of Puente la Reina

81

5

PUENTE LA REINA TO ESTELLA

21.8km
(13.5mi)

🕐 **5-6 Hours**
Difficulty: ▭☐☐
🅿 28%, 6.0km
🆄 72%, 15.8km

A Albergues:
Mañeru 5.2km
Cirauqui 7.8km
Lorca 13.4km
Villatuerta 18.1km
Estella 21.8km
Ayegui 23.4km
Villamayor 31.0km

....

⚠ **Alt. Routes:**
Split to Villatuerta
(6A Villatuerta to
Los Arcos, p. 94)

....

Scenery after Cirauqui
on the way to Estella

Revel in marvelous rolling agricultural views, enter history on a Roman road, discover a wealth of churches in "Estella la bella."

☀ A stage primarily on dirt paths with gently rolling ups and downs, passing through picturesque medieval towns. Authentic stretches of Roman road and a Roman bridge invite walkers to step back in time. Be prepared for little shade and some road noise from A-12 highway around Lorca. A day of beautiful scenery with fields and vineyards.

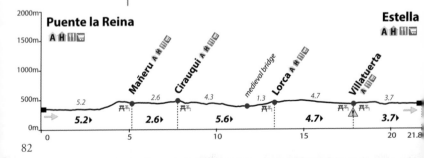

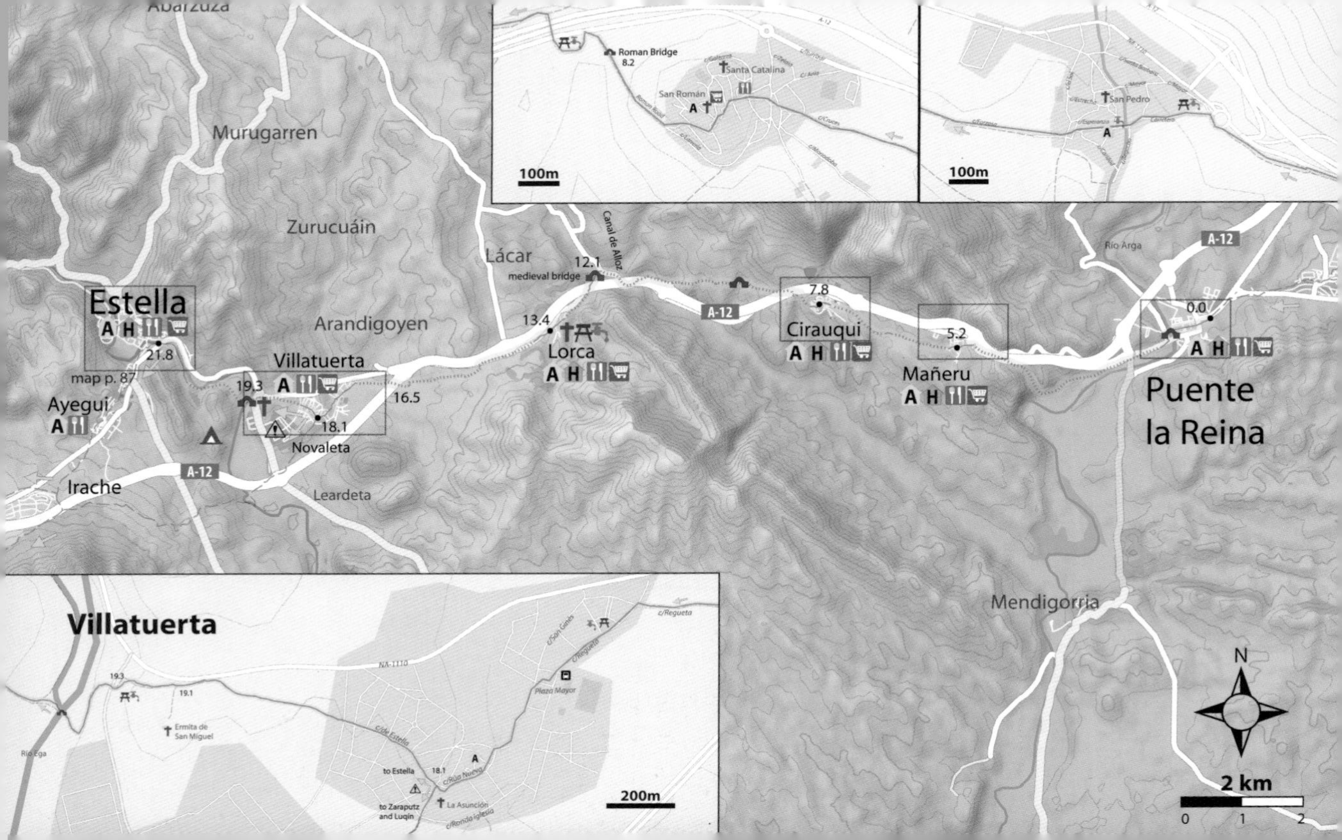
Abarzuza
Murugarren
Zurucuáin
Arandigoyen
Lácar
Canal de Alloz
12.1
medieval bridge
13.4
Lorca
A H
Estella
A H
21.8
map p. 87
Ayegui
A
Villatuerta
A
19.3
18.1
16.5
Novaleta
Leardeta
Irache
A-12
A-12
7.8
Cirauqui
A H
5.2
Mañeru
A H
0.0
Río Arga
A-12
Puente
la Reina
A H
Mendigorria
N
2 km
0
1
2
Roman Bridge
8.2
Santa Catalina
San Román
A
100m
San Pedro
A
100m
Villatuerta
NA-1110
c/Regueta
c/San Ginés
Plaza Mayor
c/de Estella
c/Rúa Nueva
A
19.3
19.1
18.1
Ermita de
San Miguel
Río Ega
to Estella
to Zaraputz
and Luqin
La Asunción
c/Ronda Iglesia
200m

5.2 **Mañeru** A H ⌂ ⬛ ✚ ⊙ ▣ Pop. 427
A **Lurgorri** (priv, ⛺12, €10 w/⬛): ▣ ⬛(free),
 c/Esperanza 5, ☎649-021705, ⊙Apr 1-Oct 31
H **Isabel** (dbl €38): ▣, c/Caridad 5, ☎948-340283

7.8 **Cirauqui** A H ⌂ ⬛ ✚ ⊙ ▣
Pop. 505, ⚑ Basque: "nest of vipers"
A H **Maralotx** (priv, ⛺28, dm €10, dbl €40): ⬛,
 c/San Román 30, ☎678-635208 ⬛,
 ⊙Mar 1-Oct 15

0.0 *Leave Puente la Reina on c/Mayor, crossing over the historic pilgrim bridge, then turning L to pass the Barrio de los Monjas (Nun Neighborhood). Cross over the N-111 highway to leave town on a dirt path, which winds along the Río Arga. After about 1km the track passes a factory and veers uphill to the R through fields and past the ruins of the 13th-century Monasterio de Bargota to reach Mañeru.*

5.2 **Mañeru:** Pass a 16th-century roadside cross coming into town. Impressive historic houses line the streets displaying coats of arms above the doors. Iglesia de San Pedro from the 18th century replaced a medieval church built by the Order of San Juan (p. 74). *Leave town on a footpath through vineyards and olive groves to the medieval town of Cirauqui.*

7.8 **Cirauqui** is a quaint medieval town set on a hill with the fascinating 13th-century **Iglesias de San Roman** and **Santa Catalina** (⊙7pm Mass often offered). Take time to appreciate the ornate Mudéjar portal over the entrance to **Iglesia San Roman** and its organic capitals, including the image of a mermaid. Pass through a Gothic arch in the historic city wall with a self-service stamp under the arch.

Picturesque Cirauqui
perched on a hill

Leaving Cirauqui descend via a Roman road to a restored Roman bridge (8.2km). Continue along a dirt path passing under the raised cement aquaduct Canal de Alloz (11.9km) and then over the Río Salado on a medieval bridge (12.1km). The trail then passes under both highways (A-12 and N-111) to enter Lorca.

13.4 Lorca: The 12th-century **Iglesia de San Salvador** features an 18th-century retablo including a Santiago Peregrino image. The *Codex Calixtinus* says that at Lorca hapless pilgrims would unknowingly water their horses in the poisonous Río Salado. Navarran men would lie in wait to skin the horses once they died. *From Lorca, follow the dirt path parallel to the highway until passing underneath (16.5km) and descending into Villatuerta.*

18.1 Villatuerta: In Villatuerta, the beautiful 14th-century **Iglesia La Asunción** is worth visiting, the retablo illustrates a battle between Moors and Christians. *[Just after the church the ⚠ alternate stage 6A via Zaraputz and Luquín veers to the L, marked by a small sign (p. 94).]*

Traditional door in Mañeru

13.4 Lorca A H ⓘ ▮▮ 🚌
Pop. 135, 🏛 Arabic: *al-aurque* "battle"
A H La Bodega del Camino (priv, 🛏30, dm €8, dbl €40): ▮▮ Ⓚ Ⓦ Ⓓ 🅿(free), c/Placeta 8, 🕐948-541162 📷, 🕐all year
A H Albergue de Lorca (priv, 🛏14, dm €7, dbl €20): Ⓚ Ⓦ 🖥 📶, c/Mayor 40, 🕐948-541190, 🕐Apr 1-Oct 31

18.1 Villatuerta A ▮▮ 🚌 ✚ 🅔 🚌 Pop. 1,122, 🏛 Latin: *vilatorta* "twisted village"
A ☆ Albergue de Villatuerta (priv, 🛏40, € 10): Ⓚ Ⓦ Ⓓ 🖥, c/Rebote 5, 🕐948-536095 📷, 🕐Apr 15- Nov, beautifully restored building, massage therapy, dog and cat on premises

Leaving Villatuerta, there is an optional detour to the **Ermita de San Miguel (19.1km, +200m)**, normally open and the table overflows with handwritten prayers to the saint in many languages. *After a picnic area, a new underpass at the highway (19.3km) was precipitated by the death of a Canadian pilgrim in 2002 who was struck by a car (above the underpass there is a memorial made by her husband). Follow a dirt path, which will cross over the Río Ega and enter Estella through a park along the river's shores. Continue straight for the municipal albergue, or cross the stone bridge for other albergues.*

☀ If taking the full alternate stage 6A via Luquín, you'll want to stay overnight in Villatuerta as there are no accommodations until Los Arcos.

21.8 **Estella** A H🏠▦☕☎✚€🅘⛺🚌 Pop. 14,251, 🅱 Basque *Lizarra:* "old church" 🅲 Latin *stellae:* "

1. **A** **Albergue de Peregrinos de Estella** (muni, 🛏96, €6): 🅺🆆🅳▦📶, c/de la Rua 50, 📞948-55020●
☉all year except Dec 19 & Jan 15, crowded rooms, outdoor patio area

2. **A** **Albergue ANFAS** (priv, 🛏34, €7): 🅺🆆🅳▦(free), c/Cordeleros 7, 📞669-114522 📱,
☉noon, May-Sept, employs developmentally challenged young adults

3. **A** **Albergue Parroquial San Miguel** (par, 🛏36, don): 🕪☕🆆, Mercado Viejo 18,
📞948-550431 📱, ☉1pm Easter-Nov, communal meals

4. **H A** **Oncineda** (youth hostel, 🛏95, dm €9.90, dbl €27): 🕪☕🆆🅳, c/Monasterio de Irache,
📞948-555022 📱, ☉closed Dec & Mar

5. **H** **San Andrés** (dbl €32-40): Plaza Santiago 58, 📞948-554158

6. **H** **Cristina** (dbl €45): c/Baja Navarra 1, 📞948-550450

7. **H** **Fonda Izarra** (dbl €30): c/Alderería 20, 📞948-550678

8. **H** **Apartamentos Gebala** (dbl €78): Plaza de los Fueros 31, 📞606-980675 📱

9. **H** **Chapitel** (dbl €90): ▦📶, c/Chapitel 1, 📞948-551090 📱

10. **⛺ H A** **Camping Lizarra** (dm €9/tent €11): 🕪📶▬, Paraje Ordoiz, 📞948-551733 📱, off-route

21.8 **Estella**: Development began under King Sancho Ramírez in the early 11th century, after a shooting star led to a Virgin Mary statue in a cave (Basílica del Puy houses the statue). Sancho encouraged French settlement and the town flourished with vibrant pilgrim business and agriculture, and textile industries of wool and leather. The town grew wealthy and important religious and civic institutions were built, giving the nickname *Estella la bella* ("Estella the beautiful").

As in Pamplona, ethnic neighborhoods grew up, separating Navarros, Francos and Jews. By the 14th century, Jews made up 10% of the population. In 1328 much of the Jewish community was massacred in a riot, and the rest were forced to convert in the 15th-century Inquisition. The Black Plague halved the population of Estella in the 14th century.

Houses line the
Ega River in Estella

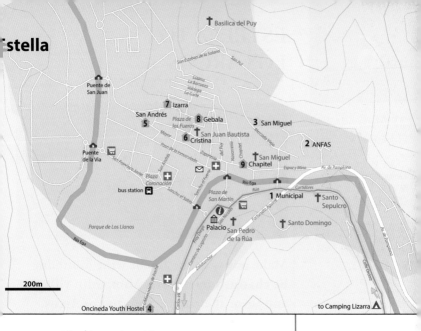

Estella

- **Basílica del Puy** †
- **Puente de San Juan** 🏛
- **7** Izarra
- **San Andrés** 🏛
- **5**
- **8** Gebala
- Plaza de los Fueros
- **3** San Miguel
- **6** Cristina
- **San Juan Bautista** †
- **Puente de la Vía** 🏛
- **2** ANFAS
- San Miguel **†** Chapitel
- **9**
- Plaza Coronación 🏥
- bus station 🚌
- Río Ega
- Rúa
- **1** Municipal
- Santo Sepulcro †
- Plaza de San Martín
- ℹ️
- **Palacio** 🏛 San Pedro de la Rúa †
- Santo Domingo †
- Parque de Los Llanos
- Río Ega
- **200m**
- 🏥
- Oncineda Youth Hostel **4**
- to Camping Lizarra ⛺

Historic Churches and Buildings:

- **Iglesia de Santo Sepulcro**: On the R as you enter town, this façade shows Santiago among the apostles.
- 🏛 **Palacio de los Reyes de Navarra/Museo Gustavo de Maeztu**: 🕐Tu-S 11am-1pm, 5-7pm; Su 11am-1:30pm 📷 Interesting example of civil Romanesque architecture, note the fine capitals that depict deadly sins and the battle of Roland and Ferragut (p. 108).
- **Iglesia de San Pedro de la Rúa**: An impressive 12/13th-century fortified church that contains important relics, such as a piece of the true cross and Saint Andrew's shoulder bone.
- **Iglesia de San Miguel**: A fortress-like 12th-century church with a spectacular north portal.
- **Iglesia de San Juan Bautista**: Built by Sancho el Fuerte and containing images of Santiago Peregrino.
- **Basílica del Puy**: Built on the spot that legend holds a Virgin was found in 1085; the wooden silver-covered statue is still on display within.

🛏 **Estella**
Aug: Patron saint San Andrés w/running of the bulls
May 25: Virgen del Puy with traditional dances
Thurs is market day.
Suckling pig is a local delicacy (*gorrín asado*).

ESTELLA TO LOS ARCOS

21.6km
(13.4mi)

⏱ **5-6 Hours**
Difficulty: ▢▢▢
🅿 22%, 4.7km
Ⓤ 78%, 16.9km

A Albergues:
Ayegui 1.6km
Villamayor 9.2km
<u>Los Arcos 21.6km</u>
Sansol 28.4km
Torres del Río 29.3km

·························

⚠ **Alt. Stage 6A:**
Villatuerta or Irache
to Los Arcos, 23.4km
(p. 94)

6A Alternate:
🅿 8%, 1.9km
Ⓤ 92%, 21.5km

A Alt. Albergues:
<u>Los Arcos 23.4km</u>

Fuente de los Moros
outside of Villamayor

Make merry at the Irache wine fountain, be charmed by historic Monjardin village and savor the remote path to Los Arcos.

🔆 More rolling red hills and vineyards lead to a place of camino legend, the Irache wine fountain. Villamayor de Monjardín provides a welcome halfway stop, with an imposing castle on the hilltop above and a historic fountain at the entrance. The last 12km are remote and beautiful, but be prepared for no services and little shade. The alternate route via Luquín offers a more remote but demanding path with hilltop views, which rejoins the main trail after Villamayor.

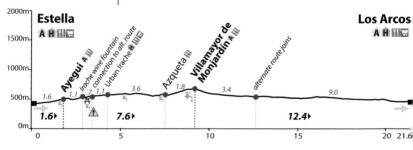

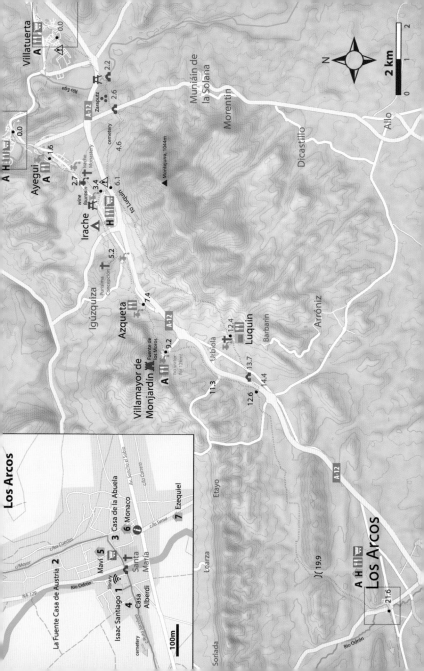

Villatuerta

A ▥ 0.0

A H ▥ 0.0

Río Ega

🚂 2.2

A-12 Zarapuz

🚂 2.6

Ayegui

A ▥ 1.6

cemetery 4.6

Irache 2.7

wine fountain Irache Monastery 3.4

fountain 6.1

a Laguna, a umbral

A H ▥

Muniáin de la Solana

Morentin

▲ Montejurra, 1044m

Dicastillo

Allo

N

2 km
0 1 2

Igúzquiza

Purísima Concepción ✝ 5.2

Azqueta ▥ 7.4

A-12

Villamayor de Monjardín Fuente de los Moros 9.2

A ▥ no water for 12km!

Urbiola 11.3

Luquin ▥ 12.4

Barbarin

12.6 14.4 13.7

Arróniz

Etayo

Ledarza

A-12

🚶 19.9

Sorlada

Los Arcos

A H ▥
21.6

Río Odrón

Los Arcos

NA-129

La Fuente Casa de Austria **2**

Isaac Santiago **1**

c/Mayor

Maví **5**

library

Casa Alberdi **4**

cemetery

c/las Cuestas

3 Casa de la Abuela

6 Monaco

Av. Sancho El Sabio

c/La Carrera

c/La Serna

Santa María

Río Odrón

7 Ezequiel

100m

1.6 **Ayegui** A ⓗ 🅿 Pop. 1,932
A **Albergue San Cipriano** (muni, 🛏70 mats, €6):
ⓘ W 🅳, 🕿948-554331 🗺, 🕐1pm all year

3.8 **Irache** ⓗ ⓘ 🍴 ⛺ Pop. 426
ⓗ **Hotel Irache** (dbl €88): Av. Prado de Irache 7,
🕿948-551150 🗺
ⓗ **Camping Iratxe** (camping/bungalows €28-95):
ⓘ 🛒 🚿, Av. Prado de Irache, 🕿948-555555 🗺

The plaque on the wall at the wine fountain reads:
"Pilgrim, if you wish to arrive at Santiago full of strength and vitality, have a drink of this great wine and make a toast to happiness."

Irache Wine Fountain

0.0 *The way out of Estella is well-marked along c/Rua to c/San Nicolás, straight through the first roundabout, and to the R at the next roundabout. Take c/Camino uphill toward* **Ayegui** *(1.6km) near the albergue, and as you descend out of town the impressive Irache monastery looms ahead.*

2.7 **The Irache monastery**
dates back to the year 958, with a pilgrim hospital added in the 11th century and cloisters added in the 16th and 17th centuries. The historic building is scheduled to become a luxury Parador hotel. *Leave town and cross N-1110 onto a dirt path, which will lead you to* **Irache Winery** *(2.7km), where a free wine fountain delights visitors* 🕐8am-8pm, *and festivities can even be watched via webcam* 🗺. *Wine museum is open* 🕐10am-2pm. *[⚠ Just after the winery, there is an opportunity to cross over to the Luquín alternate route (p. 94) or to return from that route to the main route. The main route*

turns R, while the alternate route con-
tinues straight. Anticipate this junction
as the intuitive turn is the more remote
alternate route 6A described on p. 94.]

Re-cross N-111a and pass by **Hotel**
Irache and Camping Iratxe (3.8km)
before walking through lovely shaded
forests on a dirt path. A short detour
(+450m) leads to the small Ermita de
Purísima Concepcion (5.2km) usually
closed. Pass through **Azqueta (7.4km,**
no services except a rarely open café),
and continue on dirt road through

Fuente de los Moros
near Villamayor

expansive agricultural land past the **Fuente de los Moros**
(8.8km), *a Gothic fountain associated with the moors (rebuilt*
from an earlier fountain or simply misattributed).

9.2 Villamayor de Monjardín
is a picturesque small town with a
popular café for a pick-me-up afternoon coffee or snack. Romanesque
Iglesia de San Andrés contains a
processional cross from the year
1200. Legend has it that Charlemagne battled for the town and
wrested it from the Muslim army.
Charlemange asked God which of
his soldiers would die in the battle,
and a red cross marked the heads of
150 soldiers. Charlemagne had all
the ill-fated men stay back at their
encampment, but he returned to
find they had all died in a fire.

9.2 Villamayor de Monjardín A H 🏠🔲
Pop. 139, 🖹 Latin: "Mount García" for Sancho
Garcés, first king of Pamplona

A Hogar de Monjardín (assoc, 🛏25, €7): 🍴,
across from San Andrés church, ☎948-537136,
🕓4pm, fireplace, run by Dutch Christian assoc,
simple and cozy 🖻

A H Villamayor de Monjardín (priv, 🛏20, dm
€15, dbl €40 w/ 🛁 and sheets): ❋🆆🅳🏠(free),
c/Mayor 1, ☎677-660586, 🕓1pm, Mar-Nov 🖻

H Casa Rural Montedeio (sng €30, dbl €45): ❋🆆,
c/Mayor 17, ☎676-187473 🖻

Cyclists on the path
between Villamayor
and Los Arcos

91

Leaving Los Arcos

On the way out of town, the large warehouse visible below is Castillo de Monjardín winery, known for its whites. The 🏛 **Castillo de San Esteban** looming over the town can be visited via a small road (ask at the bar for the key to the castle if you have the energy to make the trek).

⚠ Be sure to rest and fill up water in Monjardín, as the next 12km have little shade and no services. While the terrain is not very challenging, the town of Los Arcos is tucked away in a valley and not visible until arriving, this section can feel interminable!

*Continue on dirt paths, crossing a paved road (11.3km), and meet the junction of the **alternate from Luquín (12.6km)** near a highway underpass. Take dirt paths through the beautiful valley to cross a small pass (19.9km). At the entrance to Los Arcos (20.7km) is a rest stop with shelter and extensive vending machines. The municipal albergue (21.6km) is just beyond the church across the river.*

21.6 Los Arcos A H 🛏🍴➕€ⓘ🏧

Pop. 1,244, 🏴 Spanish: "the bows"
ⓘ Plaza Fueros, ☎948-640077, 📶 at library

1. **A Isaac Santiago** (muni, 🛏70, €6): 🖼🔲,
   c/San Lázaro, ☎948-441091/948-640230,
   🕐12pm, Apr-Oct 30, garden, crowded rooms
2. **A H La Fuente Casa de Austria** (priv, 🛏54,
   dm €9, dbl €30): 🖼🔲⬛📶, Travesía del Estanco 5, ☎948-640797, 🕐1pm, Feb-Dec
3. **A H ☆ Casa de la Abuela** (priv, 🛏38, dm €9,
   dbl €45): 🖼🔲📶🔲(free), Plaza de la Fruta 8,
   ☎948-640250 📱, 🕐12pm Mar-Oct, restored
   house of owner's grandmother
4. **A H Casa Alberdi** (priv, 🛏30, dm €10,
   dbl €36): 🖼🔲🔲📶, c/Hortal 3, ☎650-965250
   📱, 🕐2pm all year
5. **H Mavi** (dbl €50): 📶, c/del Medio 7,
   ☎608-934222 📱
6. **H Monaco** (dbl €55): Plaza del Coso 1,
   ☎948-640000 📱
7. **H Hostal Ezequiel** (dbl €55): 🍴, c/La Serna,
   ☎948-640107 📱

21.6 **Los Arcos** occupies an ideal location by the Río Odrón and at the crossroads of two ancient trade routes, and was once a Roman city (Curnonium). The current name comes from a battle in 914 when three Sanchos (the kings of Navarra, Castilla and Aragon) fought over the town. The Navarran army won with the help of their excellent archers, therefore the coat of arms of the city contains bows (*arcos*) and arrows. In medieval times, the city was a place for toll collection and changing money. Los Arcos flourished as a market town, becoming quite wealthy with all this pilgrim commerce.

The main historical site is the **Iglesia de Santa María de la Asunción**, which contains one of the most ornate retablos on the entire Camino Francés. *Santa María de los Arcos* occupies the central position; look also for Santiago (with crystal eyes) as well as a pelican (a symbol of Jesus' sacrifice often seen in religious art). A shaft of sunlight naturally illuminated the retablo once a year in the summer.

Luminous retablo of Iglesia de Santa María de Los Arcos

Pilgrims eating together at Casa de la Abuela

🛐 **Los Arcos**
Spring: Small bull-running festival
Aug 14-20: Santa María patron saint day
Sat is market day.
Rosquillos de Los Arcos are a local specialty of small donuts made with orange juice.

⚠ Alternate Stage 6A: Luquín Route
Villatuerta to Los Arcos (via Irache & Luquín), 23.4km

This waymarked alternate route follows an earlier pilgrim way, which later was routed through Estella as pilgrim services developed there. This route is more remote with fewer walkers and services. A short path (+350m) connects this route to the main route near the Irache Monastery (p. 90), and so it is possible to switch back to the main route there, or to sleep in Estella and take the Luquín detour from Irache. If starting this route from Villatuerta, there are no accommodations for 23.4km until Los Arcos, unless you return to the main route at Irache. Distances noted are cumulative from the split in Villatuerta.

☼ This alternate route via Luquín is 1.8km longer than stage 6 from Estella to Los Arcos with more elevation change.

The only chances to refill water between Villatuerta and Los Arcos are near Irache (6.2km, slightly off-route) and Luquín, 12.3km.

Maps for this route are primarily on the stage 6 map, with the first junction in detail on the Villatuerta map (p. 83).

0.0 **Villatuerta:** *In Villatuerta, turn L at the church toward Zarapuz (note the split shown on the blazes on the building after the church). Leave town through an industrial area on dirt paths through agricultural fields fed by cement canals. After two underpasses, cross a bridge over the **Río Ega (2.2km)**; turn R to cross the bridge (not well marked), and R again immediately on a dirt path directly after the bridge. The path will lead by agricultural fields and uphill to the ∵ ruins of Zarapuz.*

2.6 **Zarapuz** was a 15th-century medieval pilgrim albergue. *From the ruins, the trail continues upward to offer a remarkable view of Estella. Cross the highway on a **bridge (3.3km)**, and curve R on 4X4 tracks through vineyards. At a paved road by a cemetery, continue straight (4.6km, not marked), then turn L on a dirt path (5.0km, well marked) and take a quick R toward the silver water tower. Turn R at the next trail marker and pass between the line of trees on L and wheat field on R. Cross a paved road (5.4km) and enter a forested area. At the **signpost for Irache and Los Arcos (6.1km)**, either continue to the L to Los Arcos or take the underpass down to Irache to join the more traditional route (and visit the wine fountain, +1km).*

Medieval pilgrim hospital ruins at Zarapuz

Continue following way-marks toward Los Arcos through forest. After leaving the forest, turn L on a dirt road (7.7km) and note the view of Monjardín castle ahead. When the dirt road curves to the R, continue straight on smaller dirt 4X4 (8.1km). Turn L on dirt one-lane road and leave the forest to walk along the line of trees for open valley views (8.9km). Continue uphill to a ridge with some miscellaneous ruins (10.8km), and follow the footpath straight ahead downhill to the village of Luquín.

The winding trail of the Luquín route

12.4 Luquín 🏠🍴 Pop. 138

Luquín is home to the medieval Iglesia de San Martín Obispo and 18th-century Basílica de Nuestra Señora de los Remedio. The basilica houses two images of the Virgin Mary that, according to legend, were found by a farmer plowing his field. The images were initially split up in order to house one in Luquín and one in nearby Villamayor. However, the second virgin kept reappearing in Luquín with a drop of blood, so the towns decided the two must remain together.

*Pass by the Plaza de los Fueros past a natural spring, the municipal pool and a café. Cross the paved road leaving town (c/Carretera) and go straight on a cement road, which turns to dirt as you leave town. Turn R at the sign for "10.2km to Los Arcos" (13.1km), follow markings across a paved road and over a small **bridge (13.7km)**. Turn L on a gravel road parallel to the highway and use the underpass to the R (14.3km). Rejoin the main trail at **signpost "9km to Los Arcos" (14.4km)** and turn L to continue for the remaining 9km to Los Arcos on the main route on stage 6, p. 92.*

LOS ARCOS TO LOGROÑO

27.6km
(17.1mi)

🕐 **7-8 HOURS**
DIFFICULTY: ▭▭☐
🅿 41%, 11.4km
Ⓤ 59%, 16.2km

A ALBERGUES:
Sansol 6.8km
Torres del Río 7.7km
Viana 18.4km
Logroño 27.6km
Navarrete 40.2km

A pilgrim approaches
the picturesque
medieval town of
Sansol

Wander through vineyards and fields of golden wheat, visit medieval villages and sample the wine of la Rioja.

☀ Endless fields of golden wheat lead to the hilltop medieval towns of Sansol and Torres del Río. The rolling hills to Viana have a remote feel with little shade and no services. From Viana to Logroño the trail passes through a bird-watching area and enters into the autonomous region of La Rioja, best known for its superlative red wine.

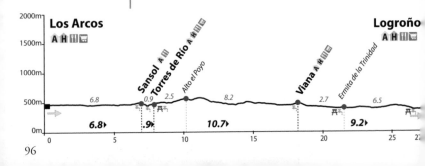

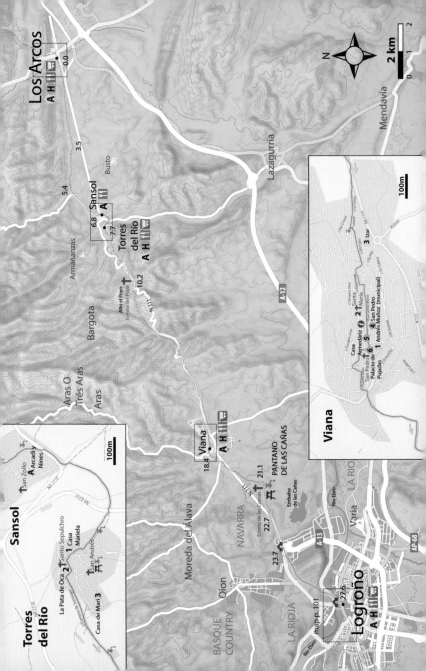

Los Arcos

A H 🏨🍴 0.0

3.5

5.4

Armañanzas

Busto

Lazagurría

Sansol
A 🏨🍴 6.8

7.7 Torres del Río
A H 🏨🍴

Aras O
Três Aras
Aras

Bargota

Alto el Poyo
Ermita del Poyo 10.2
N-111

A-12

Viana
A H 🏨🍴 18.4

21.1

22.7 Ermita de las Cuevas
PANTANO
DE LAS CAÑAS
Embalse
de las Cañas

NAVARRA

Moreda del Álava

Oion

BASQUE
COUNTRY

23.7

A-13

27.6 map p. 101
A H 🏨🍴

Logroño

Varia LA RIO

Río Ebro

LA RIOJA

AP-68

Mendavia

N

2 km
0 1 2

Viana

100m

3 Izar

Santa
María 2 1

Casa
Armendáriz
San Pedro 6 5 4 San Andrés Muñoz (municipal)
Palacio de 1 Andrés Pujadas

Sansol

100m

San Zoilo A Arcadi y
Nines

La Pata de Oca 2 Santo Sepulchro
1 Casa
Mariela

San Andrés

Casa de Mari 3

Torres del Río

6.8 **Sansol** A ▯▯✚▯ Pop. 112, ⬛ S. Zoilo, a Cordoban martyr under Diocletian persecution
  A **Arcadi y Nines** (priv, 🛏14, €6): ▯▯,
    c/Tacorena 10, ☎618-197520, ⏰12pm Apr-Oct

7.7 **Torres del Río** A ▯▯▯✚●▯▯▯
Pop. 156, ⬛ Spanish: "towers of the river"
1. A **H** **Casa Mariela** (priv, 🛏50, dm €7, dbl €35):
   ▯▯▯📶, Plaza Padre Valeriano Ordóñez 6,
   ☎948-648251 ⏰10am, all year
2. A **H** **Pata de Oca** (priv, 🛏32, dm €10, dbl €60):
   ▯▯▯▯, c/Mayor 5, ☎948-378457 📷 ⏰all year
3. A **Casa de Mari** (priv, 🛏26, €7): ▯▯, c/Casas
   Nuevas 13, ☎948-648409, ⏰10:30am all year

Iglesia del Santo Sepulcro in Torres del Río

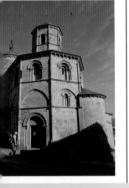

0.0 *From the municipal albergue of Los Arcos, turn R and leave town on wide dirt path past a cemetery (note cryptic inscription, "I once was what you are, you will be what I am,") and through vast vineyards. Turn R at a well-marked footpath (3.5km) before turning L on a paved road (5.4km) into the village of Sansol.*

6.8 **Sansol** has the simple Iglesia de San Zoilo, with a marvelous view of Torres del Río. *Cross the paved road outside of Sansol, and turn R to walk along the road. Turn L off of the main road (7.0km) onto a smaller road, then take a quick R onto a paved footpath, which later becomes dirt. Enter the outskirts of adjacent Torres del Río, where a natural spring 🚰 beckons pilgrims to refreshment.*

7.7 **Torres del Río**: Visit the unusual octagonal church (similar to Eunate) of **Santo Sepulchre** (€1). The origins of the church are unknown, but it is thought to be associated with the Templar Knights. The outside corbels show animals and plants, while the interior altar niche resembles a *mihrab*, or Muslim prayer niche. The 16th-century Iglesia San Andres has a picnic area and water. Torres also made an appearance in the film *The Way*, where Martin Sheen's character tries to stay in the house of Ramón, who turns out to be mentally ill (a

true story adapted from Jack Hitt's camino memoir *Off the Road*). *Leaving town, pass a cemetery with water, and the trail becomes unpaved with no shade. Continue on dirt paths near a paved road, past the hermitage at Alto el Poyo (10.2km).*

10.2 **Alto el Poyo**: **Capilla de la Virgen del Poyo** contains a statue of Mary that was said to continue returning to this spot even after being relocated many times. *Follow mostly dirt paths through rolling hills and vineyards, eventually along N-111 into Viana, passing a mural of the pilgrimage road. Take c/Algorrada through an arch to Rua de Santa Maria and to the café-lined Plaza de Fueros.*

Hikers between Torres del Río and Sansol

18.4 **Viana**, a delightful walled town with a bustling downtown and many attractive cafés, is best known as the final resting place of Navarran hero Cesare Borgia who died at the siege of Viana. Visit **Iglesia de Santa María de la Asunción**, with a retablo of Santiago in the ambulatory. Ruins of 13th-century **Iglesia de San Pedro** have been turned into an interesting municipal park with Gothic architecture. *Leaving Viana on c/Fuente Vieja, the trail continues through the pleasant wetlands of Pantano de las Cañas.*

18.4 **Viana** A H ▦▦+●❶▢ Pop. 4,018
1. **A** **Andrés Muñoz** (muni, ➽54 in triple bunks, €6): ▦▦▦▦▦, c/Ruinas de San Pedro, ☏948-645530, ☉Mar 15-Oct
2. **A** **Parroquial de Viana** (par, ➽15 mats, don): ▦▦, Plaza de los Fueros, ☏948-645037, communal meals, simple and caring, ☉June 15-Sept
3. **A** **Izar** (priv, ➽44, dm €8-10, dbl €30): ▦▦▦▦🛜, c/El Cristo 6, ☏660-071349 ☑, ☉noon Mar-Nov
4. **H** **San Pedro** (sng €30, dbl €40): c/Medio San Pedro 13, ☏948-446221 ☑
5. **H** **Casa Armendáriz** (dbl €40): c/Navarro Villoslada 19, ☏948-645078 ☑
6. **H** **Palacio de Pujadas** (dbl €80): c/Navarro Villoslada 30, ☏948-646464 ☑

99

☼ Just before the bridge, on the L is a **pilgrim information office** 🛈 w/lockers and maps. (🕐 Nov-Mar M-Sa 12-4pm, Apr-Oct 9am-2pm)

♨ **Logroño**
Sept: Fiesta de San Mateo, a wine festival featuring grape crushing exhibitions

Santiago Matamoros at Iglesia de Santiago in Logroño

21.1 **Pantano de las Cañas** an important bird migration area well known for bird watching. Pass the inviting chapel of the **Ermita de la Trinidad de las Cuevas (21.1km)** with picnic area. *The natural path soon turns to asphalt and joins N-111 (22.7km) through an industrial area. Pass the sign "2km to Logroño," which is also the boundary of entering **La Rioja region (23.7km)**. On the outskirts of Logroño, a classic camino character named Doña Felisa used to set up a table by the camino that offered "higos, agua y amor" ("figs, water and love"—the inscription on her stamp) to passing pilgrims. She died in 2003, but her daughter carries on the tradition. Cross the long 19th-century **Puente de Piedra (27.3km)** over the Río Ebro to enter Logroño. The bridge was originally built in the 11th century by Santo Domingo de la Calzada (p. 114) and rebuilt by his disciple San Juan de Ortega (p. 126).*

27.6 **Logroño** is the capital of the winemaking region of La Rioja. With its strategic location on the banks of the Río Ebro and right along the border between Aragón, Navarra and Castile y León, it's no wonder why Logroño was a much fought-over commodity. Constant warfare may be a reason that practically nothing remains of the many medieval pilgrim hospitals. Logroño is mentioned in pilgrim records as a place where a duty of two *reales* was collected.

The main churches to visit are **Iglesia de Santa María la Redonda** ("Saint Mary the Round"), with Baroque façade and stork-topped spires. **Iglesia de San Bartolomé** from the 13th century and **Iglesia de Santiago el Real**, with an impressive 17th-century Santiago Matamoros above the entrance and numerous Santiago images within. On the sidewalk just before Iglesia de Santiago, there is a large game called *Juego de Oca,* which is similar to Chutes and Ladders. *Calle Laurel* is the nightlife zone with over 60 bars and restaurants, locally known as

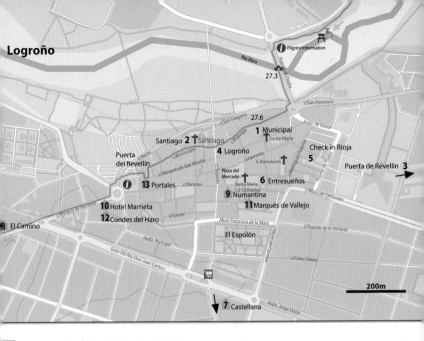

Logroño

7.6 Logroño A H 🏠🍽🍷✚€ℹ️▲🏧✈️ Pop. 152,641, 🏳️ Celtic-Latin, *ilo Gronnio*: "ford/pass"

A Municipal (↩68, €7): 🏠Ⓦ🅳♨️, Rua Vieja 32, ☎941-248686/941-275982, 🕐Mar-Oct, crowded & stuffy, no alcohol rule, courtyard with foot pool

A Iglesia de Santiago (par, ↩20, don): 🍽, 🕐Jun-Sep, sign on church door, communal meals

A Puerta del Revellín (priv, ↩40, €10.5): 🏠Ⓦ, Plaza Martínez Flamarique 4, ☎941-700832 📇, 🕐11am all year

A H Alb. Logroño (priv, ↩48, dm €10, sng €20, dbl €30): 🏠🛜, c/Sagasta 10, ☎941-254226 📇

A Check In Rioja (priv, ↩30, €10): 🏠Ⓦ🅳🛜, c/Los Baños 2, ☎941-272329, 🕐1pm Mar-Oct 📇

A Hostel Entresueños (youth hostel, ↩90, dm €14 pilgrims): 🛜, c/Portales 12, ☎941-271334 📇

H Castellana (dbl €35): c/San Anton 17, ☎941-251369 📇

H El Camino (sng €29, dbl €44): 🍽🏠🛜, Industria 2, ☎606-735862 📇

H Numantina (dbl €59): c/Sagasta 4, ☎941-251411 📇

. H Hotel Murrieta (dbl €60): 🍽🛜, Marqués de Murrieta 1, ☎941-224150 📇

. H Marqués de Vallejo (dbl €68): 🛜, c/Marqués de Vallejo 8, ☎941-248333 📇

. H Condes de Haro (dbl €70): 🍽🛜, Saturnino Ulargui 6, ☎941-208500 📇

. H Portales (dbl €75): Portales 85, ☎941-502794 📇

. H ▲ La Playa (bungalows, dbl €48, tent €12): Av. de la Playa 6, ☎941-252253 📇, +850m

"*la senda de los elefantes*" (the elephant walk), since sampling wine in too many establishments may have you walking out on all fours. The town of Clavijo, where the mythical Battle of Clavijo took place, is located about 16km from Logroño and makes an interesting side trip by bus.

LA RIOJA & CASTILLA Y LEÓN

El Cid

Rodrigo Díaz de Vivar was a medieval Spanish military leader born near Burgos in 1043, now considered the national hero of Spain. His nickname, El Cid, means "the master." Many legends tell of his exploits in battle along with his trusty warhorse Babieca and his sword, Tizona. His exploits are extolled in *El Cantar de Mio Cid*, one of the earliest examples of Spanish epic poetry.

Highlights include beautiful vineyards, superlative wine and extensive sections of Roman road.

Shortly after Viana, the camino enters the autonomous region of La Rioja and its capital, Logroño. The climate becomes more Mediterranean in La Rioja, and the deep red earth is ideal for the cultivation of wine grapes. The region has produced wine since the time of the Romans, and was improved by French immigrants who relocated here after their vines were devastated by the Phylloxera blight.

While white and rosé wines are also produced, of the 250 million liters (66 millions gallons) produced annually, 85% are reds, especially from the Tempranilla grape. La Rioja has one of the highest per capita incomes in Spain, in part thanks to its successful wine industry, with over 500 wineries in commission.

There are four classifications of Riojan wine: *Rioja* is the youngest and aged less than one year; *Crianza* is aged at least 2 with at least 1 in oak barrels, *Rioja Reserva* is aged at least 3 years with 1 in oak barrels, and *Rioja Gran Reserva* is aged at least 2 years in oak and 3 in the bottle.

The climate is also amenable to wheat, olives and vegetables, particularly the plump stalks of white asparagus common to the region. In spring and summer, huge storks seem to make their nest on every available church spire. Local culinary specialties include potato stew with spicy *chorizo* sausage, and *cordero lechal*, thick slices of young lamb roasted over a fire with grapevine in the fire for a smoky flavor. Baked apples and peaches in wine sauce are both popular desserts.

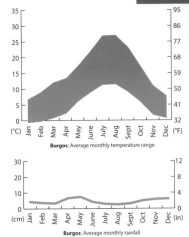

Burgos: Average monthly temperature range

Burgos: Average monthly rainfall

Shortly after Grañon, the trail enters Castilla y León, the largest autonomous region in Spain in which almost exactly half of the Camino Francés is located. With its large size of over 94,000km² and population of over 2.5 million, the region is very diverse. In this geographic section, the camino climbs the

Grapes ready for harvest

scrubby Oca mountains by historic San Juan de Ortega monastery and passes by the prehistoric site of Atapuerca to enter Burgos. The camino stays in Castilla y León until crossing into Galicia just before O Cebreiro (p. 230).

Red earth vineyard views in La Rioja (opposite)

103

29.6km
(18.4mi)

⏱ **7-9 HOURS**
DIFFICULTY: ◼️◻️◻️
🅿 40%, 11.9km
🆄 60%, 17.7km

A ALBERGUES:
Navarrete 12.6km
Ventosa 19.4km
Nájera 29.6km
Azofra 35.4km

Golden wheat between Navarrete and Ventosa

Stroll through a pleasant reservoir park, peek in the church of Navarrete with its spectacular golden retablo, lounge by the river of Nájera.

☀️ A rolling stage with a mix of natural walking paths and sections on or close to roads. After Logroño, there is a pleasant stretch through a green park with a reservoir lake. The path is close to the highway between Navarrete and Ventosa and the approach to Nájera is decidedly industrial, but before Nájera some classic Rioja red earth vineyards can be seen.

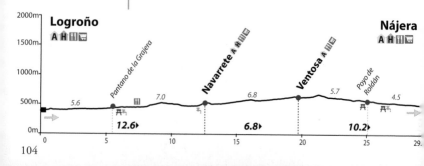

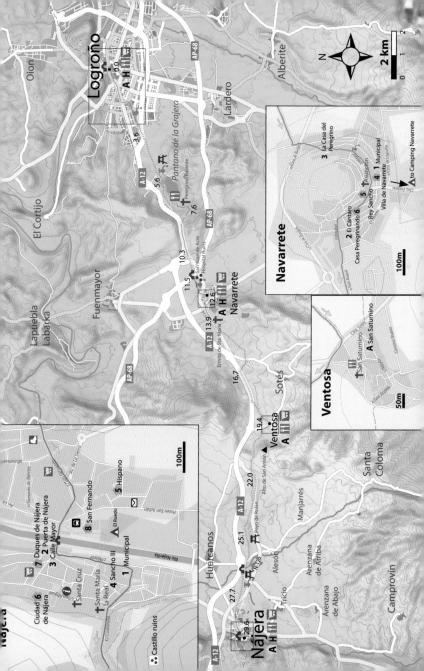

Logroño

Ojón

Alberite

Lardero

N

2 km
0 1 2

AP-68

El Cortijo

A-12

Pantano de la Grajera

0.0 A H

3.6

5.6

7.6

Peregrino/Basante

A-12

Fuenmayor

10.3

San Juan de Acre
Hospal Ruins

11.5

12.6

A-12 13.9

Ermita de Sta. María

AP-68

Lapuebla
Labarca

AP-68

Navarrete

16.7

Sotés

19.4 Ventosa
A

Alto de San Antón

22.0

A-12

Manjarrés

Huércanos

25.1

Pozo de Rolán

A120

Alesón

Tricio

Arenzana
de Arriba

Arenzana
de Abajo

Santa
Coloma

Camprovín

27.7

A-12 29.6

Nájera
A H

Navarrete

100m

3 La Casa del
Peregrino

Asunción

4 1 Municipal

5 Rey Sancho

Villa de Navarrete

2 El Cántaro

Casa Peregrinando 6

to Camping Navarrete

Ventosa

50m

San Saturnino

A San Saturnino

Nájera

Ciudad 6
de Nájera

7 Duques de Nájera

2 Puerta de Nájera

3 Calle Mayor

8 San Fernando

5 Hispano

4 Sancho III

1 Municipal

Santa Cruz

Santa María
la Real

El Ruedo

Paseo San Julián

Río Najerilla

100m

Castillo ruins

Golden retablo in
Iglesia de la Asunción
in Navarrete

🏔 **Navarrete:**
Mid-August: Fiesta del
Virgen
Wed market day.

0.0 *Leave Logroño (map p. 101) by following brass inlaid scallop shells along the sidewalk on c/Rúaviejo past Iglesia de Santiago and leave the Old City via the stone Puerta de Revellín arch (0.4km), the only remaining original entryway to the Old City. Walk L across the parking lot to the roundabout, and go R on c/Marqués de Murrieta. Turn L on c/Duques de Nájera (1.6km). Cross over the train tracks (2km) and out of town through a park. Pass under the highway (3.6km) and split off to the L through fields.*

5.6 **Pantano de la Grajera:** Soon enter a wetland park centered around a water reservoir where locals often fish on a lazy afternoon. The park contains picnic areas, an inexpensive café and public WC. *Reach **Ermita del Peregrino Pasante (7.6km)**, "Hermitage of the Passing Pilgrim," and turn R on the paved road, which leads out to parallel the highway for a stretch, where pilgrims have woven crosses of sticks and grasses into the chain link fence.* ⚠ *Cross N-120 (10.3km) and continue on the R side before splitting to the R through fields and over another highway on a green bridge (11.2km). After the bridge, the ruins of the **Hospital de San Juan de Acre (11.5km)** can be seen to the L. Continue straight to Navarrete.*

12.6 **Navarrete** A H � ⊞ ➕ ⊛ ⓘ ▲ 🅿
Pop 2,865, 🏳 "little Navarra" or "gateway to Navarra"
ⓘ c/Cuesta Caño 🕗941-441062 in summer
1. **A Municipal** (🛏50, €7): 🅺🅦🅓, c/San Juan, 🕗941-440722, 🕘2pm, Mar-Oct
2. **A H El Cántaro** (priv, 🛏22, dm €10, dbl €30): 🅐🅦, c/Herrerías 16, 🕗676-642327 ☐', 🕘all year
3. **A H La Casa del Peregrino** (priv, 🛏20, dm €8, sng €15, dbl €25): 🅚🅦🅞🅟🖥📶, c/las Huertas 3, 🕗630-982928 ☐', 🕘Easter-Oct 15
4. **H Villa de Navarrete** (dbl €40): c/La Cruz 2C, 🕗941-440318 ☐'
5. **H Rey Sancho** (dbl €70): 🆔📶, c/Mayor Alta 5, 🕗941-441378 ☐'
6. **H Casa Peregrinando** (dbl €75): 🕗941-440393 ☐'
7. **A Navarrete** (cabin €100, tent €12): 🆔🛒📺🅦📶 ▦, Crta Entrena km 15, 🕗941-440169 ☐'

12.6 **Navarrete** is an attractive town, laid out semi-circularly around the base of a hill. Doors built into the hill are *bodegas* (underground cellars) used for storing Navarrete's specialties: wine and mushrooms. Navarrete is also known for its excellent pottery made with local red clay. Enter **Iglesia de La Asunción**, one of the most impressive Baroque retablos in Spain! Spring the €1 to illuminate and prepare to be dazzled by the golden masterpiece.

*Wind through Navarrete clockwise, emerging on the paved highway (13.1km). At **Ermita de Santa María de Jesús (13.9km)**, which has a lovely Romanesque façade taken from the historic pilgrim hospital, the trail turns to dirt and heads to the L through agricultural fields. Soon the trail parallels the highway again (16.7km), until a dirt path to the L (18.2km) leads to Ventosa.*

Cyclists along the red earth path near Logroño

19.4 **Ventosa** has a church dedicated to **San Saturnino**. *From Ventosa, walk through agricultural fields. To the R, the ruins of a monastery stand on the Alto de Antón. Re-cross the highway (22.0km) to the **Poyo de Roldán picnic area (25.1km)** and monument of the famous battle with Ferragut (p. 108). Cross two small bridges and N-120 (27.7km) before entering the industrial outskirts of Nájera past a large pilgrim poem painted on the side of a building. The main albergue is located on the far side of the city, so you may wish to get groceries or anything else you need from the center before crossing the bridge (29.2km). Turn L along the Río Najerilla for the Nájera municipal albergue.*

19.4 **Ventosa** A 🏠 🛒 🚐 📮

Pop. 169, 🏴 Spanish: "windy"

A **San Saturnino** (priv, 🛏42, €9.5): 🇰 🛒 🇼 🇲 🇩 🛜,
c/Medio Derecha, 🕐941-441899 ✍️, 🕐1pm all
year, fireplace, shop with basic food

Friendly local on horseback ouside of Navarrete

29.6 Nájera A H⋕🍴⚓⛓+🛒❶ⓘ⚠🚌
Pop. 8,452, 🗎 Arabic: "between the rocks"

1. **A Municipal** (🛏90, don): 🚿🅦🅳🅾,
   🕐all year, 1pm summer, 3pm winter, crowded
2. **A H Puerta de Nájera** (priv, 🛏32, dm €10,
   dbl €40): 🅦🅳🅾📶, c/Ribera del Najerilla 1,
   📞941-362317 🗺, 🕐Easter-Oct
3. **A H Calle Mayor** (priv, 🛏17, dm €8, dbl €25):
   🍴, c/Dicarán 5, 📞941-360407, 🕐Easter-Oct
4. **A Sancho III - La Judería** (priv, 🛏10, €8): 🍴,
   c/San Marcial 6, 📞941-361138, 🕐Easter-Oct
5. **H Hispano** (sng €32, dbl €48): c/la Cepa 2,
   📞941-363615 🗺
6. **H Ciudad de Nájera** (dm €17, sng €45, dbl
   €54): Calleja San Miguel 14, 📞941-360660 🗺
7. **H Duques de Nájera** (dbl €65): c/Carmen 7,
   📞941-410421 🗺
8. **H San Fernando** (dbl €80): 📶,
   Paseo de San Julián 1, 📞941-363700 🗺
9. **⛺ Camping El Ruido**: 🍴🛒🅦🚰, Paseo de San
   Julián 24, 📞941-360102 🗺, 🕐Apr-Sept

Virgin Mary statue
discovered in 1044
by Navarran king

29.6 Nájera city is bisected by the Najerilla river, with the historic center built into the jutting red rock. The pleasant grassy banks of the river are perfect for an afternoon picnic or snooze. The main site to visit is the **Monasterio de Santa María la Real** €3, 🕐Tu-S 10am-1pm, 4-7pm, Su 10am-12:30pm, 4-6pm, 📞941-361083 🗺), an 11th-century church built by King Garcia III after a most unusual hunting trip. The story goes that as Garcia hunted partridge along the riverbank, his falcon flew into a nearby cave. Garcia followed and was amazed to find a beautiful statue of the virgin with a vase of fresh lilies and a burning oil lamp. He saw this as a blessing on the Reconquista, and used some of the money he plundered from the Moors to build a church here for the icon. The statue wore a crown of jewels, which was later stolen and divided; the Black Prince Ruby made its way to England's coronation crown!

Visit the arresting virgin statue still in the original cave (in the church), with a statue of a kneeling García outside. The church also serves as a burial place for Navarran royalty, including Garcia III as well as a particularly nice tomb of Sancho III's wife, Doña Blanca. Don't miss the fine filigree work in the arches of the cloister.

The story of **Roland and Ferragut** took place near Nájera, which closely mimics the story of David and Goliath; Ferragut is even described as a descendant of Goliath. The story goes that the giant Ferragut was sent along with 20,000 soldiers from Turkey to fight against Charlemagne's army. Ferragut came out from Nájera, challenging any of the opposition to fight him one-on-one. Many tried and failed. Finally, Roland

Río Najerilla in Nájera

insisted on having his turn and fought with the giant for three days. In between spurts of fighting the two conversed about their respective faiths, and Ferragut revealed that his one weak place (his Achille's heel if you will) was his belly button. A final battle ensued, having both agreed that the winner would be the one espousing the true faith. Ferragut tried to fall on Roland to crush him to death, but Roland stabbed him in the belly and won. Artistic renderings can be found in churches along the way, including San Pedro de Rúa in Estella.

☼ Nájera is an interesting town to explore and has good amenities, but if you have it in you to continue just 5.8km of pleasant walking to Azofra, the municipal albergue has rooms for two for only €7 per person. Worth the extra walk for a night without bunk beds or snorers!

Ornate windows in the cloister of Santa María la Real in Nájera

🏛 **Nájera**
Late June: San Juan y San Pedro festival
Sept 15-18: San Juan Mártir y Santa María la Real festival

NÁJERA TO SANTA DOMINGO

20.9km
(13.0mi)

🕑 **5-6 Hours**
Difficulty: ▭◻◻
🅿 37%, 7.7km
🆄 63%, 13.2km

A Albergues:
Azofra 5.8km
Cirueña 15.1km
S. Domingo 20.9km
Grañon 28.1km
Redecilla 32.1km

Live chickens in the
Santo Domingo
Cathedral

**Wander vineyard vistas, pass a
15th-century stone boundary marker,
find out why live chickens dwell in
Santo Domingo's cathedral.**

☀ Much of this day is on wide farm tracks through fields of
grain and grapes, far from the busy highway. Prepare for little
shade and few places to get water on this more remote day
with fewer services. A golf course and ghost town 2/3 of the
way through in Cirueña feel strangely out of place.

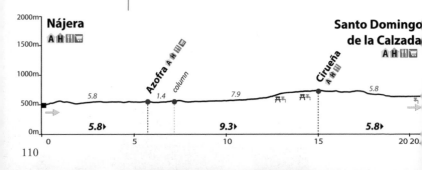

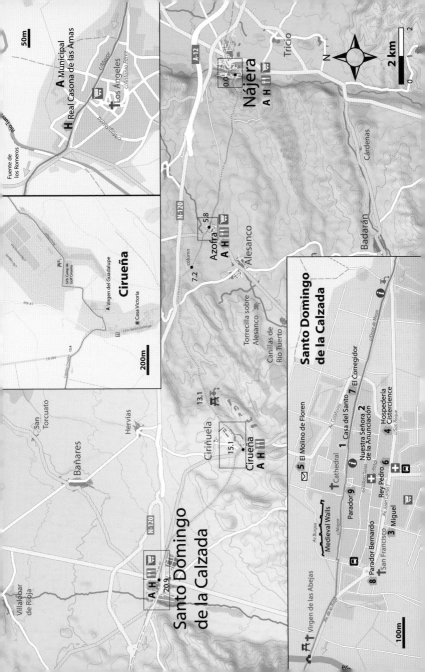

Nájera

A H 🏨 0.0

Tricio

N

2 km

0   2

A Municipal
H Real Casona de las Amas

Los Ángeles
C/Mayor

C/Antonino Pérez

50m

C/Margubete

Río San Juan

Fuente de
los Romeros

A-12

Cárdenas

Badarán

N-120

Azofra 5.8
A H 🏨

column 7.2

Alesanco

Cirueña

Ctra. Santo Domingo
Urb. Camp de
Golf Cirueña
LR-204

N-120

LR-340

Camino Cirueña 15.4

Casino Campo Cirueña

A Virgen del Guadalupe
■ Casa Victoria

200m

Torrecilla sobre
Alesanco

Canillas de
Río Tuerto

Santo
de la
Calzada

Villalobar
de Rioja

N-120

Domingo
Calzada

San
Torcuato

Bañares

Hervías

13.1 ⚕🏕

Cirueñuela

15.1 ⛪

Cirueña
A H 🏨

**Santo Domingo
de la Calzada**

A H 🏨 20.9

100m

Virgen de las Abejas

Av de la Rioja

C/San Roque

Av Juan Carlos I

8 Parador Bernardo
✝ San Francisco
3 Miguel

9 Parador

Medieval Walls
Av Burgos
C/Mayor

✝ Cathedral
Av Calahorra

C/Pinar Solar

C/Doce de Mayo

🛈

5 El Molino de Floren
1 Casa del Santo
2 Nuestra Señora
de la Anunciación
Rey Pedro **6**
4 Hospedería
Cistercience
7 El Corregidor

**Santo Domingo
de la Calzada**

Wildflowers and wheat along the path to Santo Domingo

0.0 *Leave Nájera heading west away from the river on c/Costanilla, past Iglesia de Santa Maria la Real to gently climb up out of town and turn R on a dirt road through the small pass of Nájera's western rocky hillside (0.6km). Follow pleasant dirt tracks through vineyards to arrive in Azofra via the main street.*

5.8 **Azofra's Iglesia de Nuestra Señora de los Angeles** houses a wooden statue of Santiago Peregrino. *Leaving town, follow the sidewalk along the main road briefly, turning R and then L on a small paved road (6.1km) just before the Fuente de los Romeros. The path soon becomes dirt and follows beautiful tracks through fields. Note the wayside* **15th-century columna justicia (7.2km)**, *a stone boundary marker. Cross a paved road near the highway (9.0km) and pass a rest area with water (13.1km) before arriving to Cirueña.*

5.8 **Azofra** A H 🏨🍴🛒🚌
Pop. 251, 🕮 Arabic: *as-suxra* "tribute"
A ☆ **Municipal** (🛏60, €7): 🚿🍴⊙🖥, c/Las Parras 7, ☎941-379049 ⊙all year, 2 beds per room
H **Real Casona de las Amas** (dbl €160): c/Mayor 5, ☎941-416103 🖥, spa, luxurious

15.1 **Cirueña** is basically a ghost town other than the ritzy golf club, sadly demonstrating Spain's housing bubble. *Leave Cirueña by turning R on the main road and soon L on a gravel track (15.4km). Follow rolling hills through wheat fields and sheep flocks, down toward the main road and industrial outskirts of Santo Domingo (19.3km). Stay straight on the main street to reach the main Santo Domingo albergues, just before the Cathedral.*

A shepherd tends his flock near Cirueña

Medieval boundary marker after Azofra

15.1 **Cirueña** A H 🍴 Pop. 131, internet available in bar

A Virgen de Guadalupe (priv, 🛏14, €13 w/🚿) 🍴 W,
c/Barrio Alto 1, ☎638-924069 📧,
🕐1:30pm, Mar 15-Oct 15

H Casa Rural Victoria (dbl €40): R W 🖥,
Plaza del Horno 8, ☎941-341105

113

20.9 **Santo Domingo de la Calzada** takes its name from **Saint Dominic**, born in nearby Viloria de la Rioja, who cared for and developed sections of the camino in this area in the 11th century including building bridges and clearing the road. Myths and legends abound about the saint, such as when he was clearing the forest he fell asleep and angels picked up his scythe and miraculously continued clearing!

The most famous legend associated with Santo Domingo is "the hanged innocent." A German family (father, mother and their son, *Hugonell*) were on the pilgrimage to Santiago. In Santo Domingo they stayed with a farmer's family, and the farmer's daughter tried to seduce Hugonell but, as a pious pilgrim, he refused her. She became so angry that she hid some silver items in his pack and after he left, called the authorities and accused the boy of theft. Upon finding the items in his pack, the boy was found guilty and hanged.

His grief-stricken parents continued to Santiago, but stopped to see their son's remains on the return journey (thieves were left to rot on the gallows as a warning to others). They were delighted to find that he was still alive, claiming that Santo Domingo had held him up so he did not die. The parents hurried to the magistrate and asked them to cut down their son, as he was clearly innocent. The magistrate, who

Statue of Santo Domingo in the cathedral where he is buried

114

Storks nesting outside of Santo Domingo

had just sat down to a hearty chicken dinner, shouted, "Why, he is no more alive that this roasted chicken I'm about to eat." At this, the cooked chicken stood up on his plate, miraculously brought back to life feathers and all, and crowed.

In remembrance of this story, live chickens are kept in the **Cathedral** (€3 w/*credencial*, ☉M-Su 10am-7:30pm, ☎941-340033 ☐), which are said to be the descendants of the resurrected fowl in the story. A piece of the gallows is displayed on Santo Domingo's tomb. The cathedral tower is curiously not attached to the cathedral, but across the street, and can be climbed for €2.

🏛 **Santo Domingo**
May 10-15: Fiesta del Santo
Sept 18-19: Fiestas de Gracias y Hermosilla with traditional Riojan potato dishes

Ahorcaditos (little hanged men) are sweet almond cream pastries shaped like a shell, a popular local snack.

20.9 **Santo Domingo de la Calzada**
A H▮▮✚❂❼▲🚪 Pop. 6,694, 🛈 "Saint Dominic of the Causeway" after the town's founder

1. **A Casa del Santo** (assoc, 🛏210, don): ▦▦, c/Mayor 38, ☎941-343390 ☐, ☉11:30am, new industrial-size facilities, chickens!

2. **A Nuestra Señora de la Anunciación Abadía Cistercience** (par, 🛏33, €5): ▦▦, c/Mayor 31, ☎941-340700 ☐, ☉12pm May-Sept

3. **H Pension Miguel** (sng €20, €32 shared bath): ▦, c/Juan Carlos I 23, ☎941-0343252

4. **H Hospedería Cisterciense** (dbl €54): c/Pinar 2, ☎941-340700 ☐, run by nuns same as albergue

5. **H El Molino de Floren** (dbl €59): c/Margubete 5, ☎941-342931 ☐

6. **H Rey Pedro** (€59): 📶, c/San Roque 9, ☎941-341160 ☐

7. **H El Corregidor** (€80): ▮▮, c/Mayor 14, ☎941-342128 ☐

8. **H Parador Bernardo de Fresneda** (dbl €80-140), ▮▮📶, Plaza de San Francisco 1, ☎941-341150 ☐

9. **H Parador de Santo Domingo de la Calzada** (dbl €110+): ▮▮, Plaza del Santo 3, ☎941-340300, former pilgrim hospice, historic building

10. **A Bañares camping** (bungalow, €100, tents €13): ▮▮▦▦📶▦, 2km east on N-120, ☎941-340131 ☐

115

10

SANTA DOMINGO TO BELORADO

22.9km
(14.2mi)

🕐 **5-6 Hours**
Difficulty: ▭▢▢
🄿 31%, 7.1km
🅄 69%, 15.8km

A Albergues:
Grañon 7.2km
Redecilla 11.2km
Viloria 14.7km
Villamayor 18.0km
Belorado 22.9km
Tosantos 27.8km
Villambistia 29.7km
Espinosa 31.3km
Villafranca 34.8km

A cross adorns the expansive fields of the Meseta.

Relish agricultural vistas of lush wheat fields, visit the birthplace of Santo Domingo, cross into Castilla y León.

☀ About half of this day consists of paths right next to the busy highway N-120. Luckily, there are frequent small villages that offer some respite and services. Vast corn fields characterize the landscape as the trail enters Castilla y León, the largest autonomous region of the camino.

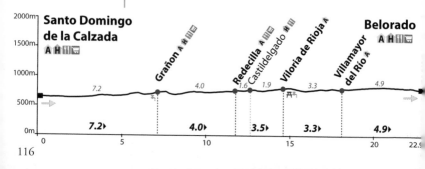

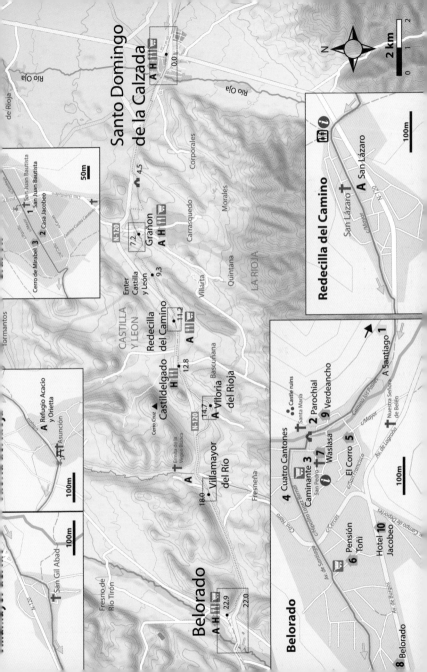

0.0 *Leaving Santo Domingo along c/Mayor, cross the **Río Oja** (from which the region derives its name) on a bridge originally built by Santo Domingo (now covered in concrete). Before the bridge to the R is the Ermita de la Puente (0.7km), where Santo Domingo is said to have resurrected a pilgrim who was crushed by an oxcart while sleeping outside the hermitage. The current building is a 1917 creation after the original was flooded. In summer, stork nests on high poles abound along the bridge. Follow paths adjacent or parallel to the highway, leaving it to the L (4.5km) and ascending a hill to arrive in Grañon.*

7.2 **Grañon's** Iglesia de San Juan Bautista houses some nice retablos. Its simple and much-loved parochial albergue has a donativo box that reads, "give what you can, take what you need." *Follow the main street through town past the church and leave on gravel roads.*

9.3 Castilla y León

A large sign indicates crossing into yet another autonomous region, and the map shows that, as the largest region in Spain, you'll be in this region for a long time (400km until Galicia just before O Cebreiro). *Pass over N-120 to reach Redecilla del Camino.*

7.2 **Grañon** A H ⛺✚💶🛏 Pop. 307
1. **A** San Juan Bautista (par, ⛺40 mats, don): 🛏🍴, ☎941-420818, communal meals, basic but well-loved for peaceful and caring atmosphere
2. **H** Casa Jacobeo (dbl €50): c/Mayor 34, ☎986-644631
3. **H** Cerro de Mirabel (dbl €55): 🍴🅦, c/Mayor 40, ☎941-420798 ☑

11.2 **Redecilla del Camino** A 🛏💶ℹ🛏
Pop. 137, Spanish: "little net," ℹ with internet for €1/hr, ☎947-588078
A San Lázaro (muni, ⛺38, €5): 🛏🍴🅦🍴, c/Mayor 24, ☎947-580283, ⊙all year, communal meals

11.2 **Redecilla** is home to the Iglesia de Nuestra Señora de la Calle that contains a Romanesque baptismal font depicting Jerusalem. *Follow N-120 to Castildelgado.*

The path leaving Santo Domingo

12.8 Castildelgado was once home to a monastery and pilgrim hospital. Today there is not much to see other than the 16th-century Gothic Iglesia de San Pedro. *Leave the town along N-120, turning L (13.6km) on a smaller paved road into Viloria de Rioja.*

14.7 Viloria de la Rioja is the birthplace of Domingo de la Calzada (p. 114), who was born in 1019. Sadly, his house has been demolished. A rundown church remains, which houses the font in which he was baptized. *Leave town on a small paved road and turn L to rejoin the side of N-120 (16.1km), following it to Villamayor del Río.*

18.0 Villamayor del Río has the 18th-century neoclassical Iglesia San Gil Abad. The tiny village is sometimes known as the "place of three lies," as the name Villamayor del Río suggests a large town on a river, and the actuality is a tiny hamlet along a creek. *Rejoin N-120 to the outskirts of Belorado, finally leaving the busy road by turning R on a dirt path (22.0km). This path leads to Belorado's center and most of its albergues and services.*

12.8 Castildelgado
Pop. 54, Named for the 16th c. bishop of Burgos
H El Chocolatero (dbl €40): ⊙947-588063, along noisy N-120 highway

14.7 Viloria de la Rioja Pop. 50
A Refugio Acacio y Orietta (assoc, 10, €5): (free), c/Nuevo 6, ⊙947-585220/679-941123, Mar 1-Oct 31, communal meals, sponsored by Pablo Coelho

18.0 Villamayor del Río Pop. 52
A San Luis de Francia (priv, 26, €5): ⊙947-580566, Easter-Oct, slightly off route

Camino symbols on the door of the parochial albergue in Grañon

119

22.9 **Belorado** A H ▮▮▮+●▮▮ Pop. 2,140
▮ local surname ❶ Plaza Mayor ☎947-580815,
🕐10am-2pm, 4-8pm

1. **A H** **A Santiago** (priv, 🛏98, dm €5-10, sng €30,
dbl €40): ▮▮▮▮▮▮, Camino Redoña,
☎677-811847 ▮, located just before town, nice
facilities with "hotel" feel

2. **A** **Refugio Parroquial de Belorado** (par, 🛏24,
don w/▮): ▮, Barrio de El Corro,
☎947-580085, 🕐May-Oct, run by volunteers

3. **A H** **Caminante** (priv, 🛏26, dm €6, dbl €40-
50): ▮▮▮▮, c/Mayor 36, ☎947-580231 ▮,
🕐Mar-Oct

4. **A** **Cuatro Cantones** (priv, 🛏62, €6): ▮▮▮▮
▮🛜▮, c/Hipólito López 10, ☎696-427707 ▮
🕐all year

5. **A** **El Corro** (youth hostel, 🛏40, €14.5):
▮▮▮, c/Mayor 68, ☎947-580683, 🕐all year

6. **H** **Pensión Toñi** (dbl €40): ▮▮▮🛜, c/Redecillo
del Campo 7, ☎947-580525/616-010808 ▮

7. **H** **Casa Waslasa** (sng €24, dbl €40): ▮▮🛜,
c/Mayor 57, ☎647-102254 ▮

8. **H** **Belorado** (sng €30, dbl €35): ▮,
Av. de Burgos 30, ☎947-580684 ▮

9. **H** **Verdeancho** (dbl €55): ▮▮▮🛜,
c/El Corro 11, ☎Elsa: 659-484584 ▮

10. **H** **Hotel Jacobeo** (dbl €60): c/Generalisimo 3,
☎947-580010 ▮

22.9 **Belorado** has been settled
since Roman times and was known
as *Bilforado* by the 10th century. After being granted a charter in 1116
that allowed for an annual fair, the
town grew in commerce and had
eight churches in the 13th century.
Belorado had pilgrim hospitals on
either side of town, while today most
albergues are concentrated around
the historic center. The **Iglesia de
Santa María** has a stone retablo with
both Matamoros and Peregrino images of Santiago.

Behind the church, caves were once
occupied by hermits, most famously
San Caprasio the patron saint of
the *Vía Francigena*, and have been
known to provide shelter for wandering pilgrims as well. At the top
of the cliff, the ruins of a medieval
castle can be seen. In modern times,
Belorado was well known for its
high-quality leather products, but
has fallen on hard times economi-
cally, though leather goods are still
for sale in many local shops.

🏛 **Belorado**
Early Sept: Thanksgiving celebration with parade
Jan 25: Virgen de Belén festival
Aug 26: Patron saint festival for San Vitores

Belorado central plaza and
Iglesias de San Pedro (above) and
Santa Maria (right)

Romanesque baptismal font in
Redecilla del Camino

11

BELORADO TO AGÉS

27.7km
(17.2mi)

⏱ **7-8 Hours**
Difficulty: ▭▭▢
🅿 12%, 3.2km
Ⓤ 88%, 24.5km

A Albergues:
Tosantos 4.9km
Villambistia 6.8km
Espinoso 8.4km
Villafranca 11.9km
San Juan 24.1km
Agés 27.7km
Atapuerca 30.2km

Ermita Virgen de la
Peña near Tosantos

Tread earthen paths through the Oca hills past the monastery of San Juan de Ortega with a remote forest landscape.

☼ This is a lovely day mostly on earthen paths and passing through frequent villages. The trail crosses through the remote Oca hills, infamous in medieval times as a dangerous route rife with thieves and ne'er-do-wells. Legend credits San Juan de Ortega, disciple of Santo Domingo, with cleaving this path through the thick oak and pine forest with its dense undergrowth. Be extra careful with traffic in Villafranca, where trucks barrel through at full speed.

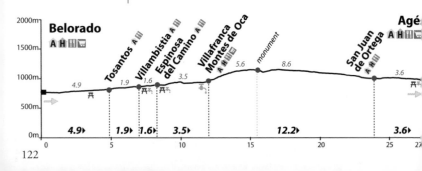

122

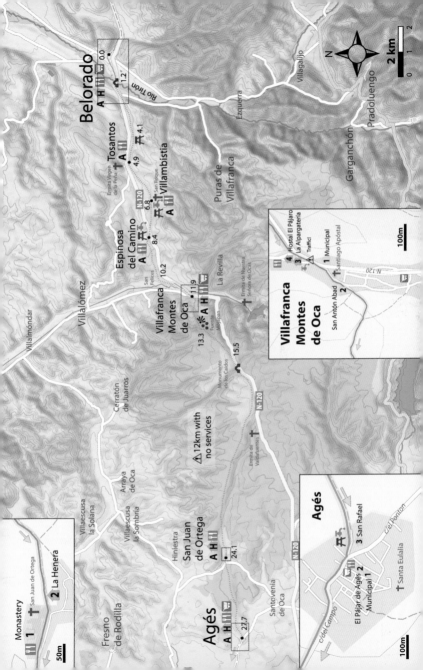

Belorado
A H ⌂⌂⌂ • 0.0

↓ 1.2'

Río Tirón

Tosantos
A ☐ • ⌂ 4.1
Ermita Virgen
de la Peña ✝ ⌂ 4.9

San Roque ✝
Villambistia
N-120 ⌂ 6.8
⌂ A H ⌂⌂

**Espinosa
del Camino**
A ⌂⌂⌂ ⌂ ⌂
8.4

San
Felices 10.2

**Villafranca
Montes
de Oca**
☐ • 11.9
A H ⌂⌂⌂

La Revilla
Ermita de Nuestra
Señora de Oca ✝

Fuente
Mojapán
13.3 ❉

15.5 ◁

Monumento
de los Caídos

N-120

⚠ 12km with
no services

Ermita de
Valdefuentes ✝

Cerratón
de Juarros

Arraya
de Oca

Villaescusa
la Solana

Villaescusa
la Sombría

Villalómez

Villalmóndar

Villagalijo

Ezquerra

Pradoluengo

Garganchón

Puras de
Villafranca

N

2 km
0   1   2

Hinlestra

**San Juan
de Ortega**
A H ⌂⌂⌂
☐ • 24.1

Santovenia
de Oca

Fresno
de Rodilla

N-120

c/del Ponton

Agés
A H ⌂⌂⌂
☐ • 27.7

**Villafranca
Montes de Oca**

4 Hostal El Pájaro
La Alpargatería
3 ⌂ Traffic!
1 Municipal
✝ Santiago Apóstol
San Antón Abad 2
N-120

100m

Agés

El Pájar de Agés 2
Municipal 1
☐ ⌂ ⌂
⌂ 3 San Rafael
✝ Santa Eulalia
c/del Campo

100m

Monastery
⌂⌂ 1
✝
San Juan de Ortega
2 La Henera

50m

Iglesia de la Asunción
in Espinosa

0.0 *Leave Belorado by crossing the Plaza Mayor and exiting on the far side via c/Hipolito Lopez Bernal. Turn R on N-120 (1.2km) and pass a small picnic area to cross the river on a wooden bridge near a stone bridge attributed to San Juan de Ortega. Continue on a dirt path parallel to the highway. Pass a picnic area (4.1km) and join the road to Tosantos.*

4.9 **Tosantos** contains the 17th-century Iglesia de San Esteban. Leaving Tosantos look to the R at the cliff north of the village to see the **Ermita Virgen de la Peña** ("Our Lady of the Cliff"), built into the rock face above the town. Legend has it an 8th-century statue of the child Jesus was hidden in this cave under a bell to protect it from invading Muslims. It may be possible to visit the hermitage by asking for the key at the house across from #18, or those staying at the parochial albergue can visit with a local guide. *Leave Tosantos on a dirt path, which brings you to Villambistia.*

4.9 **Tosantos** Ａ🍴
Pop. 53, 📖 Spanish: *todos los santos* "all the saints."
Ａ ☆ **San Francisco de Asis** (par, 🛏30, don): 🛏🚻🅺,
c/Santa Marina, 🕐947-580371, 🕐1pm Apr-mid-Nov, communal meals, prayer service with ritual of reading notes by past pilgrims

---

6.8 **Villambistia** Ａ🍴 Pop. 47
Ａ **San Roque** (muni, 🛏14, €6): 🆆🅾🍴📶,
Plaza Mayor 1, 🕐660-797011, 🕐closed on Mondays and a few weeks in winter; call ahead

---

8.4 **Espinosa del Camino** Ａ🍴
Pop. 36, 📖 Spanish: "thorny"
Ａ **La Campaña** (priv, 🛏10, €12 w/🍴):
🕐678-479361, 🕐1pm Jan 15-Dec 15

6.8 **Villambistia** has a local tradition which says that immersing your head in the fountain will cure you of tiredness, worth a try! *Follow the dirt path out of Villambistia, cross highway N-120 into Espinosa.*

8.4 **Espinosa** has the 16th-century Iglesia de la Asunción with an image of one of Santiago's disciples, San Indalecio. *Leave town via a dirt road through vast wheat fields. Pass the ruins of San Felices de Oca (10.2km), a 9th-century Mozárabic monastery, and the path joins highway N-120 (10.9km). Turn R to walk carefully* *along the road or on the faint footpath on the shoulder to Villafranca Montes de Oca.* ⚠ *Be extremely careful entering town via the busy highway N-120, which has little to no shoulder.*

11.9 Villafranca Montes de Oca
was once a Roman city named *Auca* (from which *Oca* comes), home to the 18th-century **Iglesia de Santiago** with a statue of Santiago Peregrino and baptismal font constructed of a huge shell. The historic Hospital de la Reina hosted up to 18,000 pilgrims per year in the 17th century and has been converted into a boutique hotel and albergue. *From the main street, turn R uphill to the church and continue past the San Antón hotel. Leave town on a dirt track, which is pleasantly shaded. These are the mountains of Oca that so terrified medieval pilgrims! On the steep way up you will pass the Sierra del San Millán lookout (13.2km) over the forest.*

11.9 Villafranca Montes de Oca A H 🏨🛒
🏠 Pop. 147, 📖 Latin: "French town of the hills"
1. **A Municipal** (🛏60, €6): 🚪🖥, c/Mayor, ⏰947- 582124, 🕐all year, basic
2. **A H** ⭐**San Antón Abad** (priv, 🛏26, dm €5-10, dbl €43): 🍴🚪🖥🅿🔌📶c/Hospital 4, ⏰947-582149 📮, 🕐Mar-Nov 15, restored historic pilgrim hospital
3. **H La Alpargatería** (dbl €36): 🍴🚪🖥, c/Mayor 4, ⏰686-040884
4. **H El Pájaro** (sng €20, dbl €40): c/Mayor 2, ⏰947-582029

The supermarket of Villafranca is on the main road 350m past the church turnoff—make sure you are stocked to Agés! ☀**Fill water; there is none for 12km until San Juan de Ortega.**

Steep ascent in the Oca mountains

13.3 Fuente Mójapan is found at the top, (the "bread-moistening spring") used by medieval pilgrims to gussy up their stale bread (today the spring is marked "*no potable*"). In fall, look for mushrooms, which Domenico Laffi wrote in the 1600s were "as big as a straw hat." *Continue on a wide dirt path (fire protection swathe) through thick forest with brilliant heather.*

15.5 El Monumento de los Caídos
("Monument to the Fallen") stands at the top, which remembers Franco supporters who were killed and their bodies dumped in this valley. *Continue steeply downhill, cross a small stream by a bridge (15.9km), and rise steeply back up. The flat path continues for a while before descending gradually and leaving the forest behind. As you emerge from the pine forest, a dirt path will guide you to the hamlet of San Juan de Ortega.*

24.1 **San Juan de Ortega** A H ⬛ Pop. 23,
🏷 Spanish: "St. John of the nettles," internet kiosk
1. **A** **Monastery** (par, 🛏70, €5): 🔲, ☎947-560438
   📧, ⏱Mar-Oct, basic and neglected, kitchen under
   construction, tradition of serving garlic soup
2. **H** **La Henera** (dbl €50): c/La Iglesia 40,
   ☎606-198734 📧, ⏱Mar-Nov
3. **H** **Hotel Sierra de Atapuerco** (sng €30, dbl €40):
   🚻🛏📶, ☎947-106912 📧, located 4km away but
   provide free pickup and drop off

🏛 **San Juan de Ortega**
June 2: San Juan de
Ortega festival and local
pilgrimage

Iglesia de San Juan de
Ortega and monastery

24.1 **San Juan de Ortega**,
or Juan Velásquez, was a young priest
and disciple of Santo Domingo (p.
114) who was born near Burgos. San
Juan helped Santo Domingo in the
construction of bridges in Logroño,
Santo Domingo and Nájera. After
Domingo's death, Juan went on pilgrimage to Jerusalem. On the journey, he was caught up in a shipwreck
and prayed to San Nicolás de Bari to
save him. When he survived, he re-
turned to the Burgos area determined to serve pilgrims in the
notoriously dangerous and difficult Oca mountains. He is attributed with developing the road from Villafranca to Burgos
(from which he took his name *de Ortega,* "of the nettles") as
well as a hospice and monastery in the wilderness.

Along with being considered the patron saint of innkeepers, San Juan also became known as the saint of fertility. Legend says that when his tomb was opened, the air was fragrant and a swarm of white bees flew out. Queen Isabel la Católica was perhaps the most famous barren woman to pray at his tomb. She visited twice and conceived two children, named Juan and Juana.

The **Iglesia de San Juan de Ortega** includes the saint's tomb with scenes from the legends of his life, including his shipwreck and the white bees. One capital is said to serve a calendar function and is illuminated by sunlight on certain days of the year. Another capital depicts the battle between Roland and Ferragut. An evening pilgrim mass is offered daily and one bar offers hearty *platos combinados*.

Leave San Juan de Ortega by the only road, and turn R on a dirt path (24.4km). Follow this path until a paved road brings you to the pleasant village of Agés.

27.7 **Agés**: The sweet 16th-century Iglesia de Santa Eulalia is said to have once housed the body of King García de Nájera before it was moved to the royal pantheon in Nájera. A short detour to the south from the church will take you to a small bridge attributed to San Juan de Ortega along the Río Vena.

Entering Agés

Church in Agés

27.7 **Agés** A H ⛽️🍴🛒🚌 Pop. 65
1. **A** **Municipal** (muni/priv, 🛏36, €8): 🍴 W 🅿 📶, c/ Del Medio 21, 📞947-400697 ✉️, 🕚11am all year
2. **A** **El Pájar de Agés** (priv, 🛏34, €9): W D 🅿 📶 c/Medio Paralela 12, 📞947-400629 ✉️, 🕚Mar -Oct, ask about "la casa roja" with beds for €5
3. **A H** **San Rafael** (priv, 🛏10, dm €10, dbl €45): 🍴 W D 📶, 📞947-430392 ✉️, 🕚all year, offers vegetarian and Celiac (gluten free) meals

AGÉS TO BURGOS

22.3km
(13.9mi)

🕐 **5-6 Hours**
Difficulty: ▭□□
🅿 79%, 17.7km
Ⓤ 21%, 4.6 km

A Albergues:
Atapuerca 2.5km
Cardeñuela 8.8km
Burgos 22.3km
Tardajos 33.3km

⚠ **Alt. Routes:**
Three options to enter Burgos (p. 131):
1) Villafría, 23.3km
2a) Castañares, 22.6km
2b) River, 23.1km

Gothic cathedral of Burgos

Climb the Sierra Atapuerca near prehistoric ruins. Stroll along Río Arlanzón and wander the mind-boggling Burgos Cathedral.

☼ The first half of this day consists of quiet roads between quaint villages and peaceful dirt paths through pine forests. Prepare for the second half of the day entering Burgos, which can be a long tiring walk through urban industrial zones. There are three possible approaches to Burgos; one is not completely marked. We recommend that you take the road less traveled and leave the markings behind at the town of Castañares to cross over the Río Arlanzón and walk along the river

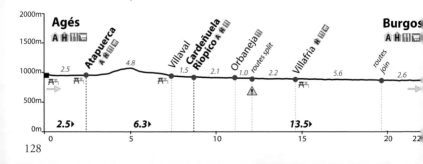

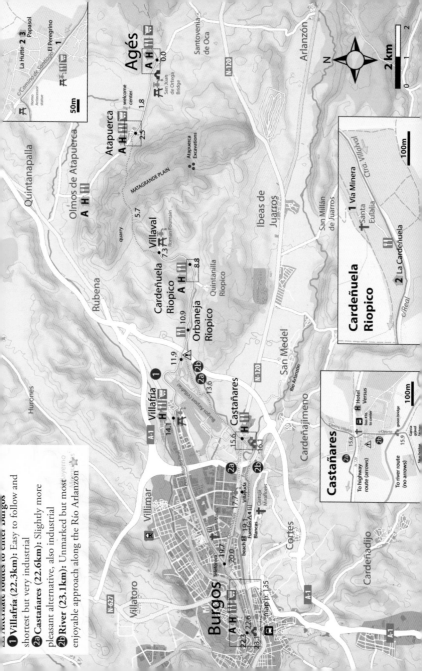

Alternate routes to enter Burgos

① Villafría (22.3km): Easy to follow and shortest but very industrial

②a Castañares (22.6km): Slightly more pleasant alternative, also industrial

②b River (23.1km): Unmarked but most enjoyable approach along the Río Arlanzón ⭐

La Hutte **2 3** Papasol

c/Camino de Santos El Peregrino **1**

Horno Antecessor statue

Agés

A H 🏪 — 0.0

San Juan de Ortega Bridge

50m

Santovenia de Oca

N-120

Arlanzón

N

0 1 2

2 km

Atapuerca
A H 🏪 — 2.5

welcome center — 1.8

Olmos de Atapuerca
A H 🏪

Quintanapalla

MATAGRANDE PLAIN

quarry

Atapuerca Excavations

Villaval 🏪 — 7.3
Roman Fountain

5.7

Rubena

Cardeñuela Riopico
A H 🏪 — 10.9

Orbaneja Riopico
A H 🏪 — 8.8

Quintanilla Riopico

Ibeas de Juarros

San Millán de Juarros

Cardeñuela Riopico

1 Vía Minera ✝ Santa Eulalia

Ctra. Villalval

🏪 **2** La Cardeñuela

c/Real

100m

11.9 ⚠

②a ②b — 13.6

Villafría
H 🏪 🏪 — 14.1

1

A-1

Rubena railway crossing

Villimar

Castañares
H 🏪 — 15.6

②a — 16.1

②b

N-120

San Medel

Río Arlanzón

Cardeñajimeno

Castañares

②b — 15.6

🏨 Hotel Versus

bus stop to station

To highway route (arrows)

green bridge

García Fernández tunnel

Vita bridge

To river route (no arrows) — 15.9

②b

100m

Cortes

Cardeñadijo

Burgos
A H 🏪 🏪

22.3
●22.6
23.1

map p.135

N-627

A-1

Villatoro

Villalonquéjar

Fuentes Blancas 🏪
19.1

beach ♨ — 19.7

②b 20.0

telefónica 19.7

Cartuja Miraflores ✝

A-1

2.5 **Atapuerca** A H 🛏🍴🛒🚌 Pop. 206

📖 Spanish: *ata* "to tie," *puerca* "pig," 🛏 ⏱Apr-Sep

1. **A H** El Peregrino (priv, 🛏36, dm €8, dbl €35): 🏧🅆🅾🛜, Crta 105, ☎661-580882 📇, ⏱1pm, Mar-Nov

2. **A** La Hutte (priv, 🛏18, €5): 🏧🛜, c/de Enmedio 38, ☎947-430320, ⏱1pm all year

3. **H** Papasol (dbl €55): 🏧🛜c/de Enmedio 36, ☎947-430320 📇

Accommodations in Olmos (+2.5km)

A Municipal (🛏24, €7): 🏧, c/La Iglesia, ☎633-586876, ⏱all year, key at Mesón Hidalgo

H Casarrota la Campesina (dbl €54 w/shared bath): c/Encimera 10, ☎616-962772 📇

Atapuerca's Prehistoric Humanoids

Excavations near Atapuerca were declared a UNES-CO World Heritage Site after revealing a tremendous wealth of prehistoric humanoid artifacts (>90% of all found in Europe!) A new species was identified, *Homo antecessor*, who are believed to have been cannibalistic. The most significant finds are in the 🏛 **Museum of Human Evolution in Burgos** (p. 134), which offers guided daily excursions to the excavation site and interpretive center near Atapuerca.

on peaceful shady dirt paths. Despite being unmarked, it's easy to navigate as the route follows the river. **All options follow the same path for the first 11.9km.**

0.0 *From Agés, take the main road out of town and cross a small stone bridge attributed to San Juan de Ortego over the Río Vena (0.6km). Pass a turnoff for the Atapuerca welcome center (1.8km, +800m), offering tours in Spanish of the archaeological park, a recreation of early dwellings. Follow the road into Atapuerca.*

2.5 **Atapuerca** is best known for the archaeological site located near the town. The looming 15th-century Gothic Iglesia de San Martín is the site of a yearly August festival recreating a famous medieval battle. *Leave via the main road to reach a statue of homo antecessor (2.8km). Turn L here on a dirt path and walk uphill along the barbed wire fence of an army base to the L. Pass through pine forest and spiny shrubs. At the hill crest cross the wide Matagrande Plain to a high point with a bench to enjoy the view down to Burgos and a first glimpse of the flat meseta (5km). At the sign for **Valle del Riopico (5.7km)**, either follow the slightly shorter local path down into the village of Villalval (water and a Roman fountain) or head R along the waymarked path, which goes another way on the west side of **Villalval (7.3km)** with a depressing view of an open strip quarry. Take the paved road to Cardeñuela.*

Matagrande Plain before Burgos

8.8 Cardeñuela de Riopico
is a quiet little town with an albergue. *Continue along the quiet
paved road through* **Orbaneja** 🍴
(10.9km). ⚠ *1km past Orbaneja arrive at a split near a housing development with two options (1 and 2a/2b).
All options to Burgos are within 1km
of each other in length.*

8.8 Cardeñuela de Riopico Ⓐ Ⓗ 🍴
1. **Ⓐ** **Via Minera** (priv, ↩26, dm €7, sng €14, dbl €16): 🍴 📶, c/La Iglesia 1, ✆630-170171
2. **Ⓗ** **La Cardeñuela** (dbl €40): 📷, c/Vía Minera, ✆610-652560

14.1 Villafria Ⓗ 🍴 🖥 🚌 📧 Pop. 926
Ⓗ **Hotel Buenos Aires** (sng €30, dbl €45): 🍴 📶, Ctra N-I, km 245, ✆877-6626988
Ⓗ **Hostal Iruñako** (dbl €45): 🍴 📶, Ctra N-1, km 245.5, ✆947-484126 📧
Ⓗ **Las Vegas** (sng €30, dbl €50): 🍴 📶, c/Vitoria 319, ✆947-484453 📧

11.9 ⚠ **Alternate Routes:**

❶ Villafría Option

This fairly well-marked option
follows the historical route,
and most people walk this way. In the present day this
means walking along the airport fence, through the
town of Villafría and almost 7km of unpleasant walking along the A-1 highway by industrial factories.
🚌 Bus #8 from Villafría skips this part (every 30 min. on weekdays). *Follow the arrows through fields and over train tracks into*
Villafría (14.1km). *From Villafría, follow N-1 all of the way
into town to where it meets N-120/Av. de la Constitution, where
the Castañares option joins from the L (19.7km). Turn R past the
Vía de la Plata mall and onto c/de las Calzadas, crossing a bridge
to enter the Old City on c/San Juan. Stay straight following signs
to reach the main albergue (23.3km).*

Castañares Option

s waymarked route provides a slightly
re attractive way to enter the city.
the junction, turn L on a dirt road to
corner of the airfield (13.6km) to pass
ugh fields to **Castañares (15.6km).**

15.6 Castañares Ⓗ 🍴 🚌 Pop. 305
Ⓗ **Hotel Versus** (dbl €90): 🍴 🖥, c/Eras, 4, ✆947-474977 📧

*n R on N-120 at the fountain. [River Route option splits into 2a/2b here, 2b instructions in the
owing section.] Follow alongside busy N-120 until signs direct you L into the suburb of Villayuda
.7km). Follow a derelict c/de Villafranca to cross railroad tracks (18.8km), turning R then L to
 Av. de la Constitución (19.1km) to join the Villafria option (20.0km) for the remaining 2.6km
he main albergue (22.6km), option 1, description above.*

Cartuja de Miraflores monastery

Cartujas Miraflores Monastery

A Carthusian monastery from the 15th century housing the exquisite alabaster tombs of Queen Isabel's parents, King Juan II and Isabel de Portugal. The golden retablo by Gil de Siloé was crafted with gold brought back from the new world by Christopher Columbus himself, and includes luminescent imagery including Santiago and Spanish monarchs. A Carthusian community still lives here, known for their white robes and vow of silence.

Free, ☉M-Sa 10:15am-3pm, 4-6pm, Sun 11am-3pm, 4-6pm, closed Wed ☎947-252586

Recommended detour: At the Fuente de Prio beach, turn L at the brick electric pole uphill to the paved road. Follow a sign up a dirt road to the entrance of the monastery. Bus #17 from the Plaza de España in Burgos passes the monastery.

➋ᵇ River Option

This is by far the most pleasant way to enter Burgos (not waymarked past Castañares, but fairly simple to navigate along the river). *From Castañares (15.6km, 2a option), cross over the N-120 highway to the south of town. Walk past a paved playground on the L and leave town on a small paved road passing over a small green bridge (15.9km), just before a T by a gravel factory "Garcia." Turn R on the gravel path, which veers L and passes over a bright blue footbridge (16.1km). After the bridge, turn R on paved path that goes through a forest and underpass (16.9km). Continue along a dirt path on the south side of the river.*

Fuentes Blancas camping area A ⛺🏕🚌🏧🛏 **(19.1km)** and **Fuente de Prio beach** ▬ provide a outdoor recreation area in summer. *For the detour to Cartujas Miraflores Monastery, turn L here (+0.8km). From Fuente de Prio beach, continue along the river on this pedestrian path all the way to the **Santa María bridge (22.6km)**, which leads through the Santa María arch into the plaza just in front of the spectacular Cathedral! The main albergue (23.1km) is on c/Fernán Gonzáles, accessible by stairs just behind the cathedral.*

Blue footbridge on the river option entrance to Burgos (above)

Gothic cathedral of Burgos (opposite)

Alabaster tomb carving in Cartuja de Miraflores

Along the Arlanzón River in Burgos

22.3 **Burgos** is a magnificent city with immeasurable wealth of historic art and architecture. A rest day to visit the sites would be well worth your time.

✝ Catedral de Burgos
(€7, €3.50 w/ credential, ☉daily 10am-6pm, free Tues after 4:30pm)

A UNESCO World Heritage site, the entrance fee includes a detailed brochure of the many naves, chapels and pieces of art. Don't miss the *Capilla del Condestable*, which contains a staggering Mudéjar-Gothic dome, unbelievably realistic 16th-century tombs, the *Retablo de Santa Ana*, created by the famous Gil de Siloé and his son, and the main retablo, also created by Siloé's son. The holiest object for local believers is

🛏 **Burgos**
Mar 17: San Antón, including a ceremony of blessing for pets
Spring: La Noche Blanca large cultural event
June: San Pedro y San Pablo festival

Queso de Burgos is a local specialty, a fresh cheese often eaten with honey, quince or walnuts.

Sacristy ceilng in the Burgos Cathedral

Santo Cristo de Burgos, a sculpture of Jesus on the cross said to be made with real skin and hair (and legend has it, needs to be shaved!) His chapel must be entered from a separate outdoor entrance, as a place of worship opposed to the rest of the cathedral, which is more of a museum. Worship areas open 🕐8:30am-1:30pm, 4:30pm-8pm and are to be visited only for prayer (no photos).

🏰 **Castillo de Burgos** (€3.70 🕐11am-1:30pm, 5-8pm 📞947-203857) The park around the castle provides a beautiful vantage point over the city; one of the few places you can take in the whole of the cathedral.

🏛 **Museum of Human Evolution** (€6 adults/€4 pilgrims, 🕐Tu-F 10am-2:30pm, 4:30-8pm, weekends, holidays, Jul & Aug 10am-8pm, closed Mon, free Wed afternoon 📞902-024246 🖥, *Paseo de la Sierra de Atapuerca*) New well-organized museum of the most important artifacts from the Atapuerca excavations. For €8, pilgrims can visit the museum and be transported to the excavation site for a tour in Spanish; €12 all-day ticket includes the museum, excavations and tour of a recreation of a prehistoric village.

🏛 **Museo de Burgos** (€1.20, 🕐Tu-Sa 10am-2pm, 5-8pm, Su 10am-2pm, 📞947-265875)

🏛 **Centro de Arte Caja de Burgos** (free modern art museum 📞947-256550)

Arco Santa María (free, 🕐M-Sa 11am-1:50pm, 5-9pm, Su 11am-1:50pm, 📞947-288868), near Puente de Santa María

On the way out of town, you may wish to visit the ✝ **Monasterio de las Huelgas** and **Hospital del Rey** (p. 140).

Hostal La Tesorera – 7

12 Puerta de Burgos

Plaza de España
San Lesmes

14 Norte y Londres
La Puebla 11
c/de San Juan

Casa de
los Cubos   1
Fernán González
San Gil
Centro
de Arte

10 Jacobeo
San Lorenzo
Peña 5   8   6 Acacia
3 Divina Pastora   Manjón
Plaza de la
Libertad   9 Carrales

Paseo de la Quinta

Mesón del Cid
13
San Nicolás
Cathedral
Plaza Mayor

Plaza del Espolón
Río Arlanzón

2b

2b

C/ del Campo
Puente de
Santa María

Museum of Human
Evolution

2 Emaús

Paseo de la Isla

Burgos Museum

La Merced

bus station

200m

22.3 **Burgos** A H [icons] Pop. 178,574, Gothic: *Baurgs* "fortified city"

. A Casa de los Cubos (assoc, ☎150, €5): [icons], c/Fernán González 28, ☏947-460922 ✍,
⊙12pm summer, 2pm winter, all year, lockers

. A Casa de Peregrinos Emaús (par, ☎20, €5): [icon], c/San Pedro de Cardeña 31, ⊙2pm, Apr-Nov

. A Divina Pastora (assoc, ☎16, €5): [icons], c/Lain Calvo 10, ☏947-207952, ⊙12pm, Apr-Oct

. A ▲ Fuentes Blancas (priv/camping, dm €8): [icons], ⊙947-486016 ✍, p. 132

. H Pensión Peña (dbl €28 shared bath): c/Pueblo 18, ☏947-206323

. H Acacia (dbl €35): [icon], c/Bernabé Pérez Ortiz 1, ☏947-205134 ✍

. H Hostal La Tesorera (dbl €40): c/Vitoria 79, ☏947-223592 ✍

. H Manjón (dbl €42): [icons], Gran Teatro 1, ☏947-208689 ✍

. H Carrales (dbl €40-55): [icons], c/Puente Gasset 4, ☏947-205916 ✍

0. H Jacobeo (dbl €55): [icons], San Juan 24, ☏947-260102 ✍, bike rental

1. H La Puebla (dbl €60): c/La Puebla 20, ☏948-200011 ✍

2. H Puerta de Burgos (dbl €50-70): c/Vitoria 69, ☏947-241000 ✍

3. H Mesón del Cid (dbl €70): [icon], Plaza Santa María 8, ☏947-208715 ✍, cathedral views

4. H Norte y Londres (dbl €85): [icon], Plaza Alonso Martínez 10, ☏947-264125 ✍

lgrim never goes without sleep

Display in the Museum of Human Evolution

135

Meseta scenery of wheat fields and big skies

Highlights include long views of big skies, vibrant cities with awe-inspiring cathedrals, massive flocks of sheep and rolling fields of grain.

The Meseta is not an autonomous region, but rather a geographical area within the region of Castilla y León—the largest region in Spain. This central high plateau makes up 40% of Spain, with elevation ranging from 400-1000m.

There is a saying that the landscape of the Meseta is not found in the land, but in the sky with its diverse colors and expansive clouds. Dreaded by some, relished by others, the Meseta has a distinct reputation for being boring, repetitive and bleak. However, the Meseta is also home to such vibrant cities as Burgos and León and there is a certain beauty and awe in the endless horizon and wide open space. To the north you will glimpse the jutting mountains of the Cordillera Cantábrica. Towns are often set down in shallow river valleys, practically invisible along the horizon until arrival.

The lack of trees means little to no shade, so be sure to wear sufficient sun protection. Medieval pilgrim records often complain of becoming hopelessly disoriented and lost in the Meseta, though recent tree planting along the trail helps to keep pilgrims heading the right direction. The Meseta can be blistering hot in summer and quite cold in winter. The flat landscape glimmers with golden wheat and flocks of sheep ramble the area along ancient sheep paths known as *cañadas*.

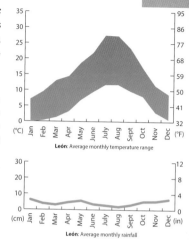

León: Average monthly temperature range

León: Average monthly rainfall

This landscape inspired such notable characters as Don Quixote de la Mancha (in the southern Meseta), and the spiritual and mystical St. Teresa of Avila and St. John of the Cross. In spite of the monotony, perhaps the Meseta can serve as a memorable "wilderness" experience.

With the lack of stone in this area, you may notice more buildings made of brick or adobe. Many towns feature *bodegas*, wine cellars dug into the earth that resemble hobbit homes, as well as mudbrick dovecotes. Some of the traditional foods include suckling pigs, snails and *morcilla*—a blood sausage stuffed with rice, onions and spices.

Bodega on the meseta

137

13

BURGOS TO HONTANAS

31.4km
(19.5mi)

⊙ **7-9 Hours**
Difficulty: ▭▭☐☐
🅿 25%, 8.0km
Ⓤ 75%, 23.4km

A Albergues:
Tardajos 11.0km
Rabé 13.0km
Hornillos 20.9km
San Bol 26.5km
<u>Hontanas 31.4km</u>
San Antón 37.0km

Meseta wheat fields
before Hontanas

Trade the urban landscape of Burgos for the peaceful Meseta, walking through field after field of wheat, past the healing San Bol stream.

☀ This day leaves behind the frantic city pace of Burgos with its whizzing cars and factories and enters the peaceful and at times monotonous landscape of the Meseta, characterized by long flat sections of wheat fields, with nothing but more fields for as far as the eye can see. This is a long stage but has enough intermediary stops with good services to take a few relaxing breaks. Be prepared for little to no shade.

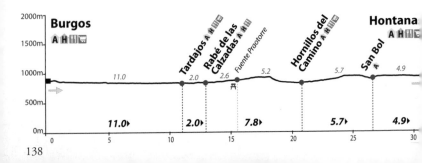

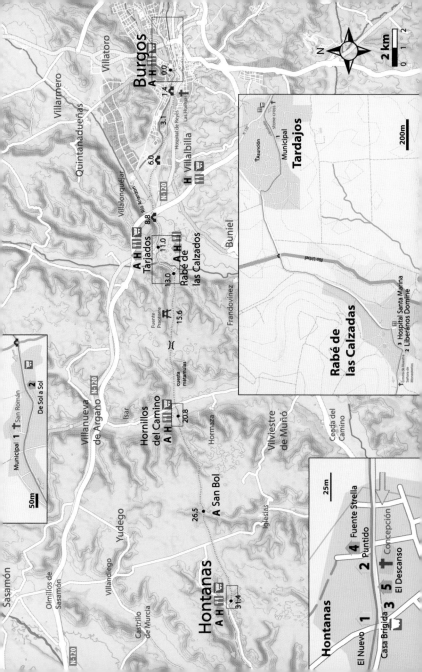

N

2 km
0 1 2

Burgos
A H

Villatoro

Villafría

Villanadueñas

Villalonquéjar

Río Arlanzón

N-120

Villalbilla
H

Hospital de Reyes
Las Huelgas

0.0
1.4
3.1
6.0

Tardajos
A H

Río Arlanzón

8.8
11.0
13.0

Rabé de
las Calzadas
A H

Buniel

Frandovinez

Fuente
Praotorre
15.6

cuesta
matamulas

Hornillos
del Camino
A H

Vilviestre
de Muñó

Ceada del
Camino

20.8

A San Bol
26.5

Iglesias

Isar

Hormaza

Yudego

Villandiego

Castrillo
de Murcia

Sasamón

Olmillos de
Sasamón

Villanueva
de Argaño   N-120

Hontanas
A H
31.4

Tardajos

Asunción

Municipal
stone cross

200m

Río Urbel

**Rabé de
las Calzadas**

Ermita de Nuestra
Señora de
Monasterio

Hospital Santa Marina
2 Liberános Dómine

Municipal 1 San Román
2 De Sol a Sol

N-120

50m

Hontanas

El Nuevo 1

2 Puntido
4 Fuente Strella

Casa Brígida 3 5 El Descanso
Concepción

25m

✝ San Nicolas de Bari
€1.50, ✆947-207095,
🕐Tu-Su 12-1:30pm,
5-7pm

Real Monasterio de
Las Huelgas

0.0 *Leave Burgos (map p. 135) via c/Fernan Gonzalez, passing* **Iglesia de San Nicolas de Bari**, *the* **Solar del Cid, Arco San Martín** *and* **Puente Malatos (1.4km)** *"bridge of the sick" through a green shady park. Pass two supermarkets 🛒 on route. After the bridge, cross highway N-120. Continue on the main route, turn through the stone door to the R and follow markings through El Parral park. [To visit* **Real Monasterio de Las Huelgas** *and/or* **Hospital de Reyes**, *continue straight to leave the marked camino route on Paseo de los Comendadores.]*

At the end of Parque El Parral, pass the Ermita de Santo Amaro el Peregrino, and turn R through the Puerta Romeros. Turn L to walk west along highway N-120. Pass under a railroad and

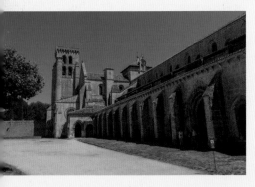

Real Monasterio de Las Huel
"Royal Monastery of the Pleasu
(€7, 🕐Tu-Sat 10am-1pm, 4-5:30p
Su 10:30am-2pm ✆947-201630
visitors must enter on a tour in Span
offered on the hour) The monastery
created by Alfonso VIII in 1175, v
transformed one of his palaces int
luxurious convent where widow nob
women could retreat from the world
decadence. Today an order of nuns
here and guide visitors on tours. A m
nificent collection of royal tombs

displayed, where they were found largely untouched in the 1940s. Some of the opulent fabr
jewelry and riches found in the tombs are on display in the museum. While the royals bur
here were heavily involved in warfare with Muslims, their final resting place draws beautifu
from the Mudéjar style, particularly the cloister roof, the walls of the *Capilla de la Asunción*,
the *Capilla de Santiago*, with amazing plasterwork and inlaid ceiling. The Santiago Matamo
statue has a jointed arm, which was used in knighting ceremonies. The final room houses a c
lection of medieval fabrics and clothing, many of which also show Islamic influence.

The late 12th-century pilgrim **Hospital de Reyes** now houses the Faculty of Law at the Univ
sity of Burgos, though the current buildings are mainly 16th-18th century. A Santiago sta
oversees the niche above the entrance. Step inside to see the remains of the 13th-century chu
to the L with Gothic paintings of pilgrim scenes. Many pilgrim graves have been unearthec
the cemetery.

turn R on c/Benito Pérez Galdós out of town (3.1km). The road soon becomes dirt and leads to a small park and bridge (6.0km) with a paved road toward Villalbilla. At the roundabout after the bridge, turn R on the paved road, then a quick L onto a dirt footpath. This footpath leads out toward the train tracks, passing under the tracks (6.8km) and across an overpass (7.6km) to turn L and continue along highway N-120 on dirt paths.

Pass under the highway near the Río Arlanzón through a green park area (8.8km, with an apology from the construction workers on a plaque) and cross the paved road by the grain tower (9.1km). Turn R on the road and pass over the Río Arlanzón for the last time (9.3km). Continue on the paved road into Tardajos, where the trail turns L on c/Mediodia (10.4km) to zigzag through town and leaves via a 1-lane asphalt road.

11.0 Tardajos was once the Roman city of *Augustóbriga*, at the junction of the *Vía Trajana* and a north-south road. Note the 18th-century **stone cross** coming into town. During medieval times, three churches were here, one said to house Saint Francis on his pilgrimage to Santiago. The **Iglesia de Nuestra Señora de la Asunción** remains, where Teresa of Ávila was said to have taken communion. *After 1km cross Río Urbel (11.9km, popular for fishing and crabbing) and veer L to Rabé de las Calzados.*

11.0 **Tardajos** A H 🍴🛏️✚🅴🅿 Pop. 856
1. **A Municipal** (🛏️10, don): c/Asunción, 📞947-451189, 🕐Mar 19-Nov 1, simple and basic, clean with friendly hospitalero

13.0 **Rabé de las Calzados** A H🍴🅿
Pop. 221, 📖 May come from "rabbi" or "riverbank"
2. **A Liberános Domine** (priv, 🛏️24, €8): 🍴🛏️📶 Francisco Ribera 10, 📞695-116901, 🕐12:30pm, all year
3. **A Hospital Santa Marina y Santiago** (priv, 🛏️8, €8): 🍴📶, Francisco Ribera 6, 📞607-664122, 🕐3pm, Apr-Oct, mixed reports

Stone crucero
outside of Tardajos

13.0 Rabé de las Calzados

The section of medieval path to Rabé was swampy and treacherous, featured in a popular pilgrim song:

De Tardajos a Rabé
no te faltarán trabajos.
Y de Rabé a Tardajos,
libéranos Domine!

From Tardajos to Rabé
you will not lack for troubles.
And from Rabé to Tardajos,
Deliver us, oh Lord!

Leave Rabé on a dirt road, passing the sweet Ermita de Nuestra Señora de Monasterios (13.4km). Begin the steady climb up onto the meseta, gaining about 125m of elevation.

🐚**Hornillos**
Late July: Celebration of the rooster story

15.6 La Fuente Praotorre (+100m) provides some shade on the way up, though unfortunately the pump for the water was broken at time of research so do not count it as a source of water. *From the high point (18.1km), experience the vast emptiness of the meseta, punctuated only by bird calls and the wailing wind. Descend again via a steep path known as the cuesta matamulas ("mule-killing incline"). At the bottom, cross a paved road and continue into Hornillos del Camino. On the way into town pass a well-equipped shop 🛒.*

20.9 Hornillos del Camino A H 🏨🍴🛒 Pop. 61, 🏛 Spanish: "little ovens [or kilns] of the camino"
1. **A Municipal** (🛏32+, €6): 🛏, Plaza de la Iglesia, 📞947-411050, 🕐closed in Feb, extra beds in the polideportivo when necessary, basic
2. **H De Sol a Sol** (sng €38, dbl €45 w/🚿): c/de Los Cantarranas 7, 📞649-876091

20.8 Hornillos del Camino was quite possibly an ancient city, but few remains have been excavated from its earliest days. Just before town, ruins of the San Lázaro hospice for lepers can be seen to the south. Ruins of a medieval pilgrim hospital have also been found. The town fountain (*fuente de gallo*) features a rooster on top because of a story that says that Napolean's troops stole all the chickens in Hornillos while the townspeople were at Mass. The soldiers killed the chickens and snuck them out of town in their drums. When confronted by the townspeople, the soldiers denied everything, but one rooster miraculously came back to life and gave a mighty crow from within the drum, proving the soldiers' guilt.

The path to Hornillos

Continue straight out of town on a dirt road, which gradually ascends and descends through shadeless wheat fields to the clearly marked turnoff to San Bol [+300m].

26.5 San Bol

Legend has it that pilgrims who soak there feet in the San Bol fountain will be cured of all foot pain. The luscious green yard is a great place to relax. Ruins scattered nearby are from the monastery of San Boadilla from the 11th century.

Fountain at San Bol

After the San Bol turnoff, the trail rises again and continues for 5km of classic meseta camino. Just when you think it can't possibly be any further, the trail will rapidly descend and the tower of the church of Hontanas will burst into view.

26.5 **San Bol A** (also called Sambol)
⛪ San Boadilla, a local saint
A Arroyo de San Bol (priv, 🛏12, €5): 🍴,
  📞609-164697/696-858770, 🕐Mar 12- Oct 31,
  dinner €6, recently renovated with electricity,
  toilets and showers, but still a rustic feel

utterflies along the
lains after Hornillos

31.4 **Hontanas** A H ▯▯

Pop. 70, ▯ Italian: "fountains"

1. **A Municipal** (▭20, 35+ overflow, €5): ▯,
   c/Real 26, ☎947-377021, ⏱1pm in summer,
   all year, interesting restored historic building

2. **A H El Puntido** (priv, ▭46, dm €5, dbl €24):
   ▯▯▯▯▯▯, c/Iglesia 6, ☎947-378597/636-
   781387 ▯, ⏱Easter-Oct

3. **A Casa Brígida** (priv, ▭14, €7): ▯▯▯▯▯,
   c/Real 15, ☎609-164697/628-927317,
   ⏱Mar 12- Oct 31, beautiful historic house

4. **H Fuente Strella** (sng €25-35, dbl €35-45):
   c/Iglesia 6, ☎947-377261 ▯

5. **H El Descanso** (dbl €35): c/Real 16
   ☎947-377035/606-137989 ▯

▬ For a summer cool-
off, walk just past town
to the **municipal pool**
(€2, 12-8pm)

31.4 **Hontanas** is named for the numerous springs and abundant water in the area. The 14th-century **Iglesia de la Inmaculada Concepción** can be found along the main road. Italian pilgrim Domenico Laffi in the 1670s complained bitterly about the dangers of packs of wolves prior to Hontanas and the inhospitable welcome he received in Hontanas:

"With God's help we crossed this deserted waste land and reached the village of Hontanas. It lies hidden in the valley of a little river, so that you scarcely see it until you have reach it... They have a strong palisade round the huts to guard against wolves which come at night to attack them... There are so many of them that you see them in packs, like flocks of sheep... So whenever you want to cross this desert you must do it in the middle of the day when the shepherds are out with their huge dogs... Having reached this wretched place by evening, we ate a little bread with garlic... Then we went to bed on the ground because there was nowhere else."

Today you'd be hard-pressed to find a wolf, and good food and beds are in abundance. Several modern pilgrim narratives mention Victorino, a camino character (now retired) who used to entertain pilgrims by drinking an entire liter of wine from a *porrón* jar in one draw. According to comedian Hape Kerkeling, "He pours a liter of red wine over his hair, inhales it through his nose, and blows it into his mouth while warbling a tune."

Entering Hontanas

HONTANAS TO BOADILLA DEL CAMINO

28.5km
(17.7mi)

🕐 **6-8 Hours**
Difficulty: ▭◱◻
🅿 32%, 9.0km
🆄 68%, 19.5km

A Albergues:
San Antón 5.6km
Castrojeriz 9.4km
San Nicolás 18.3km
Itero 20.3km
<u>Boadilla 28.5km</u>
Frómista 34.3km

Approaching
Castrojeriz

Visit the enigmatic ruins of San Antón and the medieval castle of Castrojeriz, sleep in a church in San Nicolás or go for a swim in Boadilla.

☀ Most of this day is on pleasant dirt tracks with two towns offering pilgrim services. The hill after Castrojeriz is especially steep (both up and down) so be sure to reserve energy and take plenty of water for this shadeless section. After San Nicolás, the path crosses from Burgos province into Palencia. Note that Boadilla does not have a shop, so bring any supplies you may need for an overnight there.

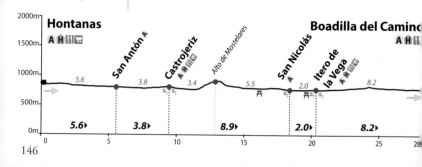

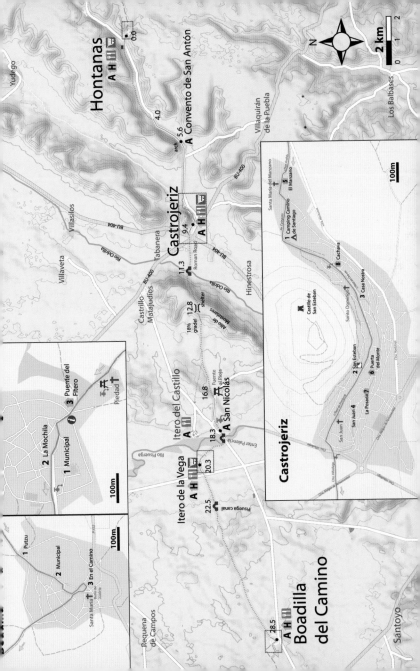

Hontanas
A H [icons]

0.0

4.0

5.6 A Convento de San Antón

Castrojeriz
A H [icons]

9.4

11.3 Roman Road

12.8 16% gradel

shelter

Alto de Mostelares

Fuente

16.8 A San Nicolás

Itero del Castillo
A [icons]

18.3 A San Nicolás

Enter Palencia

20.3

Itero de la Vega
A H [icons]

22.5 Pisuerga canal

28.5

Boadilla del Camino
A H [icons]

N

2 km
0 1 2

Yudego

Los Balbases

Villaquirán de la Puebla

Villasilos

Villaveta

Tabanera

Castrillo Matajudios

Hinestrosa

Requena de Campos

Santoyo

BU-400
BU-404
BU-404

Río Odrilla
Río Odrilla
Río Pisuerga
Río Pisuerga

Castrojeriz

100m

Santa María del Manzano

5 Camping Camino de Santiago
El Manzano

8 Cachava

Castillo de San Esteban

3 Casa Nostra

2 San Esteban

6 Puerta del Monte

San Juan 4

La Posada 7

San Juan 1

Santo Domingo

1 Municipal
2 La Mochila
3 Puente del Fitero
Piedad

100m

1 Putzu
2 Municipal
3 En el Camino

Santa María

100m

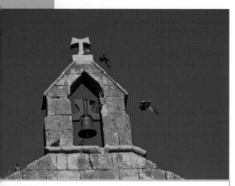

0.0 *Leave Hontanas on the main road, continuing onto a dirt path (hot weather alternative is to walk the shaded paved road). The path rejoins the road (4.0km), and continues to the ruins of the Convento de San Antón. Walk around to the back of the convent and peek in if the door is open.*

5.6 **San Antón** church complex was started by the Order of St. Anthony, a 11th-century order dedicated to the 3rd-century Egyptian hermit whose relics it held. A man brought his daughter to the relics and she was healed of a particularly pernicious disease reminiscent of leprosy. This disease became known as St. Anthony's Fire, which caused a terrible burning feeling, loss of circulation and eventually gangrene. This disease was in fact likely ergotism, caused by a fungus that grows on rye bread. The order developed a reputation for healing this disease, though serendipitously, pilgrimage was an excellent antidote to the disease as vigorous exercise and plenty of wine helped to overcome it.

Notice the niches outside the church as you pass, which used to hold food for the poor. St. Antón is the patron saint of animals, and across Spain people bring their pets to be blessed on his saint's day. The church ruins include a high archway over the camino path, and the remains of rosette windows featuring the *Tau* cross (t-shaped), used as a symbol of the order. An unusual but beloved albergue now exists in the ruins.

5.6 **Convento de San Antón** **A**

A **Hospital de Peregrinos de San Antón** (priv, 🛏12, don): 🍴, 🕐May to Sept 📷, in ruins of convent, communal meals by candlelight, no electricity or hot water, basic, special experience

Tau on the bell tower of Convento de San Antón (above)

Camino marker entering Castrojeriz

Colorful flowers in Castrojeriz

The trail continues on the paved road right through the Arch of San Antón and follows a pleasant quiet shaded road to **Castrojeriz (9.4km)**, easily identifiable with its imposing castle ruins on the hill above. The trail winds through this classic medieval city, which seems to be perpetually on siesta with hardly a soul out on the street.

9.4 **Castrojeriz** occupies a perfect position for defense along the steep mesa topped by the 🏰 **Castillo de San Esteban**. The Romans used the castle, said to be founded by Julius Caesar, to protect the roads to Galicia's lucrative gold mines. The city changed hands frequently until coming under Christian rule in the 10th century. The charter for the city was progressive for its day—the punishment for killing a Jew was the same as for killing a Christian.

9.4 **Castrojeriz** A H 🏠🍴🛒🔌➕🛈🏧
Pop. 873, 🏛 Latin: *Castrum Sigerici* "Castle of (King) Sigerici," 🛈 Plaza Mayor, 3, 🕐947-377001

1. **A Camping Camino de Santiago** (priv, 🛏35, €6): 🍴🚿🧺🔌📶, c/Virgen del Manzano, 🕐947-377255 📱, 🕐Mar 15-Nov 15
2. **A San Esteban** (muni, 🛏30, don w/🛏): 🛏, Plaza Mayor, 🕐947-377001 📱, 🕐12:30pm, all year, historic building using solar energy
3. **A Casa Nostra** (priv, 🛏26, €6.50): 🔌🍴🚿🧺, c/Real de Oriente 52 📱, 🕐11am Feb-Dec
4. **A San Juan** (muni, 🛏28, don): c/Cordón, 🕐947-377400 📱, 🕐Apr-Oct, basic facilities
5. **H El Manzano** (dbl €35): 🍴, c/Colegiata, 🕐620-782768
6. **H Puerta del Monte** (dbl €54): 🍴, Plaza Puerta del Monte, 🕐947-378647 📱
7. **H La Posada/Mesón de Castrojeriz** (dbl €33-58): 📶, c/Cordón 1, 🕐947-377400 📱
8. **H La Cachava** (dbl €72): 🍴, 🕐947-378547 📱

149

Iglesia de Santa María del Manzano just before Castrojeriz

Franks and Jews settled in the town, which became a way station on the pilgrimage road with five churches and seven pilgrim hospitals along the "long road" through the city. Don't miss the impressive 13th-century Gothic **Iglesia de Santa María del Manzano**. Legend has it that Mary appeared to St. James from an apple tree and he was so startled that his horse reared up and came down heavily, leaving hoofprints in the stone outside the entrance.

✝ **Iglesia de Santa María del Manzano** (🕐Jun 15- Sep 30, 10am-2pm, ☎947-377001)

On the way through town, pass the 16th-century **Iglesia de Santo Domingo**—note the ominous carved skulls along the wall with the message *O Mors* (Latin: Oh death). The 13th-century **Iglesia de San Juan de los Caballeros** features an ornate Mudéjar ceiling. The castle looming above Castrojeriz goes back to pre-Roman times, used and built upon by the Romans, Visigoths, Moors and Christians. The view is well worth the climb, but probably only practical if you are staying the night in town.

Leaving Castrojeriz, cross highways BU-404 and BU-400 and continue straight on a gravel path that joins a restored Roman road before passing over a marshy area on a wooden bridge over the **Río Odrilla (11.3km)**. *Thousands of tons of stone were brought here to create a Roman causeway through the swampy Odrilla Valley for transporting gold and other minerals. The remains of Roman mines are still visible to the R, as well as a seam of mica running up the hill. The path climbs steeply up to the* **Alto de Mostelares (12.8km)**. *At the top is a small shelter for shade.* ⚠ *The downhill has been paved in cement and reaches a grade of 18%; proceed with caution. The path continues as gravel through more shadeless wheat fields.*

🏛 **Castrojeriz**
Late May: Garlic festival

16.8 Fuente al Pioja

Relief comes at Fuente al Pioja (the "Flea's fountain") where local fellows regularly offer coffee, fruit and other snacks along a shady picnic area. A natural spring offers untreated water, though locals say it is safe to drink. *Follow a paved road and turn L onto a dirt path, with Itero del Castillo visible amongst the trees in the valley off route.*

+1.0 **Itero del Castillo** A ⬛ Pop. 105

A Municipal (1.0km off-route, 🛏7, €5): Plaza del Ayuntamiento, ☎608-977477, 🕐all year, ask for key in Bar El Castillo

---

18.3 San Nicolás Chapel

Pass the friendly San Nicolás chapel and albergue, who practice footwashing for pilgrims that stay overnight. Clean restrooms are behind the chapel in the yellow modern building.

18.3 **San Nicolás Chapel** A

A ☆ **San Nicolás** (assoc, 🛏12, don): ⬛, 🕐June-Sept, to the L before the bridge, communal meals, 13th-c. church restored and run by an Italian Confraternity, no electricity [except in WC/shower house in back], ritual of foot washing

---

Dawn view near Castrojeriz

151

A cyclist passes through wheatfields before Boadilla

After San Nicolás cross over the **Río Pisuerga (18.5km)** on a paved bridge, turning R past a picnic area and welcome sign to **Palencia** (river is the border between Burgos and Palencia provinces). A pilgrim bridge was first commissioned here in the 11th century by Alfonso VI to unify the territories of Castile and León.

The *Codex Calixtinus* provided ambiguous information about *Tierra de Campos*, the territory you are entering. It is "full of royal treasure, of gold and silver, fabrics and the strongest horses, and flush with bread, wine, fish, milk and honey. It is however lacking in firewood and the people are evil and vicious."

🏔 Itero de Vega
Aug: Itero Rock heavy metal festival 📱

20.3 **Itero de Vega** A H 🍴🚌📧
Pop. 177, 🗺 Spanish: "boundary of the meadow"
1. **A Municipal** (🛏12, €5): 📷📶,
   Plaza de las Iglesias, 🕐605-034347, 🔄all year
2. **A La Mochila** (priv, 🛏20, €6-8): 🍴📧📧,
   c/Santa Ana 3, 🕐979-151781, 🔄all year
3. **H Puente de Fitero** (sng €28, dbl €38): 🍴📧,
   c/Santa Maria 3, 🕐979-151822

20.3 **Itero de Vega**: Reaching the outskirts of town, the road becomes paved. To the L is a the 13th-century Ermita de la Piedad, with a picnic area and water. *Continue through town and leave via a wide dirt road. Cross the* **Pisuega canal (22.5km)** *on a small bridge. Arrive to Boadilla del Camino after a long desolate road over a gentle hill on a mesa.*

28.5 Boadilla del Camino

is built in a circular plan, suggesting that it was fortified in medieval times. The Gothic **Rollo de la Justicia** outside of the **Iglesia de Santa María de la Asunción** symbolizes the independence granted to Boadilla in the 15th century, as they were then permitted to publicly torture and hang their own criminals. At its largest, the town supported a monastery and four churches. The **Canal de Castilla** begins here, which the camino follows to Frómista.

The Canal de Castilla was built from 1753-1859, covering 207km. The canal was used for ships that were pulled by mules on tow paths. Today the canals are used to irrigate agricultural fields.

28.5 Boadilla del Camino A H

Pop. 124, Latin: *boava* "ox."

1. **A** Putzu (priv, 16, €7): (free), c/las Bodegas 9, all year, mixed reports
2. **A** Municipal (12, €3): c/Escuelas, 979-810390, very basic
3. **A H** ☆ En el Camino (priv, 48, dm €6, dbl €26-31): , Plaza el Rollo, 979-810284/619-105168 , Mar-Nov, large green garden with small pool, good pilgrim menu

Rollo de la Justicia in
Boadilla del Camino

15

BOADILLA TO CARRIÓN DE LOS CONDES

24.5km
(15.2mi)

🕒 **6-7 HOURS**
DIFFICULTY: ▭▢▢
🄿 16%, 4.0km
Ⓤ 84%, 20.5km

A ALBERGUES:
Frómista 5.8km
Población 9.1km
Villarmentero 14.8km
Villalcázar 19.0km
Carrión 24.5km
Calzadilla 41.5km

⚠ **ALT. ROUTE:**
Río Ucieza Route,
+1.5km (p. 156)

Almost halfway to
Santiago!

Meander along canals, gaze at stunning column capitals, see the miraculous Virgen Blanca and sing with nuns in Carrión.

☀ This day begins along the Canal de Castilla to Frómista, then along the road to Población. Then choose between two alternates, the more obvious and better-marked path along a gravel path parallel to the highway or a river route that follows the small Río Ucieza and provides more shade and peace and quiet, but is not as well marked. The routes meet in Villalcázar for the last slog to Carrión parallel to the road.

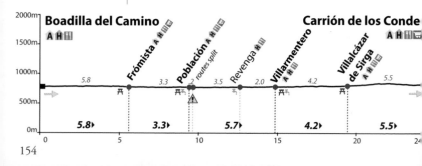

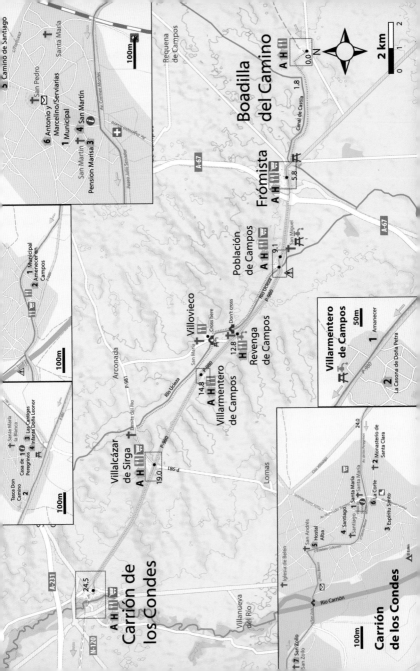

5 Camino de Santiago

Santa María

✝ San Pedro

6 Antonio y
Marcelino/Serviarias

1 Municipal

San Martín ✝ **4** San Martín

San Martín ✝ **3**
Pension Marisa

100m

Requena
de Campos

✝ **Boadilla**
del Camino

A H ⊞ 0.0 N

1.8

Canal de Castilla

A-67

Frómista

A H ⊞ 5.8

San Miguel ⚓

Población
de Campos

A H ⊞ 9.1

Río Ucieza
P-980

⚠

2 km

0   1   2

---

1 Municipal en
Campos

2 Amanecer

⊞ ⊞

100m

⚠

Arconada

Río Ucieza

Ermita del Río
P-981

Villalcázar
de Sirga

A H ⊞

186-d

19.0

Santa María
la Blanca

Tasca Don
Camino **2**

Casa de **1** ⊞ **3** Las Cantigas
Peregrinos   ✝ Infanta Doña Leonor

100m

Villovieco

✝ San María

✝ Cross here

12.8 ✝ Don't cross

H ⊞

Revenga
de Campos

14.8 A H ⊞ P-980

Villarmentero
de Campos

Lomas

Villarmentero
de Campos

⚓

50m

1 Amanecer

2

La Casona de Doña Petra

Carrión de
los Condes

A-231

A H ⊞ 24.5

N-120

Villanueva
del Río

Carrión
de los Condes

Río Carrión

✝ San Andrés

24.0

✝ Santa María
Santa María

✝ **4** Santiago **1**

5 Hostal
Alba

6 La Corte

3 Espíritu Santo

2 Monasterio de
Santa Clara

100m

✝ **7** San Zoilo
San Zoilo

Iglesia de Belén

0.0 *From Boadilla, follow the trail out of town via a dirt road that veers L by a fence and barn. The trail joins the **Canal de Castilla (1.8km)** and follows the flow all the way to Frómista. Entering Frómista, the trail passes over a dam complex and under the railroad tracks into town. The trail passes Av. Ingeniero Rivera, which has a variety of services* 🅾️🍴🛏️.

5.8 **Frómista** has been a breadbasket farming area since Celtic times until being destroyed by the Moors and later rebuilt in the 12th century. When the Jews of Castilla y León were systematically attacked in 1391, Frómista absorbed some of the Jewish refugees, though the Jewish population was exiled in 1492. In spite of being a successful market town in the 15th century, the town declined until a revival in 1773 when the canal brought water and enabled agriculture to again thrive. Visit the Romanesque **Iglesia de San Martín** (€1, 🕐10am-2pm, 4-8pm) for its amazing series of capitals and corbels, with the overall construction based on the cathedral of Jaca.

Sunrise over Canal de Castilla (upper)

Iglesia de San Martín in Frómista (lower)

⚠ Alternate: Río Ucieza Route, +1.5km

*This route is not well marked but is easy to navigate because it closely follows the river. The scene[ry] is more natural than the primary route along the road. Turn R immediately before the bridge aft[er] Población and follow the faint 4X4 track closest to the river. This track is often overgrown wi[th] flowers, grass and thistles so be sure to wear long pants. Don't cross the first bridge unless to visit t[he] town of Revenga and/or cross over to the primary path. Continue to the town of **Villovieco**, whic[h] has a fountain and church. Turn L and cross over the bridge. There is a picnic area, small snac[k] stand and water. The trail continues to the R directly after the bridge (before picnic area) on a we[ll] marked dirt road. Follow this road until you meet a paved road with the **Ermita de Nuestra S[e]ñora del Río** to the L, which houses a Mary statue said to have swum upstream to the spot during [a] flood! Turn L and follow the paved road (P-981) to rejoin the main trail in **Villalcázar de Sirg[a]**.*

🏛 **Fromista Cheese Museum:**
free, ©979-810012, ⊕10am-2pm,
5-8pm weekdays

🧹 **Friday** is Frómista's market day.

The trail leaves Frómista on the sidewalk over a bridge, which becomes a dirt track parallel to the highway for 3.3km to Población de Campos, with 13th-century Ermita de San Miguel off to the L when the trail turns R into town.

9.1 Población de Campos

has existed since the 11th-century and housed two pilgrim hospitals. ⚠ Just after Población, the alternate route splits to the R at the small bridge. *See sidebar opposite for alternate river route. For the standard route, continue straight on a gravel track next to the highway, with the river on the R. Pass through* **Revenga de Campos** 🍴 *(12.8km). Continue straight to Villarmentero.*

14.8 Villarmentero

has a Mudéjar-style ceiling in the 16th-century Iglesia de San Martín de Tours. *Follow the same path along the road to Villalcázar de Sirga.*

19.0 Villalcázar:

Turn R if you wish to enter Villalcázar and visit the church (retablo of St. James and an image of Mary said to perform miracles) or continue straight to bypass the town on dirt road parallel to highway.

5.8 Frómista A H🍴🚆✚🕭ℹ🚌🛈
Pop. 846, 📖 Possibly from Latin *frumentum* "grain"
1. **A Municipal** (🛏56, €7): 🚾🅳, Plaza de San Martín, ©979-811089, ⊕summer opens noon, winter 3:30pm, all year except Dec 24-Jan 30
2. **A Estrella del Camino** (priv, 🛏34, €8): 🍴🅳, Av. del Ejército Español, ©979-810053 📱, ⊕noon in summer, 1:30pm in winter, Mar-Oct
3. **H Pensión Marisa** (dbl €30): Plaza San Martín 3, ©979-810023 📱
4. **H San Martín** (sng €38, dbl €48): 🍴🛜, Plaza San Martín 7, ©979-810000 📱
5. **H Camino de Santiago** (sng €25, dbl €48): 🍴🛜 c/Francesa, ©979-810053/979-810282 📱
6. **H Antonio y Marcelino/Serviarias** (quad €85): 🍴, c/Magistral Aguado 14, ©626-959079 📱

9.1 Población de Campos A H🍴🚆
Pop. 140, 📖 Spanish: "town of the fields"
1. **A Municipal** (🛏18, €4): 🍴, Paseo del Cementerio, ⊕all year, very basic, administrated by CTR Amanecer, nicer rooms available in hotel for €10
2. **H Amanecer en Campos** (dbl €45): 🍴🛜, c/Fuente Nueva 5, ©979-811099📱

14.8 Villarmentero A H🍴 Pop. 11
1. **A H Amanecer** (priv, 🛏36, dm €6, dbl bungalow €18, teepee €5, hammock €3): 🍴, c/José Antonio 2, ©662-279102 📱, ⊕Mar-Oct
2. **H Casona Doño Petra** (dbl €50): 🍴🛜, c/Ramon y Cajal 14, ©979-065978

19.0 Villalcázar de Sirga A H🍴🚆 Pop. 174
📖 Latin: *villa* (town), Arabic *cazar* (castle), *sirga* (road)
1. **A Casa de Peregrinos** (muni, 🛏20, don): Plaza de Peregrino, ©979-888041, ⊕4pm, Apr-Oct
2. **A Tasca Don Camino** (priv, 🛏20, €7): 🍴🚾🅳, c/Real 23, ©979-888053, ⊕1:30pm all year
3. **H Hostal Las Cantigas** (sng €30, dbl €40): 🍴🛜, Av. de Condes Toreno 1, ©979-888027 📱
4. **H Infanta Doña Leonor** (dbl €45): 🛜, Av. de Condes Toreno, ©979-888118 📱

Evening singing with the nuns of Santa María in Carrión

According to tradition, Villalcázar was under the protection of the Knights Templar (p. 163). The camino did not originally pass through this town, but later detoured when the fame of the **Virgen Blanca** ("white virgin") and her many miracles spread. She is on display in the 13th-century **Iglesia de Santa María la Blanca** (☉10:30am-12pm, 4:30-7pm). A 1530 retablo has scenes from the life of Saint James, including his legendary run-in with the magician Hermogenes, who later converted to Christianity and burned his magic books.

⛪ **Carrión**
Aug 22: San Zoilo patron saint day
Thurs is market day, faithfully held since 1618.

Continue on the path along the road, and when Carrión de los Condes comes into view, cross the highway to the L and enter the city on Av. de los Peregrinos (24.0km). The trail is marked through the old town just past ❶ *Tourist Information. Santa María albergue is in the center, just off the Plaza de Santa María.*

24.5 Carrión de los Condes

was a wealthy and important camino town, with as many as 10,000 citizens in the Middle Ages and no less than 14 pilgrim hospitals. According to legend, Charlemagne camped here in his campaign against the Moors, who had succeeded in building a castle in Carrión in the 8th century (now **Iglesia de Belén**). It was also home to famous medieval poet Sem Tob, a Jewish rabbi known for his epic poem *Proverbios Morals*.

The **Iglesia de Santiago** was reconstructed in 1845 after the original 12th-century structure was lost in a fire. The original façade remains and the building houses a small art museum. **Iglesia de Santa María del Camino** commemorates the legend of the 100 virgins, in which the Moor rulers demanded 100 Christian virgins each year from the Christian ruler Mauregato. The Christians prayed that this travesty would end, and the Moors were chased away by a herd of bulls. Look for two bulls on each of the jambs. Evening pilgrim Mass is offered.

The 13th-century **Monasterio de Santa Clara**, which now offers an albergue, was said to house Saint Francis on his pilgrimage.

The town is named for a legend that the Cid's daughters married counts in this area, whom the Cid had killed after they tried to rob him (hence *Los Condes*, "the counts"). See El Cid (p. 102).

☼ Be sure to procure enough supplies for the 18km stretch without services on the trail tomorrow.

Crosses in Carrión de los Condes

24.5 Carrión de los Condes A H 🛒⛲

✚●🛈▲⛺ Pop. 2,221, 🛁 nearby Carrión river

1. **A** ☆ **Santa María** (par, ☎52, €5): 🖥️Ⓦ🅓🅑🖥️,
   ☏979-880500 ✉, ⊖Mar-Oct, next to Iglesia Santa María, nuns offer an evening session of folk singing

2. **A H Monasterio de Santa Clara** (par, ☎16, dm €5, sng €21, dbl €42): 🖥️, c/ Santa Clara 1, ☏979-880837, ⊖11am Mar-Nov

3. **A Espíritu Santo** (par, ☎90, €5): 🖥️Ⓦ🅓🅑🖥️, c/San Juan 4, ☏979-880052, ⊖all year

4. **H Santiago** (dbl €40): Ⓦ🅓🛜, Plaza de los Regentes 8, ☏979-881052

5. **H Hostal Albe** (dbl €28, €34 w/kitchenette): c/Esteban Collantes 21, ☏979-880-913 ✉

6. **H La Corte** (dbl €45): 🍴, c/Santa María 36, ☏979-880138 ✉

7. **H Real Monasterio San Zoilo** (dbl €90): Obispo Souto, ☏979-880049 ✉

8. **Δ Camping El Edén** (tent €20, bungalows €80): c/Tenerías 11, ☏979-880200 ✉

CARRIÓN DE LOS CONDES TO TERRADILLOS DE LOS TEMPLARIOS

26.6km
(16.5mi)

⏱ **6-7 Hours**
Difficulty: ▭☐☐
🅿 28%, 7.6km
Ⓤ 72%, 19.0km

A Albergues:
Calzadilla 17.0km
Ledigos 23.3km
<u>Terradillos 26.6km</u>
Moratinos 29.8km
San Nicolás 32.4km

⚠ **Alt. Route:**
Small detour after
Calzadilla de
la Cueza (p. 162)

Fields of sunflowers
after Carrión

**Pass fields of blooming sunflowers,
trace ancient Roman roads,
step back into Templar history.**

☀ This day begins with a long, straight slog on the *Via Aquitana*, an ancient Roman route that has been restored. This is one of the longest stretches between towns on the Camino Francés: 17km to Calzadilla de la Cueza, no water sources and very minimal coverage for any bathroom breaks. The only respite and services are a seasonal snack stand, Oasis, offering drinks and sandwiches at about the halfway point to Calzadilla.

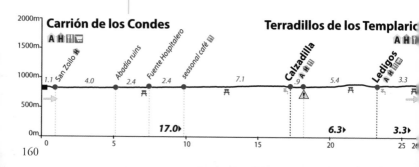

Carrión de los Condes · A H ▦▦
Terradillos de los Templarios · A H ▮
San Zoilo · 1.1 · 4.0 · Abadía ruins · 2.4 · Fuente Hospitalero · 2.4 · seasonal café · 7.1 · **Calzadilla** · .9 A ▦▦ · 5.4 · **Ledigos** A ▦▦ · 3.3

17.0▶ · **6.3▶** · **3.3▶**

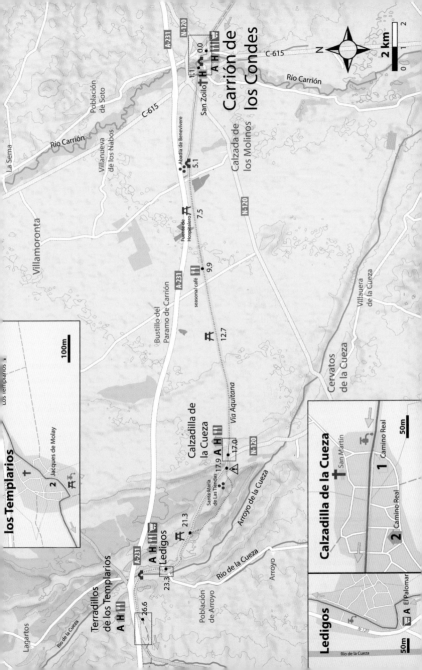

Carrión de los Condes

N

2 km

Río Carrión

C-615

N-120

A-231

0.0

1.1

San Zoilo

Calzada de
los Molinos

Población
de Soto

Río Carrión

C-615

Villanueva
de los Nabos

La Sema

Villamoronta

Bustillo del
Paramo de Carrión

A-231

Abadía de Benevivere
5.1

Fuente de
Hospederos
7.5

seasonal café
9.9

12.7

Vía Aquitana

Cervatos
de la Cueza

Villaquera
de la Cueza

los Templarios

Los Templarios

Jacques de Molay

100m

Calzadilla de
la Cueza

Santa María
de las Tiendas
17.9

A H
17.0

N-120

21.3

Ledigos

A H

23.3

A-231

Calzadilla de la Cueza

San Martín

Camino Real
1

2
Camino Real

50m

Ledigos

El Palomar
A

N-120

Río de la Cueza

50m

Terradillos
de los Templarios
A H

26.6

Lagartos

Río de la Cueza

Población
de Arroyo

Río de la Cueza

Arroyo

Arroyo de la Cueza

0.0 *Leave Carrión de los Condes from the Plaza de Santa María and follow the shells in the sidewalk out of town. Cross over the Río Carrión bridge and note the* **Monasterio de San Zoilo (1.1km)** *to the L, now a luxury hotel. The monastery holds relics of San Zoilo, a 4th-century martyr killed under the Diocletian persecution. At a large roundabout, cross N-120 and continue straight onto a 1-lane asphalt road (there is a bicycle detour marked to L). Follow this paved road to an equally straight dirt road (the historic Roman road). Look to the R for the ruins of the* **Abadía de Benevívere (5.1km)**, *a 11th-century Augustinian abbey. Pass fields of sunflowers (girasoles), stunning in summer when they are blooming. Sunflowers are a prime agricultural product; the oil is used as a cheaper substitute for olive oil.*

Pilgrims on the straight Roman route to Calzadilla

7.5 **Fuente de Hospitalero**, a historic spring that is usually dry, provides a welcome break from the monotony. Unfortunately, the shady picnic area is often overrun with trash and toilet paper. Pass a small **snack stand** 🏠 **(9.9km),** ☺ Apr-Oct, 7am-3:30pm. *Cross a paved road (10.2km) with graffiti intended to motivate you—bar, pool, albergue, 9km, ánimo! Continue to a rest area with shelter and picnic tables (12.7km), but unfortunately the water pump is not drinkable. Finally see the church tower of Calzadilla and enter the hamlet.*

☀️ Do a little dance, you are halfway to Santiago!

A welcome snack shop

17.0 Calzadilla de la Cueza

has Iglesia de San Martin with a 16-century Renaissance altarpiece. *The rest of the standard way to Ledigos is on a dirt path parallel to N-120. [⚠ There is also an option to turn off to the L for short alterate routes, which are slightly longer than the primary route. The "Palomar route" passes an adobe dovecote, common in this area as the doves were useful for pest control, fertilization and for food. This one was particularly ornate but is largely eroded away.] The main route passes the ruins of Santa María de las Tiendas, a former monastery and pilgrim hospital. Cross the highway one more time and arrive to Ledigos.*

17.0 **Calzadilla de la Cueza** A H 🚽🍴⭘
Pop. 54, 📖 Spanish: "little road on the Cueza river"
1. **A Camino Real** (priv, 🛏80, €7): 🍴 🅆 🅾 🔲,
   c/Mayor, 📞979-883187 ⭘all year
2. **H Camino Real** (dbl €40): 🍴, Trasera Mayor,
   📞979-883187

23.3 **Ledigos** contains Iglesia de Santiago with a lovely image of the saint, but the church is rarely open. *From Ledigos, the path passes back over the highway and onto another dirt path parallel to the highway, across the* **Río de la Cueza (24.5km)** *and into Terradillos.*

23.3 **Ledigos** A H 🚽🍴⭘ Pop. 74
A H El Palomar (priv, 🛏52, dm €6, dbl €18):
🍴 🅺 🅆 🔲 🛜 🔲, c/Ronda de Abajo,
📞979-883605, ⭘Feb-Nov, bar/shop in albergue

26.6 **Terradillos de los Templarios** was once home to a 13th-century church belonging to the **Knights Templar**, but is one of the few pilgrimage towns that never had a pilgrim refuge until modern times. Iglesia de San Pedro contains a Gothic crucifix but is rarely open. The church is built of brick rather than stone, as this area has very little local stone. Set aside from the N-120 highway, Terradillos has a peaceful sleepy town feel.

The Knights Templar were a medieval military order responsible for protecting pilgrims. While the order was popular and successful for almost 200 years, grand master Jacques de Molay was arrested in 1307 (on Friday the 13th, possibly the origin of this superstitious date) and burned at the stake for heresy and a variety of trumped-up charges. The order was disbanded in disgrace, though many think the charges had more to do with politics than any actual wrongdoing.

26.6 **Terradillos de los Templarios** A H 🍴
⭘ Pop. 78, 📖 Spanish: "small Templar terraces"
1. **A H Los Templarios** (priv, 🛏52, dm €7-9,
   sng €28, dbl €36): 🅆 🅾 🔲, 📞667-252279 🔲,
   ⭘Mar-Oct
2. **A Jacques de Molay** (priv, 🛏49, €8-10):
   🍴 🅴 🅆 🅾 🔲, c/Iglesia, 📞979-883679 🔲,
   ⭘all year except Dec 25-Jan 2

17

TERRADILLOS TO CALZADILLA DE LOS HERMANILLOS

26.4km
(16.4mi)

🕒 **5.5-7 Hours**
Difficulty: ▭□□
🅿 17%, 4.6km
Ⓤ 83%, 21.8km

A Albergues:
Moratinos 3.2km
San Nicolás 5.8km
Sahagún 12.8km
Calzada 18.0km
Calzadilla 26.4km
Reliegos 44.0km

⚠ **Alt. Stage 17A:**
Terradillos to Burgo
Mansilla, 30.9km
(p. 170 🅿Ⓤ)

A Alt. Albergues:
Same to Calzada
Bercianos 23.3km
Burgo Ranero 30.9km
Reliegos 44.1km

The regal arch of San
Benito in Sahagún

See small-town Meseta life with mudbrick buildings, view impressive ruins in Sahagún, enjoy big sky scenery.

☀ From Terradillos to Sahagún, the trail largely parallels the N-120 road through Meseta scenery and small towns with mudbrick houses. Sahagún has a wealth of historic buildings. At the split in Calzado, choose between the more remote northern route along the Roman *Via Trajana* to Calzadilla (recommended) or stay on the southern *Real Francesa* route, which parallels the paved road on a gravel track.

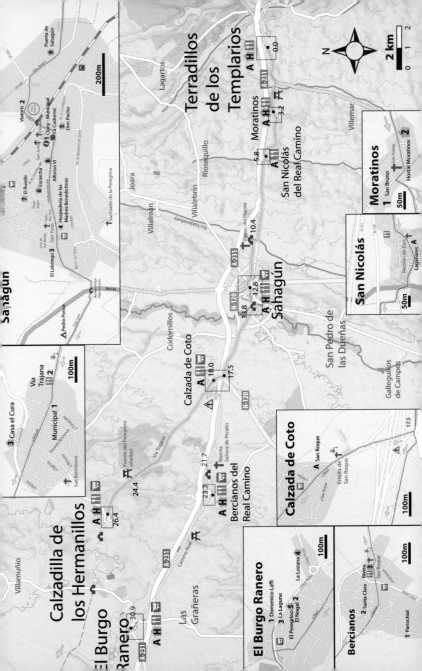

Sahagún

9 Puerta de Sahagún
10 La Codorniz
Don Pacho
1 Cluny · Municipal
8 Alfonso VI
6 Escarchia
7 El Ruedo
4 Hospedería de las Madres Benedictinas
El Labriego **3**

Santuario de la Peregrina

Viatoris **2**

200m

Rio Cea

Pedro Ponce

Calzadilla de los Hermanillos

3 Casa el Cura

Vía Trajana **2**
Municipal **1**

100m

26.4

San Bartolomé

Villamuñío

El Burgo Ranero

30.9

Las Grañeras

A-231

Camino Real

24.4

Vía Trajana

Fuente del Peregrino (shelter)

21.7

Nuestra Señora de Perales

Bercianos del Real Camino

23.3

El Burgo Ranero

1 Domenico Laffi
5 El Peregrino
2 La Laguna
3 La Laguna
2 El Nogal
La Lozana **4**

100m

Bercianos

2 Santa Clara
3
Ribera
San Roque

1 Parrochial

100m

Terradillos de los Templarios

0.0

A-231

3.2

Lagartos

Villamar

Moratinos

5.8

Riosequillo

San Nicolás del Real Camino

Villalebrín

Villalmán

Río Valderaduey

Joara

Codornillos

Calzada de Coto

18.0

17.5

N-120

Virgen del Puente
10.4

N-120

13.8

12.8

Sahagún

N-120

A-231

San Pedro de las Dueñas

Gallegillos de Campos

Moratinos

1 San Bruno

50m

Hostal Moratinos **2**

San Nicolás

Nicolás de Bari

Lagañares · A

50m

Calzada de Coto

A San Roque

Ermita de San Roque

17.5

100m

N

2 km

0   1   2

3.2 **Moratinos** A H 🛏️ Pop. 68
1. A H San Bruno (assoc, 🛏️18, dm €9, dbl €45):
   🍴 W 🖥️, c/Ontanón 9, ☎979-061465 ✉️,
   🕐Jan 16-Nov 14, run by Italian Association
2. H Hostal Moratinos (sng €30, dbl €45): 🍴 W 🛜,
   c/Real 12, ☎979-061466 ✉️ jacuzzi

5.8 **San Nicolás del Real Camino** A 🍴 🛏️
Pop. 48, 🏴 Spanish: "St. Nicholas of Royal Camino"
A H Albergería Laganares (priv, 🛏️22, dm €8,
dbl €25): 🍴 W 🖥️ 🛜 🖥️(free), Plaza de la Iglesia,
☎979-188142/629-181536 ✉️, 🕐Mar 15-Oct

0.0 *Leave Terradillos by a dirt track lined with poplar trees south of highway N-120 and continue to the village of Moratinos.*

3.2 **Moratinos**: The name suggests that this village may have once been Muslim or had a significant Muslim population. Many *moriscos* (Muslims who converted to Catholicism) settled as farmers in the flat areas of Castilla, only to be removed in 1609. There's not much to see in the 16th-century Iglesia Parroquial de San Tomás, but the roofed porch provides a shady spot for a break. *After town, rejoin the dirt track south of the highway to San Nicolás del Real Camino.*

5.8 **San Nicolás del Real Camino** was also under Templar control until the late 12th century. The mudbrick Iglesia de San Nicolás de Bari was rebuilt in the 18th century but has a Baroque retablo inside. *Continue to the dirt track parallel to the highway. At the **Río Valderaduey (10.0km)**, cross and leave the highway to the R and continue perpendicular away from the highway to **Ermita Virgen del Puente (10.4km)**,*

Bridge leading to Ermita Virgen del Puente before Sahagún

built in Sahagún Mudéjar style. From here, the route approaches Sahagún by dirt path. The trail is waymarked through Sahagún in a way that avoids the most interesting churches and monuments, so be sure to check the city map (p. 165) to detour to points of interest.

12.8 Sahagún

Looking at Sahagún today you would never guess its great significant in medieval times, second in the kingdom of León only to León city. King Alfonso VI was educated in Sahagún and sought refuge there while warring with his brother and richly rewarded the city when he emerged victoriously. He invited the Benedictines of Cluny to run the monastery, and the city became a center of Cluniac development (hence the name of the municipal albergue, Cluny). The city thrived with a diverse populace including Muslims and Jews. Sahagún's historic architecture illustrates the Romanesque-Mudéjar style, which incorporated Islamic decorative motifs and was built primarily out of brick rather than stone.

After crossing the railroad tracks into town, the first churches on the way are the modern **Iglesia de la Trinidad**, an imposing mudbrick building housing the municipal albergue and 🛈 Tourist Information office, and next to it the bright **Iglesia de San Juan de Sahagún**, a Neoclassic structure that holds the remains of the martyred saints Facundo and Primitivo. From the albergue turnoff, the camino is marked through Sahagún in a way that misses most of the architectural treasures, staying straight on *c/Arco*, then R on *c/Antonio Nicolás* through the city.

To detour to the historic sites, turn R past the albergue and take *c/El Arco* out to visit **Iglesia de San Lorenzo**, a 13th-century Romanesque-Mudéjar church with horseshoe arches and an interesting 1730 retablo. Turn L and head down through the *Plaza Mayor* to *c/Constitución* and *Plaza San Tirso,* which features numerous historical monuments.

12.8 Sahagún A H ⚑🍴🛒🚲🅿🛈🛈▲🚌🚉

Pop. 2,820, 🏛 *San Facundo*, a martyr killed nearby

1. **A Cluny** (muni, ⚑64, €4): 🅿 W 🖥,
   Iglesia de la Trinidad, 📞987-782117 🖼

2. **A H Viatoris** (priv, ⚑50, dm €7, sng €25, dbl €45): 🅿 W D 🖥 📶, c/Arco Travesía 25, 📞987-780975 🖼, 🕒Mar-Oct, bike rental

3. **A El Labriego** (priv, ⚑10, €9): 🍴📶, c/Antonio Nicolás 42, 📞987-781057 🖼, good location

4. **A H Hospedería de las Madres Benedictinas** (dm €5, dbl €20, dbl €30): 🅿 W D 📶, 🖥(free), Av. Bermejo y Calderón 10, 📞987-781139 🖼

5. **H Don Pacho** (dbl €35): Constitución 84, 📞987-780775

6. **H Escarcha** (sng €20, dbl €40): c/Regina Franco 12, 📞987-781856 🖼

7. **H El Ruedo** (dbl €55): 🖥, Plaza Mayor 1, 📞987-781834 🖼

8. **H Alfonso VI** (sng €30, dbl €40): 🖥(free): c/Antonio Nicolás 4, 📞987-781144 🖼

9. **H Puerta de Sahagún** (sng €60, dbl €85): 🍴, c/Burgos, 📞987-781880 🖼

10. **H La Codorniz** (sng €40, dbl €50): 🖥📶, c/Av. Constitución 97, 📞987-780276 🖼

11. **▲ Camping Pedro Ponce** (tent €6): 📶, Crta León 1, 📞987-780415

🏛 **Sahagún**
July 2: Festival de Peregrina
Late Oct: Leek festival (*feria de puerro*)
Sat is market day.

Iglesia San Tirso in Sahagún

Little remains of the once-great Clunian Monasterio de San Facundo, which in its heyday controlled over 100 monasteries throughout Tierra de Campos. Most of the remains were destroyed in the 19th century, first by the Peninsular War, then by fire. An 1835 clock tower looms above the ruins and the 1662 **Arco de San Benito** looks particularly regal with its lions and massive coat of arms.

On the other side of the ruins is **Iglesia de San Tirso**, another early 12th-century Mudéjar style church, whose impressive tower was rebuilt after a 1945 collapse. The nearby **Convento de las Madres Benedictinas** contains a 🏛 small museum featuring the Virgen de la Peregrina, patroness of Sahagún, brought to the museum from the Santuario de la Peregrina, a 13th-century church once part of a Franciscan monastery. This pilgrim virgin motif comes from a legend that lost pilgrims were guided here by a woman with a lighted staff.

⚠ Stage Options: 17 and 17A

☆ **Via Trajana (via Calzadilla), 26.6km (17)**
Recommended as the route is farther from the highway, more remote and follows a Roman road. Shorter distance than alternate, but **4.4km farther** to Mansilla in the next stage.

Real Francesa (via Burgo Ranero), 30.9km (17A)
Alternate route that shadows the highway but has more intermediary services (description p. 170). Allows shorter next stage.

Routes reconvene in Reliegos on stage 18 (p. 174).

*Leave Sahagún via the marked route on c/Antonio Nicolás and cross the **Río Cea (13.8km)** on the Puente Canto ("the singing bridge"), first built by Alfonso VI. Look for a grove of poplars to the R near the campground of Pedro Ponce; these are said to correspond to the Legend of the Flowering Lances, in which Charlemagne's troops stuck their lances in the ground while they slept. By morning they found that the lances had become trees and sprouted leaves and bark, which was considered an inauspicious sign. Many were lost in the battle after they had to hew down their own lances.*

Continue parallel to the highway on a dirt track. ⚠ *At the junction of N-120 and N-601 (17.5km), two route options diverge and reconvene in Reliegos in stage 18. The recommended route description is below, and the alternate is on p. 170.*

17.5 Via Trajana Route via Calzada de los Hermanillos
(alternative via el Burgo Ranero, p. 170)

The northern route follows the original Roman route, the *Via Trajana*. While today the straight path and planted shade trees make navigation easy, in medieval times this desolate area of the camino was a notorious place to get lost as one could lose all sense of direction in the monotonous, featureless landscape. *At the split, take the R option and cross over A-231 on an overpass and enter Calzada de Coto.*

18.0 Calzada de Coto was one of many
villages under the control of the monastery in Sahagún. Today it contains a church dedicated to Saint Stephen. *Pick up a dirt path on the outskirts of town, and continue straight to cross train tracks (20.3km) and on to the **Fuente del Peregrino (24.4km)**, with a shady rest area and playground. Keep straight to enter Calzadilla de los Hermanillos.*

26.4 Calzadilla de los Hermanillos
was named for the Benedictine monks sent from Sahagún who built the Ermita de la Virgen de los Dolores with Mozárabic brick details. Iglesia de San Bartolomé was built in the 16th-17th centuries, and features a statue of Saint Bartholomew wrestling with a demon.

Stone crucero in Calzadilla

18.0 Calzada de Coto A 🏠🛒 Pop. 259
📖 Spanish: "boundary road"
A San Roque (muni, 🛏24, don): c/Real, ☎987-78123, ☺all year, basic, ask for key in bar

---

26.4 Calzadilla de los Hermanillos A H
🏠🛒 Pop. 146, 📖 Spanish: "little road of the little brothers"
1. **A Municipal** (🛏22, don): 🄺Ⓦ🅾, c/Mayor 28, ☎987-330023, ☺all year
2. **A H Via Trajana** (priv, 🛏20, dm €15, dbl €35): 🄷Ⓦ🅾🖥, c/Mayor 55, ☎987-337610 🖋, ☺Mar-Nov
3. **H Casa el Cura** (dbl €45): 🄷Ⓦ, c/la Carretera 13, ☎987-337647 🖋

Walking parallel to the road on the alternate route

⚠ Alternate Stages 17A-18A: Real Francesa
17A: Terradillos to Burgo Ranero, 30.9km
18A: Burgo Ranero to Mansilla (via Reliegos), 19.2km
*distances measured from Terradillos

STAGE 17A
🅿 13%, 4.0km
Ⓤ 87%, 26.9km

17.5 *From the split, follow arrows L at the roundabout after crossing N-120. Pass a sign showing the route and a small monument before continuing on a dirt track parallel to a small quiet road. Pass the* **Ermita de Nuestra Señora de Perales (21.7km)** *"Our Lady of the Pear Trees," site of a former pilgrim hospital just east of Bercianos del Camino.*

23.3 Bercianos del Real Camino Ⓐ Ⓗ 🏨🍴
Pop. 195, 🏛 *Bercianos* likely refers to people from Bierzo region settled here after the Reconquista
1. **Ⓐ ☆ Bercianos** (+500m, par, 🛏46, don): 🍴Ⓦ, c/Santa Rita 11, 📞987-784008, 🕐1:30pm Apr-Oct, communal meals and singing
2. **Ⓐ Santa Clara** (priv, 🛏8, don): 🍴🛏Ⓦ◯🛜, c/Iglesia 3, 📞605-839993, 🕐July-May, plans to expand to 24 beds
3. **Ⓗ Rivera** (dbl €25 shared bath, €35 private bath): c/Mayor 12, 📞987-784287

23.3 Bercianos del Camino was also administrated by the monastery of Sahagún. The town has one small chapel of San Roque since the main Iglesia de San Salvador collapsed in 1998. The tower has been reconstructed in metal and can be seen off to the R on the way into town. *Leaving Bercianos, continue on the now-familiar parallel dirt track to Burgo Ranero.*

30.9 **El Burgo Ranero** was a wool-producing town, the biggest business of Castilla during the Middle Ages. Huge flocks of sheep (up to 40,000) were tended. They grazed in the mountains in summer while the Meseta fields were occupied with wheat, and returned in winter via specially developed sheep roads known as *cañadas*. Even today you may have the privilege of witnessing a flock of sheep blocking your path as they cross the camino on an ancient *cañada*. If coming from Terradillos, El Burgo Ranero is the most logical town for overnight. Below is the route description for the following stage, which reconnects with the main route in Reliegos, corresponding to the map on p. 173.

30.9 **El Burgo Ranero** A H 🍴🛒➕🏧🚲
Pop. 826, 🏛 Spanish: "town of frogs," or perhaps a distortion of *burgo granero*, or "town of wheat"
1. **A** **Domenico Laffi** (muni, 🛏28, don): 🅚 Ⓦ Ⓓ 🖥, Plaza Mayor, 🕿987-330023 📝, ⊙all year
2. **A** **El Nogal** (assoc, 🛏30, €10): Ⓦ, c/Fray Pedro 42, 🕿627-229331, ⊙Easter-Oct
3. **A** **H** **La Laguna** (priv, 🛏18, dm €8, dbl €40): 🅚 Ⓦ Ⓓ, c/La Laguna 12, 🕿987-330094, ⊙Mar-Nov
4. **H** **Lozana**: c/Fray Pedro 19, 🕿987-330060
5. **H** **El Peregrino** (dbl €45): c/Fray Pedro 36, 🕿987-330069

STAGE 18A
🅿 6%, 1.2km
Ⓤ 94%, 18.0km

To continue on alternate stage 18A to rejoin the main route, follow the gravel path next to a quiet paved road. Be prepared for few services and little shade to **Reliegos (13.0km)**. *A few picnic areas are present, but no water sources. At Reliegos, this alternate route joins with the recommended route coming from Calzada de los Hermanillos (p. 174). The distance from El Burgo Ranero to* **Mansilla de las Mulas** *is 19.2km.*

Mudbrick albergue Domenico Laffi in Burgo Ranero

171

18

CALZADILLA DE LOS HERMANILLOS TO MANSILLA DE LAS MULAS

23.6km
(14.7mi)

⏱ **6-7 HOURS**
DIFFICULTY: ▭▭▢
🅿 22%, 5.4km
Ⓤ 78%, 18.2km

A ALBERGUES:
Reliegos 17.6km
Mansilla 23.6km
Villarente 29.6km
Arcahueja 33.9km

⚠ **ALT. STAGE 18A:**
Burgo Ranero to
Reliegos, 19.2km
(p. 171 🅿Ⓤ)

A ALT. ALBERGUES:
(from Burgo Ranero)
Reliegos 13.2km
Mansilla 19.2km
Villarente 25.2km
Arcahueja 29.5km

Priests along the Roman road to Reliegos

Tread remote Roman paths and climb medieval walls in Mansilla de las Mulas, enjoy the freedom of the open road.

☀ This is an isolated day, far from towns and paved roads, along one of the best sections of Roman road in all of Spain. Be sure to bring sufficient water and food for the 17.6km without services until Reliegos, where this route joins the southern route from El Burgo Ranero (details in stage 17, p. 171) and continues into Mansilla parallel to a paved road.

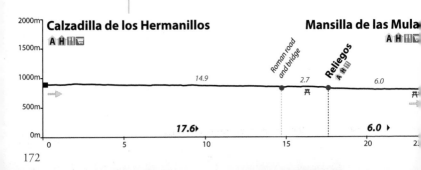

Calzadilla de los Hermanillos
A H ▦▦

Mansilla de las Mula
A H ▦▦

Roman road and bridge

Reliegos
A H ▦

14.9   2.7   6.0

17.6▸   6.0 ▸

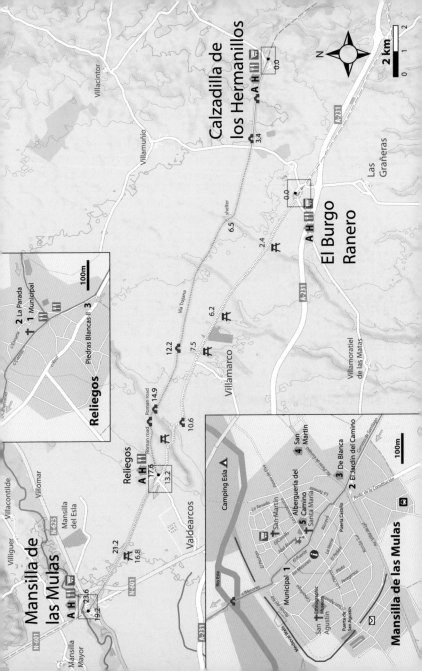

Calzadilla de los Hermanillos

A H ![] 0.0

3.4

N

2 km
0   1   2

A-231

Las Grañeras

shelter
6.5

2.4

0.0
A H ![]

El Burgo Ranero

Villamoratiel
de las Matas

A-231

Via Trajana

6.2

7.5

12.2

Villamarco

10.6

14.9
Roman road

Roman road
17.6
13.2
Reliegos
A H ![]

Reliegos

2 La Parada
1 Municipal ![]
Piedras Blancas II 3

c/Real

100m

16.8

21.2

Mansilla de las Mulas

Mansilla
del Esla

N-625

Villamontilde

Villómar

Villiguer

N-601

A-231

Mansilla
Mayor

N-601

N-601

23.6
A H ![]
19.2

Camping Esla △

4 San Martín
3 De Blanca
2 El Jardín del Camino

Albergería del
5 Camino

Santa María
1 Municipal

San Martín

La Tenada
El Corralón

Puerta Castillo

Avda. de la Constitución

Camino de Santiago

Río Esla

c/Mesones

San
Agustín
Ethnographic
Museum

Puerta de
San Agustín

100m

Mansilla de las Mulas

0.0 *Leave Calzadilla on c/Mayor, where the path leaves asphalt and continues on a dirt path along the same route the Romans used to transport gold from Galicia to Rome. To the north on a clear day the Cantábrica Mountains will be visible, with the Picos de Europa peeking out from behind.*

⚠ Routes join in Reliegos; see p. 171 for information on route via Burgo Ranero

⚠ Routes join in Reliegos; see p. 171 for information on route via Burgo Ranero

*Continue straight on the dirt path, crossing multiple bridges over small canals and streams. After the final bridge crossing **Arroyo del Valle de Valdearcos (14.9km)**, pass sections of original Roman road fenced off to either side of the path. Begin to see bodegas (underground cellars) carved into the slight hillside. At a 4-way junction, continue straight to Reliegos.*

17.6 **Reliegos** A H 🍴 Pop. 237
1. **A Municipal** (🛏50, €5): ⛶ 🖥, c/Escuela, 📞987-317801, 🕐all year
2. **A H La Parada** (priv, 🛏36, dm €7, dbl €30): 🍴⛶Ⓦ🅳🖥, c/Escuela 1a 7, 📞987-317880 📧, 🕐 all year except Dec 20-Jan 15, small 🛒
3. **A Piedras Blancas II** (priv, 🛏8, dm €9, dbl €45): 🍴Ⓦ🅳📶, c/Cantas, 📞607-163982, 🕐 Mar-Oct

23.6 **Mansilla de las Mulas** A H 🍴🛒➕€ℹ
🚌 Pop. 1,950, 🗝 Latin: *mansella* "small estate" and Spanish "of the mules" refers to historic mule markets
ℹ Plaza del Pozo 12, 📞987-310012
1. **A ☆ Municipal** (🛏76, €5): 🍴⛶Ⓦ🅳🖥📶, c/del Puente 5, 📞661-977305, 🕐12pm, Jan-Nov
2. **A El Jardín del Camino** (priv, 🛏32, €8-10): 🍴Ⓦ🅳🖥📶, c/Camino de Santiago 1, 📞987-310232 📧, 🕐all year
3. **H Pension de Blanca** (dbl €40): 📶, Av. Picos de Europa 4, 📞626-003177/676-191829 📧
4. **H San Martin** (sng €20-25, dbl €40-50): 🍴📶, Av. Picos de Europa 32, 📞987-310094 📧
5. **H Albergueria del Camino** (dbl €52): c/Concepción 12, 📞987-311193 📧
6. **⛺ Camping Municipal Esla** (tent €6.5): Ⓦ🛒, c/Fuente de los Prados, 📞630-212114

17.6 **Reliegos**: Brick bodegas mark the entrance of Reliegos, once the Roman town of *Palantia* located at the convergence of three Roman military roads. Its modern claim to fame is being struck by a meteor in 1947. The 17.3 kilo (38lb) meteor is on display in the natural science museum in Madrid. *Leaving Reliegos, the path follows parallel to the quiet paved c/Cantas, which then joins the paved road into Mansilla.*

23.6 **Mansilla de las Mulas** was once a Roman town, likely a stopping point on the *Via Trajana*. The city was fortified with walls in the 12th century and rebuilt in the subsequent two centuries. Today, more than half of the medieval walls remain, some as tall as 14m and as thick as 3m. It is possible to climb the stairway up into the rounded towers, and two of the original gates still stand.

Mansilla with grazing
sheep near the
historic city walls

Iglesia de Santa María was the only church in Mansilla until 1220 when five churches were added, and Santa María has outlasted them all (though it was rebuilt in the 18th century). The church contains a Baroque retablo and a Gothic Virgin Mary. Ruins of the 14th-century **Iglesia de San Martín** have been incorporated into a government building, the **Casa de Cultura**. The former 🏛 **Convent of San Agustín** has been converted into an attractive ethnographic museum beautifully displaying over 3,500 local artifacts, such as farming implements, textiles and traditional costumes (🕒Oct-Mar 10am-2pm & 4-7pm; Apr-Sep 10am-2pm & 5-8pm, closed Mon 🕒987-311923, *c/San Agustín 1*).

Mansilla is also the backdrop of the famous 1605 novel *La Pícara Justina*. The Río Esla provides a shaded pleasant area for a walk or wade in the evening.

🏛 **Mansilla de las Mulas**
Nov 11: San Martín patron saint day
Early Sept: Pilgrimage from León
Bacallao mansillés, cod in a special garlic sauce, is a local specialty.

175

MANSILLA DE LAS MULAS TO LEÓN

17.9km
(11.1mi)

🕐 **4-5 Hours**
Difficulty: ▭▭▭▢
🅿 42%, 7.6km
Ⓤ 58%, 10.3km

A Albergues:
Villarente 6.0km
Arcahueja 10.3km
León 17.9km
Virgen 25.6km

Luminous stained glass
in the León Cathedral

Stand in awe of León's luminous Gothic cathedral and Romanesque Real Colegiata de San Isidoro, splurge on a night at San Marcos Parador.

☀ If you were going to skip one day of the camino, this would be it. Much has been done to improve the safety of the pilgrim approach to León, with pedestrian bridges and overpasses, but the route still involves a lot of industrial walking. Be on alert for trail markers, detours and traffic! The effort is well-rewarded with the fascinating sites and history of the vibrant city of León.

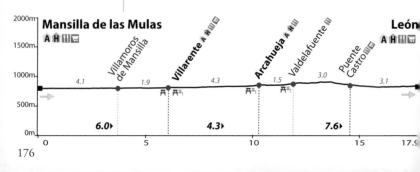

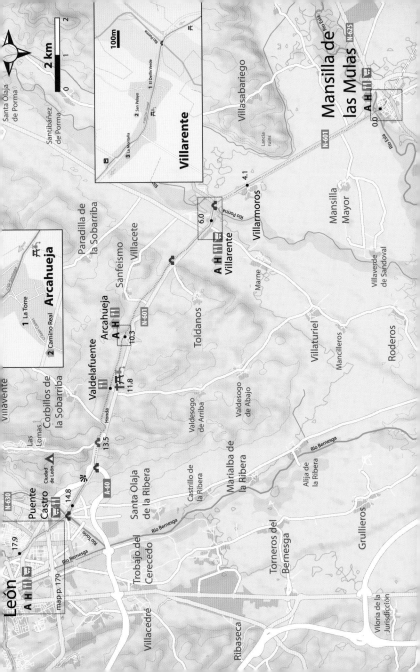

N

2 km

Santa Olaja
de Porma

Santibáñez
de Porma

Paradilla de
la Sobarriba

Sanfeismo

Villacete

Villarente

100m

Río Porma

1 El Delfín Verde

2 San Pelayo

3 La Montaña

Villarente

4.1

6.0

A H

Villarente

Villarmoros

Río Porma

Villasabariego

**Mansilla de
las Mulas**

N-601

A H

0.0

Río Esla

N-625

Lancia
ruins

Mansilla
Mayor

Villaverde
de Sandoval

Villaverde
de Sandoval

Roderos

Villavente

Corbillos de
la Sobarriba

Las
Lomas

Arcahueja

1 La Torre

2 Camino Real

Arcahueja

A H

10.3

N-601

Valdelafuente

Honda

A

11.8

Toldanos

Marne

Valdesogo
de Arriba

Valdesogo
de Abajo

Villaturiel

Mancilleros

Puente
Castro

N-630

A H

13.5

A-60

14.8

León

17.9

A H

map. p.179

Ciudad
de León

Río Torío

Río Bernesga

Santa Olaja
de la Ribera

Trobajo del
Cerecedo

Villacedré

Castrillo de
la Ribera

Marialba de
la Ribera

Alija de
la Ribera

Río Bernesga

Torneros del
Bernesga

Grullieros

Ribaseca

Vilória de la
Jurisdicción

6.0 **Villarente** A H 🛒➕🚍🅿 Pop. 342

1. **A** **El Delfín Verde** (priv, 🛏24, €6): 🍴,
Crta 601 km 15, ☎987-312065 📧, 🕐Mar-Oct

2. **A H** **San Pelayo** (priv, 🛏56, dm €8, dbl €30):
🄺 🅆 🄾 🖥, c/El Romero 9, ☎650-918281/987-312677 📧, 🕐noon, all year,

3. **H** **La Montaña** (dbl €45):
Camino de Santiago 17, ☎987-312161 📧

10.3 **Arcahueja** A H 🍴🅿 Pop. 194

1. **A H** **La Torre** (priv, 🛏22, dm €8, dbl €35,
trp €45): 🍴 🅆 🄾 🖥 📶, c/La Torre 1,
☎669-660-914 📧, 🕐Mar-Jan

2. **H** **Camino Real** (dbl €58): 🖥,
Ctra Valladolid km 320, ☎987-218134 📧

0.0 *Leaving Mansilla de las Mulas, cross the Río Esla and continue on a dirt path parallel to highway N-601. The ruins of Lancía, an ancient Celtic city, are visible to the R of the highway and can be visited by detour [+1.2km]. Pass through the outskirts of **Villarmoros de Mansilla (4.1km)** and continue on a dirt path until joining the highway to cross a pedestrian bridge over Río Porma into Villarente.*

6.0 **Villarente** contained several pilgrim hospitals and perhaps the camino's first ambulance—a donkey service for sick pilgrims to be transported to León (no longer in service). The town is named for the bridge with 20 arches that spans the Río Porma. A picnic area to the L after the bridge beckons, near one of the historic pilgrim hospitals. *On the far side of Villarente, leave busy N-601 to the R onto a gravel path (7.2km) uphill toward Arcahueja.*

10.3 **Arcahueja** is a small town near the outskirts of León. *Continue along the highway past the northern edge of **Valdelafuente** 🍴 **(11.8km)**, meeting the highway again at a Honda dealership. At the crest of the hill, watch for views of León with the mountains of behind. Cross a massive blue footbridge over the highway (13.5km) before descending to Puente Castro.*

14.8 **Puente Castro** 🍴🛒 was the site of a Roman fort and bridge (bridge has been rebuilt). Hebrew grave markers suggest a Jewish community here as far back as 905. The hill used as a vantage point in 1196 when Aragón and Castile attacked León, taking the castle, destroying the Jewish quarter and enslaving the Jewish population. *Cross Río Torío on a footbridge to enter León (15.9km). The marked path into León brings you to a large roundabout of major roads. Stay straight on Av. Alcalde Miguel Castaño for the parochial albergue and downtown. Cross Plaza de Santa Ana to enter the Old City with its cobblestone streets and ancient walls.*

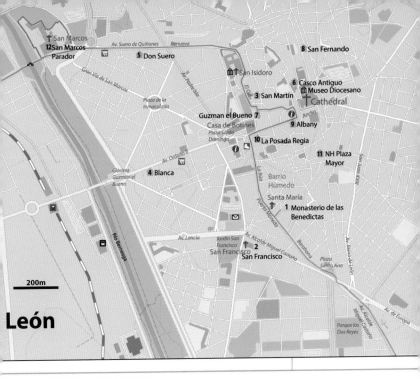

León A H ⛏🍴🛒🛏️✚🎵ℹ️⛺🚌♟✈️

4,305, 📖 In Spanish, *León* means "lion," but the name comes from the Latin military term for legion.

Monasterio de las Benedictinas (par, 📞142, €5 w/🍴): 🔲🅃🅓, Plaza Santa María del Camino, 987-252866 📧, 🕐Feb 1- Dec 15, evening Mass and pilgrim blessing, stuffy dorms

San Francisco de Asis (priv, 📞54-156, dm €10, dbl €36): 🔲🅓🍴📶, Av. Alcalde Miguel Castaños 4, 987-215060, 🕐all year, laundry and internet is free

Hostal San Martín (dbl €31): 📶, Plaza de Torres de Omaña 1, 📞987-875187 📧

Pension Blanca (sng €22-27, dbl €35-43): 🎫📟📶, c/Villafranca 2, 📞987-251991 📧

Hostal Don Suero (sng €24, dbl €40): 📶, c/Suero de Quiñones 15, 📞987-230600 📧

Hostal Casco Antiguo (dbl €50): 📶, c/Cardenal Landázuri 11, 📞987-074000 📧

Guzmán el Bueno (dbl €50): 📶, c/Lopez Castrillón 6, 📞987-236412 📧

Hospederia Fernando I (dbl €60): Av. de los Cubos 32, 📞987-220731 📧

Albany (dbl €68): 🍴📟(free), c/de la Paloma 13, 📞987-264600 📧

Hotel La Posada Regia (dbl €70): 🍴 📶, c/Regidores 9, 📞987-213173 📧

NH Plaza Mayor (dbl €70-100): 🍴 📶, Plaza Mayor 15-17, 📞987-344357 📧

Parador de San Marcos (dbl €130-200): 🍴 📶, Plaza de San Marcos 7, 📞987-237300 📧

Ciudad de León (tent €10, cabin €45): 🍴🛒🅦📶▬, 📞987-269086 📧, 3km out of city

Historic walls of León

17.9 **León** began as a Roman military encampment in 29CE and developed into a permanent settlement charged with protecting Galician gold on its journey to Rome. Visigoths took the city in 585, only to lose it to Muslim invaders in 712. The city was reconquered by Ordoño I around 850, who initiated a building boom and welcomed Mozárabic refugees (Christians living under Muslim rule). The city was leveled in 988 by Al-Mansur's troops. Rebuilding began soon after, and León flourished as a wool industry center. In 1188, the city hosted the first Parliament in Europe under Alfonso IX and became wealthy enough to construct the astonishing cathedral.

☀ León has a wealth of dozens of other churches and historical buildings. Head to ❶ **Tourist Info** for additional information (opposite cathedral at Plaza de Reglas 4, ☎987-237082).

León's finest treasure is its sublime Gothic **cathedral** (€5, 🕑M-Sa 9:30am-1:30pm, 4-8pm Su 8:30am-2:40pm, 5-8pm/ winter closed 1hr earlier ☎987-875770 📧) featuring 1,800m² of magnificent stained glass windows from the 13th-15th century. Without a flashy central retablo, the cathedral lets the streaming light steal the show. This is the fourth church on this spot, began in 1205 and completed in record time (about 100 years). From across the square, the whole of the west façade can be taken in. The serene *Virgen Blanca* welcomes from below the central tympanum. Choir stalls are intricately carved with biblical characters along with some humorous depictions of creative vices. The seven chapels contain Gothic tombs such as that of Ordoño II, with a scene of the crucifixion. El Cid (p. 102), an epic knight born in Burgos in 1040, is buried in the center of the cathedral.

Virgen Blanca (left) at the west entrance of the León cathedral (right)

The 🏛 **Museo Diocesano** (€5, ⊙M-F 9:30-2pm, 4-7:30pm Sa 9:30-2pm, 4-7pm, Su closed, reduced hours in winter) houses almost 1,500 pieces of sacred art, including Hispano-Islamic textiles, Hebrew funerary stones and a 1576 sculpture, *Christ on the Cross*.

The impressive **Real Colegiata de San Isidoro** (⊙987-876161 📷) is one of the premier Romanesque structures, setting the standard for all of northern Spain. The 11th-century complex was commissioned by the pious Fernando I to house relics returned by Muslims after their defeat in the Reconquista. The relics of San Isidoro of Seville (ca. 560-636) are housed in the basilica.

The **Panteón de los Reyes** and 🏛 **Museo de San Isidoro**, across the plaza from the basilica, can be visited on a guided tour in Spanish (€5, ⊙summer: M-Sa 9am-8pm, Su 9am-2pm). The 12th-century fresco paintings in the pantheon are a highlight, with remarkable representations of the 12 months on its arches. There are 44 tombs, including 23 kings, demonstrating the site's importance. Doña Urraca's jeweled chalice

⛪ **León**
Late June: Trout festival
October 5: Patron saint day, Sunday before celebrates the medieval Christians being freed from giving 100 virgins to their Muslim over-lords (p. 159)
Wed and **Sat** are market days in the Plaza Mayor, ⊙9am-2pm

A pilgrim statue rests outside off Hostal San Marcos Parador

is another must-see of the museum. The impressive library contains texts from as far back as the 10th century and a particularly lovely illuminated Bible. The basilica also features a *Puerta del Perdón,* which pilgrims who were unable to continue to Santiago could walk through to receive substitute indulgences.

Nightlife in the historic *Barrio Húmedo*

For evening entertainment, check out León's **Barrio Húmedo** (literally "wet neighborhood") in the Old City, known for its high concentration of bars and tradition of free tapas with drinks.

Antonio Gaudí's Modernist Casa de Botines (1893) incorporates Gothic elements but retains Gaudí's unique whimsical style. The building originally housed a department store and is now a bank.

Shell motif on Hostal San Marcos

On the way out of town, pass **Hostal San Marcos**, a sumptuous 15th-century pilgrim hospital now restored as a modern Parador hotel, which was featured in the film *The Way* as the place where Martin Sheen's character treats his friends to a night of luxury. A dozing pilgrim statue rests barefoot in the plaza facing San Marcos.

Wedding in the León Cathedral

LEÓN TO VILLAR DE MAZARIFE

21.5km
(13.4mi)

⏱ **5-6 HOURS**
DIFFICULTY: ▭☐☐
🅿 73%, 15.6km
🆄 27%, 5.9km

🅰 **ALBERGUES:**
Virgen 7.7km
Mazarife 21.5km
Villavante 31.1km
Hospital 36.7km

⚠ **ALT. STAGE 20A:**
León to Villadangos,
20.8km (p. 188 🅿🆄)

🅰 **ALT. ALBERGUES:**
Virgen 7.7km
Villadangos 20.8km
San Martín 25.4km
Hospital 32.8km

Colorful house in Villar
de Mazarife

Visit the legendary church of Virgen del Camino, abandon pavement for earthen paths, visit mudbrick churches.

☀ The exit from León is no more glamorous than the entrance with about 8km of city walking including some highly industrialized area. These can be skipped with bus M1 to Virgen de Camino, where the path leaves the León metro area. The path splits again, with the recommended route to the south and a northern route (p. 188) parallel to the N-120 road. The recommended route is longer but much more scenic. The routes converge in Hospital and again before Astorga.

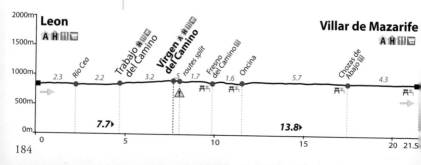

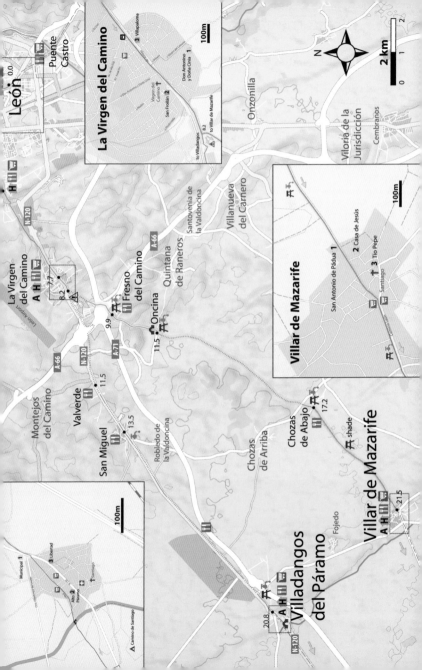

La Virgen del Camino

100m

③ Villapaloma

Don Antonio y Doña Cinia ①

Virgen del Camino ②

San Froilán

8.2 to Villar de Mazarife

to Villadangos

N

2 km

0 1 2

Onzonilla

Viloria de la Jurisdicción

Cembranos

León 0.0

Puente Castro

N-120

La Virgen del Camino
A H ⛪
7.7
8.2

León Airport

Montejos del Camino

A-66

N-120

A-71

Valverde
11.5

San Miguel
13.5

Robledo de la Valdoncina

Fresno del Camino
9.9

Oncina
11.5

Santovenia de la Valdoncina

Quintana de Raneros

A-66

Villanueva del Carnero

Villar de Mazarife

100m

San Antonio de Pádua ①

Casa de Jesús ②

Santiago

③ Tío Pepe

Chozas de Arriba

Chozas de Abajo
17.2

shade

Villar de Mazarife

Villadangos del Páramo

20.8
A H ⛪

N-120

Fojedo

Villar de Mazarife
21.5
A H ⛪

Villadangos del Páramo

100m

Municipal ①

③ Libertad

Alto ② Páramo

Santiago

⛪ Camino de Santiago

4.5 Trobajo del Camino 🏠🍴🚐€📖📷
Pop. 21,378
🏠 **Hostal Gárgola** (dbl €32): 🍴, c/Gran Capitán 7,
  📞987-806180 📱
🏠 **El Abuelo** (dbl €45): 🍴, c/Los Mesones 6-8,
  📞987-801044 📱

7.7 Virgen del Camino Ⓐ🏠🍴🚐➕📖
Pop. 4,820
1. Ⓐ **Don Antonino y Doña Cinia**
  (muni, 🛏40, €5): 📶🅦🄳📖, Villacedré 16,
  📞987-302213 📱, 🕛noon, Apr-Sept
2. 🏠 **San Froilán** (sng €25, dbl €40):
  Av. de Pablo Díez, 📱
3. 🏠 **Villapaloma** (dbl €53): 🍴, Av. Astorga 47,
  📞987-300990 📱

0.0 *From the parochial albergue, take c/Ancho and walk to the cathedral (map p. 179). Turn back to wind your way west to reach c/Renueva. Follow this road to San Marcos and continue across* **Río Bernesga (2.3km)** *on a 16th-century stone bridge to head straight through the suburb of* **Trobajo del Camino (4.5km)** *and onward to Virgen del Camino.*

7.7 Virgen del Camino
The **Basílica de la Virgen del Camino** is a modern church (1961) of artistic significance, unique along the camino. The location stems from a legend that in 1505 the Virgin appeared to a shepherd here. The shepherd went to the bishop to build a hermitage on the spot, but the bishop was not convinced. The Virgin Mary told the shepherd to use a slingshot to throw a stone and build the shrine wherever the stone landed. The shepherd obeyed, and the small stone became a boulder, a miracle that convinced the bishop to build the church.

One legend says that a Christian was being held captive inside a strong box in North Africa in 1522. The Virgin Mary knew of this man's plight and his desire to visit her church, so she miraculously transported him here, box, chains and all. The sacristy of the current church houses the box and chains.

Basílica de la
Virgen del Camino

The church became a local pilgrimage site and was recently elevated to the rank of a minor basilica. The modern façade features the 12 disciples, and the interior includes the Baroque retablo from the former church.

⚠ *Just past Virgen del Camino near a small park with a Santiago statue, the trail splits into two options (8.2km). The recommended route via Villar de Mazarife to the far L on gravel, and the alternate route via Villadangos along the N-120 road (p. 188).*

Villar de Mazarife Route

*The recommended route to Villar de Mazarife crosses over highways A-66 and A-71 and onto a quiet country road to **Fresno del Camino** 🍴 **(9.9km)** and follows the same road over the railroad tracks and Río Oncina to **Oncina de la Valdoncina (11.5km)**. Leave town on a small paved road that becomes a pleasant dirt path through fields, with some slight incline to a flat plateau into **Chozas de Abajo** 🍴 **(17.2km)**, known for its fall potato festival. The path becomes paved again through town and follows a paved road to the outskirts of Villar de Mazarife past a pilgrim mosaic into the town.*

21.5 Villar de Mazarife

is a friendly pilgrim town with the mudbrick **Iglesia de Santiago** featuring several images of the saint. There's even an eclectic museum of art and local artifacts called 🏛 **Casa Museo Antolín** (free 📷). A medieval-style mosaic greets visitors at the entrance.

21.5 Villar de Mazarife A H 🍴 🛒

Pop. 391, 🏷 Mozarabic surname

1. **A H San Antonio de Pádua** (priv, 🛏50, dm €8, dbl €30): 🍴 🔲 💿 🖥, c/Leon 33, 📞987-390192 📷 🕐all year

2. **A Casa de Jesús** (priv, 🛏60, €5): 🍴 🔲 🔲 🖥, c/Corujo 11, 📞987-390697, 🕐all year

3. **A H Tío Pepe** (priv, 🛏26, dm €9, dbl €40-50): 🍴 🔲 🖥 📶, c/El Teso 2, 📞987-390517 📷, 🕐Mar-Jan 15

Iglesia de Santiago in Villar de Mazarife

Pilgrim statue in Villar de Mazarife

⚠ Alternate Stages: Villadangos Route

20A: León to Villadangos, 20.8km
🄿 55%, 11.4km
🅄 45%, 9.4km

While this route was the historic Camino Francés, today it follows a monotonous path next to highway N-120 with whizzing traffic and industrial stretches. The route is about 5km shorter over the course of two stages and has slightly less pavement, but is much less scenic than the recommended route. *From the split after Virgen del Camino, stay R uphill past a cemetery and straight through the highway junction and along the N-120 road.*

Valverde de la Virgen 🅸🄱 **(11.5km)** is the first town with services. Soon afterwards the path passes through **San Miguel del Camino** 🄷 **(13.5km)**, which had a 12th-century pilgrim hospital. Today a local man offers candy and nuts to passing pilgrims. *The track parallel to the highway continues all the way to Villadangos del Páramo through industrial areas.*

20.8 **Villadangos del Páramo** is the site of an 1111 battle between Queen Urraca of León and Alfonso I of Aragón (who were married at the time). Their marriage was meant to unite the kingdoms but instead resulted in civil war. The modern **Iglesia de Santiago** has a chancel depicting the Battle of Clavijo and a Santiago Matamoros image appears to leap out from the altar. The town straddles the highway and provides good pilgrim services and is the logical overnight stop if starting in León.

20.8 **Villadangos del Páramo** A H 🄸🖶🚰➕€
🄰🄴 Pop. 1,140 🎒 Spanish: "town of Angos [a French surname] of Páramo [this region]."
1. **A Municipal** (🛏72, €5): 🄱🆆🅾🖩🛜,
   Crta a Villadangos del Páramo, ☎987-390003,
   🕐all year, call in winter
2. **H Alto Páramo** (sng €21, dbl €31):
   N-120 km 18, ☎987-390425
3. **H Libertad** (sng €35, dbl €45):
   c/Padre Ángel Martínez 25, ☎987-390640
4. **A Camping Camino de Santiago**: N-120 km
   324, ☎987-680253 🖂, 🕐Apr 15-Sept 25

21A: Villadangos to Astorga, 27.1km
🅿 49%, 13.5km
Ⓤ 51%, 13.6km

*From **Villadangos (map p. 191)**, follow the main street and leave town via a dirt path that crosses a small footbridge past the ruins of a former pilgrim hospital. This shady dirt path goes out to highway N-120 and across onto a path on the L side of the highway next to a canal. Note camping area to L. Enter **San Martín del Camino (4.6km)**. Be careful crossing the busy N-120 highway.*

4.6 San Martín del Camino

is a village from the 13th century, which housed a pilgrim hospital in the 17th century. *Continue on the dirt path parallel to highway. Rejoin the recommended route in **Hospital de Órbigo (12.0km, p. 193)**.*

⚠ *From Hospital, follow the recommended route (p. 193) or turn L at the outskirts of Hospital to follow a marked track along highway N-120.*

*The routes rejoin in 10.3km at the **Crucero de Santo Toribio (22.3km, p. 194)** outside of Astorga, saving 1.2km, but sacrificing scenery. The shortest distance from Villadangos to Astorga is 27.1km, using this road route.*

4.6 San Martín del Camino A H 🍴🛒📮
Pop. 517

1. **A Municipal** (🛏68, €4): 🍴❄🖥💻, ☎616-354331, ◷11am, all year, under the water tower, use of kitchen costs €1.5, basic and not very clean
2. **A H Santa Ana** (priv, 🛏96, dm €6, dbl €30): 🍴❄🌐💻🖥, ☎987-378653 ✉, ◷all year
3. **A H Vieira** (priv, 🛏60, dm €7, dbl €25): 🍴❄🌐💻, Av. Peregrinos, ☎987-378565 ✉, ◷11am Feb-Oct

A stone arrow marks the way to Villar de Mazarife

21

VILLAR DE MAZARIFE TO ASTORGA

31.5km
(19.6mi)

🕐 **7-9 HOURS**
DIFFICULTY: ▭▭☐
🅿 48%, 15.0km
Ⓤ 52%, 16.5km

A ALBERGUES:
Villavante 9.6km
Hospital 15.2km
Villares 17.6km
Santibañez 20.2km
Astorga 31.5km
Valdeviejas 34.3km

. . . .

⚠ **ALT. STAGE 21A:**
Villadangos to
Hospital to Astorga
(p. 189 🅿Ⓤ)

A ALT. ALBERGUES:
(from Villadangos)
Hospital 12.0km
Astorga 27.1km
Valdeviejas 29.9km

Pilgrim statue in
Astorga

Imagine the excitement of a medieval joust in Hospital de Órbigo. Visit Roman ruins and a chocolate factory in Astorga.

☀ The first half of this stage offers the last of flat Meseta scenery before the path becomes more rolling and green in preparation for the Cantabrian Mountains in the next stage. Hospital de Órbigo is a pleasant halfway point to enjoy medieval ambiance. The alternate routes meet in Hospital, but split again at the far end of town, with the slightly longer recommended route to the north. The two reconvene just before Astorga at a marvelous viewpoint into the city.

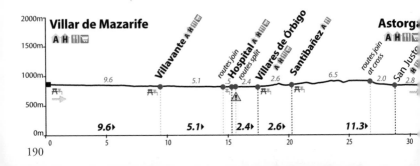

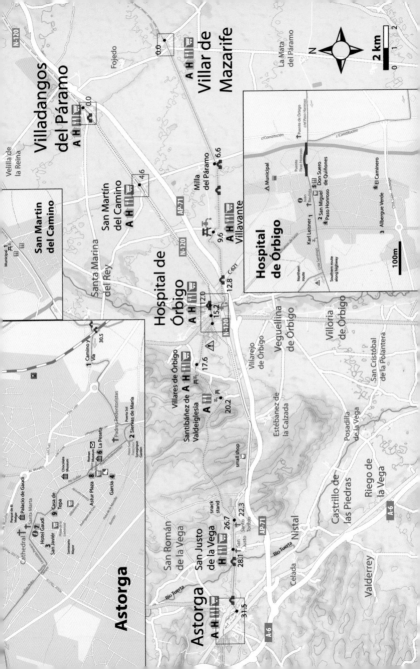

Villadangos del Páramo

Villar de Mazarife

N-120

2 km
0 1 2
N

Velilla de la Reina

Foledo

0.0

A H

0.0

A H

La Mata del Páramo

4.6

San Martín del Camino

San Martín del Camino

A H

A-71

Milla del Páramo

6.6

Santa Marina del Rey

San Martín del Camino

Municipal

9.6

Villavante

A H

N-120

Hospital de Órbigo

Hospital de Órbigo

c/Construción

Puente de Orbigo
(el Passo Honroso)

c/Construción

Puente

A Municipal

Northern route

Southern route along highway

Karl Leisner 1

San Miguel
Don Suero
de Quiñones

Paso Honroso

El Caminero

Albergue Verde 3

100m

12.8 C-601

2.0

15.2

A H

Hospital de Órbigo

A H

N-120

Vegüellina de Órbigo

Villoria de Órbigo

San Cristóbal de la Polantera

Villarejo de Órbigo

Villares de Órbigo A H

Camino y Vía 1 30.5

Santibáñez de A H
Valdeiglesia

17.6

20.2

Estébanez de la Calzada

Posadilla de la Vega

Castrillo de los Piedras

Riego de la Vega

A-6

Astorga

Cathedral

Palacio de Gaudi
Parque de El Melgar

Santa Marta

San Javier 3

Hotel Gaudi 7

Casa de Tepa 9

La Peseta 6

Astur Plaza 8

García 4

Chocolate Museum

Roman Museum

2 Sierras de María

Padres Redentoristas 1

Synagogue Garden

Fuente Sol

Santiago Mayor

small shop

San Román de la Vega

snack stand

San Justo de la Vega H

22.3

26.7

San Justo

Santo Toribio

28.1

Río Tuerta

Celada

Nistal

A-71

Río Tuerta

Valderrey

Astorga

A H

31.5

A-6

A Santa Lucía (priv, 📞32, dm €7, dbl €20):
🏨🐾Ⓦ🖥📶, c/Doctor Vélez 17, 🕐692-107693 📱,
🕐Mar-Oct

H Molino Galocha (sng €40, dbl €55 w/🚿):
🕐987-388546 📱

Paso Honroso bridge in Hospital de Órbigo

0.0 *Leave Villar de Mazarife on a long quiet country road through agricultural fields. Cross over a canal just south of **La Milla Del Páramo (6.6km)**. Turn R into the village of **Villavante (9.6km)**. Wind through town and cross over a railroad (10.4km), joining road C-621 to turn R on another railway overpass (12.8km). Turn L almost immediately and skirt a water treatment plant to turn R. Cross the busy N-120 (14.1km) and continue straight until the historic bridge into Hospital de Órbigo, meeting the other route coming from Villadangos.*

15.2 Hospital de Órbigo: The impressive Gothic bridge over the Río Órbigo is the site of a legendary medieval jousting competition. Don Suero de Quiñones, a wealthy Leonese knight, was rejected by the woman he loved. In his heartbreak, he locked his neck in an iron collar and swore he would not take it off until he had defeated 300 knights in jousting. The call went out, and knights from all over the kingdom came in the Holy Year of 1434. Quiñones succeeded in his quest, freeing him from the torment of love. He took off the collar and made a pilgrimage to Santiago where he left a bejeweled bracelet, which can still be seen in the cathedral museum. The bridge became known as **El Paso Honroso** "the Honorable Pass." Looking south from the bridge into a grove of poplars, one can imagine the brilliant flags, trumpets blowing and excitement of a medieval joust. *Follow the main road through Hospital, and at the edge of town, ⚠ turn R at the option to continue on the recommended route to Villares de Órbigo or stay straight to take the **alternate route** (description p. 189). The recommended route is 0.8km longer, but has nicer scenery.*

17.6 Villares de Órbigo is a friendly town with a church featuring a Santiago Matamoros. *After Villares, you'll see rolling hills again! Pass over a small hill into **Santibañez de Valdeiglesias (20.2km)**, where Iglesia de la Trinidad has a Santiago Matamoros. From Santibañez, continue on a lovely dirt path through oak groves and orchards. Pass a seasonal snack stand (25.1km). Climb up to the magnificent view of Astorga at a large stone cross.*

15.2 Hospital de Órbigo A H 🛏🛒➕€🅿
Pop. 1,031
1. **A Karl Leisner** (par, 🛏90, €5): 🇰,
   c/Álvarez Vega 32, ⏰987-388444 🕚11am all year
2. **A San Miguel** (priv, 🛏40, €7): 🇰🇼🇩🇴🇪,
   c/Álvarez Vega 35, ⏰987-388285 📧, 🕚Apr-Nov
3. **A ☆ Albergue Verde** (priv 🛏26, €9): 🇮🇱🇼🇩🇴
   🇪🇷, Av. Fueros de León 76, ⏰689-927926 📧
   🕛12pm Easter-Oct, solar heating, organic local
   vegetarian meals, yoga classes
4. **H Paso Honroso** (dbl €47): 🍴, N-120 km 335,
   ⏰987-361010 📧
5. **H Don Suero de Quiñones** (sng €45,
   dbl €65): c/Álvarez Vega, ⏰987-388238
6. **H El Caminero** (dbl €70): 🍴,
   c/Sierra Pambley 56, ⏰987-389020 📧
7. **▲ Municipal Camping** (tent €6): 🏕,
   N-120 km 31, ⏰987-361018 📧

17.6 Villares de Órbigo A H 🛏🛒➕🅿
A H Villares de Orbigo (priv, 🛏36, dm €7,
dbl €20): 🇰🇼🇩🇴🇪🇷, c/Arnal 21,
⏰987-132935 📧, 🕚11am, Feb-Dec

20.2 Santibañez de Valdeiglesias A 🍴
A Parochial (par, 🛏60, €6): 🍴, Caromonte 3,
⏰626-362159, 🕐1:30pm, Mar-Oct

Snack stand after
Santibañez

Crucero de Santo Toribio above Astorga

26.7 **Crucero de Santo Toribio** is named for the 5th-century bishop of Astorga who was said to have fallen to his knees at this spot when he was banished from his beloved city. Look for the spires of the cathedral and beyond the city to the Cantabrian Mountains on the camino ahead.

28.1 **San Justo de la Vega** 🏠 🍴 ♨ 🛒 ➕ 🏧
🏠 **Hostal Juli** (dbl €45): c/Real 56,
📞987-617632 📧

*Continue on a paved road down to **San Justo (28.1km)**, where the Iglesia de San Justo contains a 17th-century retablo. From San Justo, continue on the sidewalk next to the highway, crossing over the **Río Tuerta (28.7km)** and then over the train tracks on an elaborate maze of a footbridge (30.5km). Continue uphill to enter Astorga Old City through the Puerta Sol into the Plaza de San Francisco.*

Pilgrims crossing the train tracks to enter Astorga

31.5 **Astorga** is a pleasant city with interesting and varied historical buildings, just the right size to not be too overwhelming with main sites confined to the small Old City. First a Celtic settlement, Astorga developed into an important Roman city at the crossroads of the *Via Trajana* and the *Vía de la Plata*, as well as an important center for Christianity. According to legend, both St. James and St. Paul preached here. The bishopric of Astorga was one of the earliest Christian titles. The city passed to the Visigoths in the 5th century and was destroyed by the Muslims in 714, then reconquered by Ordoño I in the mid-9th century. After León was destroyed by Al-Mansur's army, Astorga acted as the capital of the kingdom. The city flourished with the pilgrim trade and housed 21 pilgrim hospitals, the second most on the Camino Francés (after Burgos). One of these hosted Saint Francis of Assisi on his pilgrimage in 1214.

The 15th-century **Cathedral** (free, ☾winter 9:30-1pm, 4:30-6pm; summer 9-12pm, 5-6:30pm, ☎987-615429) features an impressive Baroque façade and one of the best Renaissance retablos on the route, completed by a disciple of Michelangelo and Raphael (Gaspar Becerra). Next

Inside Astorga's awe-inspiring cathedral

31.5 Astorga A ♁ ▥▤▦▧♁⊙❶▨▣
Pop. 12,078, ▣ Latin: *Asturicus* regional name of the ancient Astur tribe, ❶ c/Eduardo de Castro 5 across from Gaudí building, ☎987-618222, free 🛜
1. **A Camino y Via** (priv, 🛏22, €6): ▨▦▣,
   ☎987-615192
2. **A ☆ Siervas de María** (assoc, 🛏156, €5): ▨▦
   ▣▤(free), Plaza San Francisco 3, ☎987-616034
   ▣, ☾all year, foot care offered in evenings
3. **A St. Javier** (priv, 🛏95, €8): ▨▦▣▤🛜,
   c/Portería 6, ☎987-618532, ☾Apr-Nov
4. **H Pensión Garcia** (sng €20, dbl €30 shared
   bath): 🛜, Bjda Postigo 3, ☎987-616046 ▣
5. **H Hostal San Narciso** (sng €25, dbl €39): ▥🛜,
   c/León 81, ☎987-6165001 ▣
6. **H La Peseta** (dbl €62): 🛜,
   Plaza de San Bartolomé 3, ☎987-617275 ▣
7. **H Hotel Gaudí** (dbl €65): ▥▦,
   Eduardo Castro 6, ☎987-615654 ▣
8. **H Astur Plaza** (dbl €80): Plaza de España 2,
   ☎987-618900
9. **H Casa de Tepa** (dbl €108): 🛜, c/Santiago 2,
   ☎987-603299 ▣

to the cathedral is the **Iglesia de Santa Marta**, connected by a plain 14th-century cell historically used to imprison prostitutes. Passing pilgrims would share food through the bars as an act of charity. The inscription above the window still reads, "*Acuérdate de mi juicio, porque así será el tuyo. A mí ayer, a ti hoy.*" ("Remember how I was judged, for your judgement will be the same. Yesterday to me, today to you.")

In the same plaza stands the **Palacio de Gaudí**, which was a palace for Archbishop Juan Bautista Grau Villespinós until his death, when it sat empty until serving as a military headquarters for the Falange movement. In 1963, the current 🏛 **Museo de los Caminos** (€3, ⊙Tu-Sa 10am-2pm, 4-8pm, Su 10am-2pm, ☎987-616882)

Astorga Cathedral interior

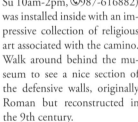

was installed inside with an impressive collection of religious art associated with the camino. Walk around behind the museum to see a nice section of the defensive walls, originally Roman but reconstructed in the 9th century.

🏛 **Museo Romano**
(⊙11am-2pm, 5-8pm, closed Sun afternoon and Mon ☎987-616937) features artifacts from the Roman period, including an interesting gravestone that is explained in a short film displayed in a Roman tunnel known as an *Ergástula*. The ❶ Tourist Information offers a guided tour of the Roman ruins called the *Ruta Romana* (€4, ☎987-618222, 2 hours, Spanish language). Mosaics and ruins are displayed in the Plaza San Francisco.

Chocolate lovers should visit the 🏛 **Museo del Chocolate** (€1, ⊙Tu-Sa 10:30am-2pm, Oct-Apr 4-6pm, May-Sep 4:30-7pm, Sun 11am-4pm 🖼), which documents the chocolate industry that flourished in Astorga in the 18th-19th century. The museum features a modest collection of antique machinery and wrappers, an interesting film (in Spanish) on chocolate making and (the best part) a tasting session with a variety of chocolate, including one made with the local *cecina* sausage.

☀ Before leaving, make sure you have enough cash to get you to Ponferrada as there are no ATMs in between. Astorga is also the last place to get any warmer clothing you may need for the colder mountains ahead tomorrow.

⚑ **Astorga**
Late July: Fiesta de Ástures y Romanos, celebrating Asturian and Roman culture
Aug 22: Santa Marta patron saint day with gladiator fights and chariot races
Tues is market day.

Gaudí's Bishop's Palace now houses the Museo de los Caminos.

Roman mosaics in Astorga

CANTABRIAN MTNS & EL BIEZO

A view of Villafranca del Bierzo from the *Camino Duro* to Pradela

Highlights include magnificent mountain scenery, enigmatic Maragato culture, quaint stone villages and the towering cross at Cruz Ferro.

This section is characterized by the wild and rocky Cantabrian Mountains and the sheltered microclimate in the valley of El Bierzo.

The trail passes through a region of the *Maragato* culture, centralized in about 40 villages around Astorga. This mysterious group is rumored to be descended from the Berbers of North Africa, who arrived with the Muslim conquest in the 8th century and later converting to Christianity. Maragato men traditionally worked as *muleteers*, mule drivers who transported goods (especially fish and gold) around the peninsula.

Restaurants in the area offer *Cocido Maragato*, an extremely filling meal that is served in a kind of "reverse order," beginning with a hearty meat dish (incorporating a dizzying array of meats: blood sausage, chicken, pork, pig's ear, pig's snout, bacon, chorizo), followed by the vegetables (usually chickpeas and cabbage) and finished off with a thick noodle soup and dessert.

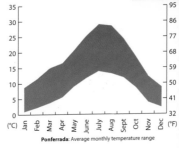

Ponferrada: Average monthly temperature range

Ponferrada: Average monthly rainfall

The Bierzo region has come into its own as a wine region and in 1989 became its own DOC (*Denominacion de Origen*). The low altitude makes it possible to harvest the grapes up to one month earlier than other regions. You can ignore the advice given by 15th-century German pilgrim Hermann Künig con Vach regarding El Bierzo: "When you get there, drink wine sparingly as it burns like a candle and can scorch your very soul."

Local architecture becomes quite interesting as the trail enters regions with Celtic influence. Look for circular thatched stone buildings, called *pallozas*. You will also see plenty of *hórreos*, rectangular stone corncribs that are elevated off the ground to protect the corn from vermin. Common trees include holly, birch and maple, and fauna includes wild boar, roe deer, badgers and wolves.

Passing over the Cantabrian Mountains

22

ASTORGA TO FONCEBADÓN

25.9km
(16.1mi)

⊙ 6.5-8 Hours
Difficulty: ▬◻◻
🅿 26%, 6.8km
Ⓤ 74%, 19.1km

A Albergues:
Valdeviejas 2.8km
Murias 5.1km
Santa Catalina 9.4km
El Ganso 13.7km
Rabanal 20.5km
Foncebadón 25.9km
Monjarín 30.3km

The ruins of Guacelmo's pilgrim hospital near Foncebadón

Explore the mysterious Maragato culture and experience the ambiance of tiny stone villages nestled in the mountains.

☀ Today begins the slow steady climb toward the high point of the camino, reached in the following stage. The landscape and buildings change as the camino draws nearer to the wild hills of Galicia. Vegetation becomes more scrubby, typical houses are low stone structures with thatch or slate roofs and the weather becomes more dreary and overcast.

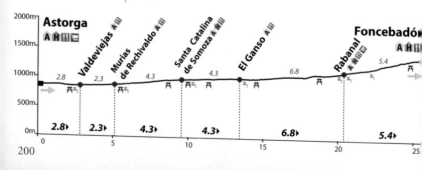

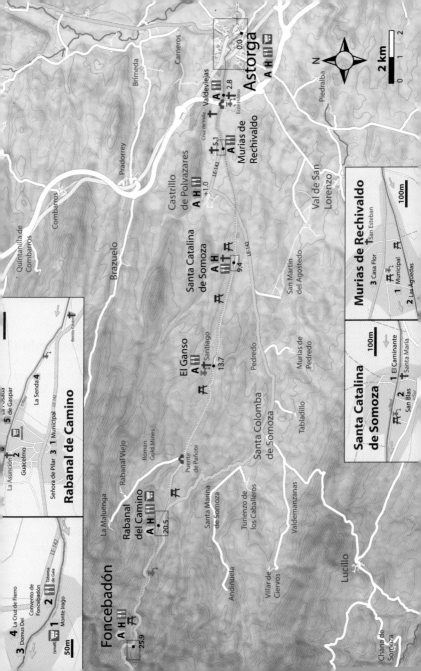

2 km

N

0 1 2

Astorga
A H 🏨
0.0

Carneros

Piedralba

Valdeviejas
A 🏨
2.8
Ecce Homo

Brimeda

Cruz de Valle

Murias de
Rechivaldo
A 🏨
5.1
LE-142

Pradorrey

Combarros

Quintanilla de
Combarros

Castrillo
de Polvazares
A H 🏨
+1.0

Val de San
Lorenzo

Brazuelo

Santa Catalina
de Somoza
A H 🏨
9.4
LE-142

San Martín
del Agostedo

El Ganso
A 🏨
Santiago
13.7

Pedredo

Murias de
Pedredo

La Maluenga

Rabanal Viejo

Roman
Gold Mines

Puente
de Pañote

Santa Marina
de Somoza

Santa Colomba
de Somoza

Tabladillo

Foncebadón
A H 🏨
25.9

Rabanal
del Camino
A H 🏨
20.5

Andiñuela

Turienzo de
los Caballeros

Valdemanzanas

Villar de
Ciervos

Lucillo

Chana de
Somoza

Rabanal de Camino

3 Domus Dei

5 Señora
de Gaspar

La Senda 4

La Asunción 1
Guaicelmo
2

Señora de Pilar 3 1 Municipal

Benito Cristo

Murias de Rechivaldo

† San Esteban

3 Casa Flor

1 Municipal

2 Las Águedas

100m

Santa Catalina de Somoza

1 El Caminante

† Santa María

2
San Blas

100m

Foncebadón

4 La Cruz de Fierro

3 Domus Dei

1 Monte Irago

Convento de
Foncebadón

2 Taberna
de Gaia

50m

0.0 *Leave Astorga by following arrows through town (map p. 191) past the cathedral and turning L onto c/Leopoldo Panero and leaving on c/Puerta Obispo. Turn R on c/San Pedro past a church with interesting mosaics. Arrive to minor highway LE-142 on the northwest edge of town. Follow this road, passing through Valdeviejas.*

2.8 **Valdeviejas** houses the Ermita del Ecce Homo, a former pilgrim hospital. To access the simple albergue and Iglesia de San Verésimo, turn R at the Ermita. *Follow the road to Murcias de Rechivaldo, veering L (4.7km) to pass by the municipal albergue.*

5.1 **Murias de Rechivaldo** is a Maragato village (p. 198) with many traditional stone buildings and the 18th-century **Iglesia de San Esteban** with a *Virgen de Pilár* image and outside staircase to the bell tower. Most building are from the late 19th century as many constructions were destroyed in an 1846 flood.

*Follow the marked wide dirt path past the albergue and fountain out of town to **Santa Catalina (9.4km)**, or detour 1km on the road to first visit the picturesque Castrillo de Polvazares.*

2.8 **Valdeviejas** A Pop. 156
A **Ecce Homo** (muni, 10, €5): 620-960060, Mar-Oct, all beds-not bunks

5.1 **Murias de Rechivaldo** A Pop. 108
1. A **Municipal** (20, €4): , Carretera Santa Colomba, 987-691150, Apr-Oct 15
2. A **Las Águedas** (priv, 40, €9): , c/Camino de Santiago 52, 636-067840, Mar-Nov
3. A **Casa Flor** (priv, 15, €10): , c/Carretera Santa Colomba 54, 609-478323

Stone arrow on the path after Santa Catalina

+1.0 Castrillo de Polvazares is a traditional Maragato village whose stone buildings have been sensitively restored as a tourist attraction. Author Concha Espina used the location as the backdrop to her novel *La Esfinge Maragata*.

9.4 Santa Catalina de Somoza is another traditional village, all but deserted, with a modern Iglesia de Santa María. *Walk down the central c/ Real and continue on a dirt path along the road to el Ganso.*

13.7 El Ganso: The tiny crumbling hamlet of El Ganso once held the Hospital de San Justo, a 12th-century Benedictine pilgrim shelter as well as a 13th-century monastery, but nothing remains of either. The architecture today is very traditional with some now rare thatched roofs. Iglesia de Santiago has a 16th-century statue of the saint. The ghost-town feel today is somewhat enlivened by Mesón Cowboy, a Tex-Mex bar, as well as an albergue that at maximum capacity basically doubles the town's population.

Continue parallel to the road, passing a venerable old tree with a bench under its branches, affectionately called el Roble del Peregrino "the pilgrim's oak," said to watch over weary pilgrims. Pass the remains of a Roman gold mine known as La Fucarona and the 18th-century Ermita del Bendito Cristo de la Vera Cruz at the entry to Rabanal.

+1.0 Castrillo de Polvazares A H 🚌
Pop. 70, Off route +1.0km
A Municipal (🛏7, €4): 🔲, c/Jardín, ☎655-803706, ⏰12pm, Apr-Oct
H Cuca la Vaina (dbl €70): 📶, c/Jardín, ☎987-691034/987-691078 📧
H Casa Coscolo (dbl €58): 🍴, c/El Rincon 1, ☎987-691984/619-280540 📧

9.4 Santa Catalina A H 🏠 Pop. 60
1. **A El Caminante** (priv, 🛏22, €6): 🍴 w 🅳 💻, c/Real 2, ☎987-691098 📧, ⏰all year
2. **A H San Blas** (priv, 🛏20, dm €5, dbl €35): 🍴 w 🅳 💻, c/Real 11, ☎987-691411 📧, ⏰all year

---

13.7 El Ganso A 🍴 Pop. 30, 📖 Spanish: "goose"
A Gabino (priv, 🛏28, €8 w/🚿): 📶 w 📶, c/Real, ☎660-912823, ⏰Easter-Nov

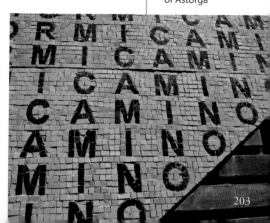

Camino mosaics on a church on the way out of Astorga

20.5 Rabanal del Camino A H ⬛⬛ 🛒
Pop. 73, Small shop (closed in winter)

1. **A Municipal** (⌂34, €4): 🔲 W 🔲,
   Plaza de Jerónimo, ☎987-631687, Apr-Oct

2. **A ▲ ☆ Guacelmo** (assoc, ⌂46, don w/🔲):
   🔲 D 🔲, c/Calvario 4, ☎987-691901, ☺2pm,
   Apr-Oct, friendly volunteers prepare English tea

3. **A H Nuestra Señora de Pilar** (priv, ⌂74,
   dm €5, dbl €35): 🔲 W 🔲, Plaza de Jerónimo,
   ☎987-631621 📱, ☺all year

4. **A La Senda** (priv, ⌂34, €5-7): 🔲 W D 🔲 📶,
   c/Real, ☎650-952721/696-819060 📱,
   ☺Apr-Oct 20, formerly called "el Tesín"

5. **H La Posada de Gaspar** (sng €41, dbl €54): 🍴,
   c/Real 27, ☎987-631629 📱

6. **H Hostería el Refugio** (sng €35, dbl €50): 🍴,
   c/Real, ☎987-631592 📱

The monks at Santa María de la Asunción also offer
accommodations, which must be arranged in
advance by calling ☎987-631528 between 10am
and 1pm or emailing monteirago@gmail.com.

☀ Rabanal makes a
nice overnight stop,
but pushing on to Fon-
cebadón will shorten the
already-long day tomor-
row. Be forewarned that
it is all uphill!

Pilgrims socialize at
Guacelmo albergue in
Rabanal

20.5 Rabanal del Camino
is another beautiful and isolated
Maragato village brought back to life
by modern pilgrim traffic. This was
the end of the 9th stage of the *Codex
Calixtinus,* and many pilgrims
stopped to rest from the ascent and
find refuge from the wolves and bandits that plagued the León mountains. The Knights Templar ran a fort
here to protect passing pilgrims. A
legend says that one of Charlemagne's knights married a Muslim
woman in Rabanal.

The heavily reconstructed **Iglesia de
Santa María de la Asunción** contains a 12th-century image of San
Roque. The church is currently operated by the Benedictine Abbey of
San Salvador del Monte Irago and
offers a moving Vespers service with Gregorian chant and an
evening pilgrim blessing. The 12th-century Hospital de San
Gregorio has been converted into a modern albergue by the
British Confraternity, named Guacelmo after the 10th-cen-
tury monk who founded a hermitage in nearby Foncebadón.
*Follow c/Real out of Rabanal onto a dirt track coming alongside
the paved road. The entrance to Foncebadón is marked with a
wooden cross.*

25.9 <u>Foncebadón</u>: Practically deserted in the 1980s, Foncebadón has made a comeback as a stopping point for modern pilgrims. Amidst crumbling stone buildings and cold weather even in summer, some of the wildness of the Irago Mountains of old can be felt. The traditional stone houses with slate roofs or thatched with local broom provide a timeless ambiance. The Roman road went through this pass, and its protected location below Cruz Ferro made Foncebadón a logical pilgrim stop.

Monte Irago albergue in Foncebadón

Paolo Coelho's *The Pilgrimage* describes his mystical experience in Foncebadón in which he wrestles with a large black dog. In Shirley Maclaines' *The Camino*, she also encounters vicious dogs in Foncebadón. Today the village offers several albergues and cafés and a rustic, timeless atmosphere.

25.9 <u>Foncebadón</u> A H 🍴 Pop. 13

1. **A Monte Irago** (priv, 🛏35, €8): 🍴⬜🔲🔵⬛, ☎695-452950 📇, ⊙all year, good meals, small shop, fireplace, moderate hippie vibe, offer yoga
2. **A H El Convento de Foncebadón** (priv, 🛏20, dm €7, sng €36, dbl €46): 🍴⬛, ☎658-974818, ⊙Feb-Nov
3. **A Domus Dei** (par, 🛏18, don): ⬛⬜, 📇, ⊙Apr-Oct
4. **A La Cruz de Fierro** (priv, 🛏40, €7): ⬛⬜🔲⬛, c/Real, ☎987-691093, ⊙Apr-Oct

FONCEBADÓN TO PONFERRADA

27.1km
(16.8mi)

⊙ **6-8 Hours**
Difficulty: ▭▭☐☐
🅿 32%, 8.6km
Ⓤ 68%, 18.5km

A Albergues:
Monjarín 4.4km
El Acebo 11.5km
Riego 14.7km
Molinaseca 19.5km
Ponferrada 27.1km
Cacabelos 43.6km

⚠ **Alt. Route:**
Shortcut to
Ponferrada albergue,
saves 1.4km (p. 211)

Enjoy mountain
scenery in the Irago
Mountains

Place a stone at Cruz Ferro, have coffee with modern-day Knights Templar at Monjarín, visit a Templar castle in Ponferrada.

☀ This stage begins with more climbing to Cruz Ferro and the high point of the Irago Mountains before the steep descent down to Ponferrada. Typical Maragato mountain villages with slate-roofed houses like El Acebo offer services. On a clear day, the mountain views are superb. Be prepared for the possibility of cold, rain and wind.

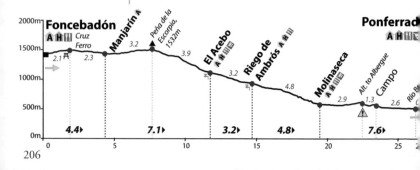

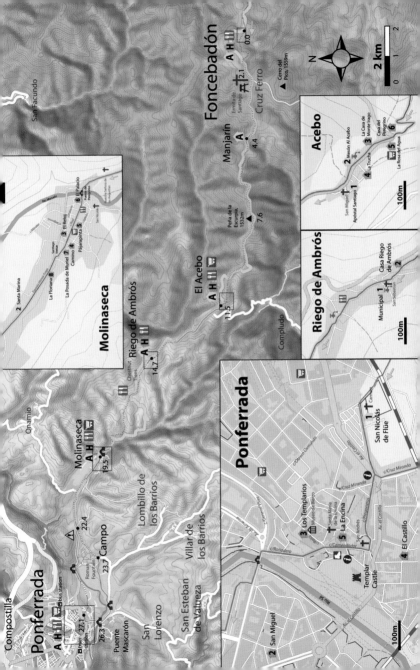

0.0 *Leave Foncebadón on the main dirt road, passing horse pastures and the ruins of Guacelmo's medieval pilgrim hospital. Ascend through scrubby heather and gorse, cross the road and arrive at a camino highlight, the Cruz Ferro.*

2.1 **Cruz Ferro** occupies nearly the highest point of the entire Camino Francés (there's a slightly higher pass after Manjarín). The site consists of a tall wooden pole topped with an iron cross. This is said to be an ancient monument, first erected by the ancient Celts, then dedicated by the Romans to their god Mercury (protector of travelers) and later crowned by the cross and renamed as a Christian site by the 9th-century hermit Guacelmo. For centuries, pilgrims have brought a stone to the place (either from home or the flatlands below) to represent their burden. The stone and the burden are left here, leaving the pilgrim lighter (literally and figuratively) for the journey ahead. Today all sorts of symbolic items are left behind, and some stones bear written messages. The small modern **chapel of Santiago** provides a good place for a rest. *Continue downhill to Manjarín.*

Pilgrims at Cruz Ferro

Signs at Manjarín

4.4 **Manjarín** **A**

A **Refugio de Manjarín** (priv, 🛏35, don): 🍴, 🕑all year, communal meal, no electricity or running water, a truly rustic experience with Thomas, a "modern-day Templar"

4.4 **Manjarín**: This enigmatic little spot features a most unusual albergue, administered by Tomás who considers himself a modern-day Templar, last of his order. Drinks and snacks are available as well as a none-too-private outhouse. Recognizable by bright flags and signs with the distance to Santiago among other cities. *After continuing through beautiful heather fields, arrive at the true high point of the camino (1520m) where a radio tower is visible to the R (7.6km). [Go off route*

here on the wide dirt path up to a large cairn for a breathtaking view of Ponferrada in the valley below.] Descend sharply for 3.9km to El Acebo.

Approaching the slate roofs of El Acebo

11.5 **El Acebo** is a typical camino town with a church at the center and houses with wooden balconies flanking the pilgrim route. The town was larger in medieval times and received a tax break for maintaining the pilgrim road markers over the Foncebadón pass. The 15th-century **Iglesia de San Miguel** contains an image of John the Baptist. On the way out of town is a statue in remembrance of 70-year-old German cyclist Heinrich Krause who died of a bicycle accident there in 1987. *Follow the road until a dirt path to the L (13.6km) leads into Riego de Ambrós.*

11.5 **El Acebo** A H 🏠🖼️
Pop. 37, 🏠 Spanish: "holly"
1. **A Apóstal Santiago** (par, 🛏24, don): 🖼️🖼️, Plaza de la Iglesia ⏰Apr-Oct, shared meals
2. **A H Mesón El Acebo** (priv, 🛏18, dm €5, dbl €20): 🖼️🖼️, c/Real 16, ☎987-695074 🖼️, ⏰ Jan 22-Dec 21
These 2 albergues only open if the others are full:
    A Elisardo Panizo (muni, 🛏10, €5): basic
    A La Taberna de José (priv, 🛏7, €5): ☎987-695074
3. **H La Casa del Monte Irago** (dbl €40): c/Real 45, ☎639-721242
4. **H La Trucha** (dbl €42): 🍴, c/La Cruz, ☎987-695548, excellent vegetarian meals
5. **H La Rosa del Agua** (sng €35, dbl €50 w/🛁): 🖼️🖼️, c/Real 52, ☎616-849738 🖼️
6. **H Casa del Peregrino** (sng €40, dbl €50 w/🛁): 🍴🖼️(free), c/Real 67, ☎987-057875 🖼️

209

Walking through the scrub brush before Molinaseca (above)

14.7 Riego de Ambrós A H ⏰ Pop. 42, 📷
Spanish: "irrigation of Ambros," likely a family name
1. **A Municipal** (30 🛏, €5): 🔒WD, c/Real, ☎987-695190, ⏰12:30pm, Apr-Nov
2. **H Casa Riego de Ambrós** (dbl €35-€40): 🔒W, c/Astorga 3, ☎986-95198/616-123557 📷

14.7 Riego de Ambrós is another typical camino town, whose 16th-century Iglesia de San Sebastián features a Baroque retablo. After Riego you will pass a spectacular grove of massive chestnut trees (15.6km), which practically beg you to take a rest stop under their wise branches. *A picturesque dirt footpath leads down to Molinaseca.*

🐻 **Molinaseca**
Aug: Virgen de las Angustias procession
Aug 17: Fiesta del Agua—huge city-wide water fight

Iglesia de San Nicolás in Molinaseca (right)

Venerable chestnut tree after Riego (left)

19.5 **Molinaseca:** On the way into Molinaseca pass the **Santuario de Nuestra Señora de las Angustias**, built into the rock to the R with a 18th-century Baroque retablo. Medieval pilgrims carved off slivers of the wooden door for good luck, though today the doors are iron plated. Turn L to cross the medieval **Puente del Peregrino** over the Río Meruela. The water to the R of the bridge is dammed up for refreshing summer swimming. Pass the **Iglesia de San Nicolás**, which contains a 17th-century retablo. ☀ Molinaseca is a pretty, quiet town with good pilgrim facilities and makes a great overnight spot if you prefer to avoid the crowded albergue of Ponferrada.

Leave Molinaseca on the paved road. After the albergues at the far side of town, turn R at the tennis courts (scarcely marked) and a quick L on a gravel path to avoid the road. Rejoin and cross the paved road (22.2km).

[⚠ For a shortcut directly to the Ponferrada albergue saving 1.4km, continue on the main road following faint arrows (22.4km, map p. 207).] Otherwise follow markers downhill to the L on a dirt road turning paved into **Campo (23.7km)**, *with its Roman fountain and parish church next to a massive oak tree. Continue on the road to cross* **Puente Mascarón (26.3km)**. *Continue straight on c/Cruz Miranda to the albergue, or follow markings to access the downtown area and castle, and/or continue along the camino.*

19.5 **Molinaseca** A H ⏹⏹⏹⏹⏹⏹⏹
Pop. 854, ⛯ Spanish: "dry mill"
1. **A Municipal** (⛺44, €5): ⏹⏹⏹, Av. Fraga Iribarne, ☎987-453077/615-302390 ✉, ⏱1pm, all year, in summer extra beds on the porch
2. **A Santa Marina** (priv, ⛺56, €7): ⏹⏹⏹⏹, Av. Fraga Iribarne, ☎987-453077, ⏱1pm, Mar- Nov
3. **H El Reloj** (dbl €35-40): ☎987-453124 ✉
4. **H Camino** (dbl €40): ☎653-504330 ✉
5. **H Pájarapinta** (dbl €40-50): ☎987-453040 ✉
6. **H El Palacio** (dbl €50): ⏹, c/El Palacio 19, ☎987-453094
7. **H La Posada de Muriel** (dbl €50-80): ⏹, Plaza del Santo Cristo, ☎987-453201 ✉
8. **H Floriana Hotel** (dbl €72): ☎987-453146 ✉

27.1 Ponferrada A H ⊞ 🍴 ☕ ♨ ✚ ⊖ ▣ 🏱
Pop. 68,508 🏳 Latin: *pons ferrata* "iron bridge"
ℹ️ c/Gil y Carrasco 4, 📞987-424236, 🕐M-Sa 10am-2pm, 4-8:30pm, Su 10am-2pm

1. **A San Nicolás de Flüe** (par, ↪174 , don):
   🄺🅆🄾🅂, c/de la Loma, 📞987-413381 📱,
   🕐 1-3pm all year, can get very crowded, evening Mass offered
2. **H Hostal San Miguel** (sng €25, dbl €36):
   c/Juan de Lama 14, 📞987-426700 📱
3. **H Hotel Los Templarios** (dbl €50):
   c/Flores Osorio 3, 📞987-411484 📱
4. **H El Castillo** (dbl €60): ⊞ 🛜,
   Av. el Castillo 115, 📞987-456227 📱
5. **H Hostal La Encina** (dbl €63): ⊞,
   c/Comendador 4 📱

27.1 Ponferrada started off as a Celtic settlement, followed by a Roman mining town. The city was destroyed first by the Visigoths and then Muslim invaders. After the Reconquista, Bishop Osmundo of Astorga commissioned a pilgrim bridge here, which was unusually constructed with steel beams, giving the city its modern name. Ponferrada was a booming pilgrimage town, with diverse merchants including Franks and Jews, who were protected during a 15th-century restriction that called for segregating communities. The railroad came to the city in 1882 and in the 1940s the town grew with the coal industry.

While the historic center retains its charm, much of the new city is modern and industrial. The most impressive site is the 🏰 Templar castle (€6, 🕐Tu-Sa 11am-2pm, 4-6pm, Su 11am-2pm), built in the 13th century over a destroyed Visigoth fort, which was built over a Roman fort, which was built over a pre-Roman castro. Soon after its completion, the Templars were banished. The entrance is impressive with a coat of arms over the door. According to legend, the castle holds all kinds of secret Templar symbolism, such as the 12 towers representing the 12 months or the 12 disciples.

Historic center of Ponferrada (above)

Shell adorning a fence outside of Ponferrada (left)

† **Iglesia de Santa María de la Encina** (🕘9am-2pm, 4:30-8:30pm), on the Plaza Encinas, houses an image of Mary said to be originally in the Astorga cathedral, but it was hidden in the 9th century for protection from invading Muslims. Years later, the image was miraculously found in an oak tree, hence the name "Our Lady of the Oak." There is a statue in the plaza depicting the miracle.

🏛 **Museo de Bierzo**
(🕘Tu-Sa 11am-2pm, Oct-Apr 4-7pm, 5-8:30pm May-Sept, Su 11am-2pm, 📞987-414141, *c/del Reloj 5*), housed in the former jail, displays artifacts ranging from pre-Roman to ethnographic and features an in-depth display of the archaeological theory of how the castle was built.

🍺 **Ponferrada**
Summer: Noche Templario medieval festival with costumed knights
Sept: Virgen de la Encina patron saint day
Wed/Sat are market days.

Templar Castle in Ponferrada (above)

Refreshing drinks served at Ponferrada albergue

PONFERRADA TO VILLAFRANCA DEL BIERZO

24.2km
(15.0mi)

🕐 **6-7 HOURS**
DIFFICULTY: ▭□□
🅿 69%, 16.8km
🆄 31%, 7.4km

A ALBERGUES:
Cacabelo 16.5km
Pieros 18.0km
Villafranca 24.2km
Pereje 29.8km
Trabadelo 34.2km

⚠ **ALT. ROUTE:**
Shortcut to approach
Villafranca, saves
1.0km, (p. 217)

Villafrana del Bierzo on
the Río Burbia

Stroll through vineyards and fruit orchards, experience Medieval and Rennaisance history in Villafranca del Bierzo and dip your feet in the Río Burbia.

☀ After leaving Ponferrada's urban area, the trail soon enters the Bierzo region with its temperate microclimate, ideal for viticulture. The scenery is green with vineyards, cherry orchards, wildflowers and trees. The mountains of Galicia loom ahead, and beautiful Villafranca lies nestled among the foothills long the Río Burbia.

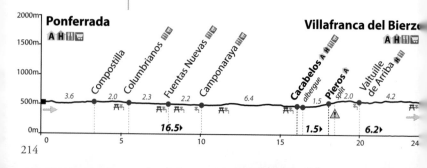

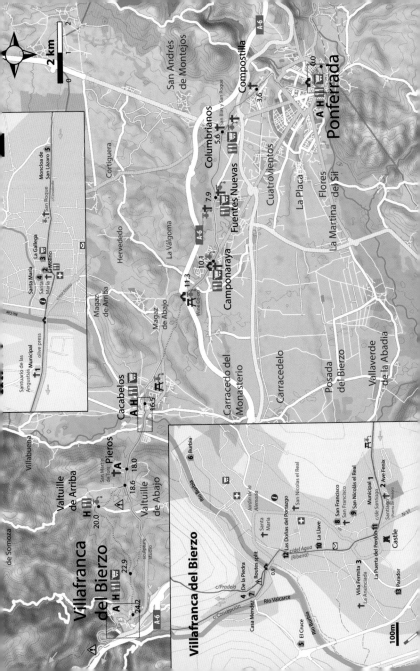

1. **A H Municipal** (⚑70, €5): 🔲🔳📶📋(free),
   Plaza del Santuario, 📞987-546151, ⊕noon,
   May-Oct, all rooms with 2 beds
2. **H El Molino** (dbl €35): c/Santa María 10,
   📞987-546 979
3. **H La Gallega** (dbl €40): 📋🔲📋,
   c/Santa Maria 23, 📞987-549476 📧
4. **H Santa María** (dbl €45): c/Santa María 20,
   📞987-549588 📧
5. **H Hotel Moncloa de San Lázaro** (dbl €70): 📋,
   Cimadevilla 97, 📞987-546101

Walking through
vineyards before
Villafranca

0.0 *From the Ponferrada Albergue,
make your way to the castle (map p.
207) and turn R to walk through the
downtown area. Turn L over the Río
Sil on a bridge, then turn R on c/Río
Ardieles. Turn R at a park, then R
again at a plaza with a statue of a
large drop of blood honoring blood do-
nors. Pass through a roundabout, then
L at signs for Compostilla and walk
through the suburb of **Compostilla**
(3.6km). Stay straight through an underpass to **Columbrianos** 📋🔳✚
(5.6km), then stay L at Ermita San Blas y San Roche leaving
town. Pass a cross and drinking fountain entering **Fuentes Nuevas** 📋🔳 (7.9km), then stay straight until **Companaraya** 📋🔳
(10.1km), where the trail turns R on the main road passing
vending machines with free 📶, cafés and a 🔳 mini market. On
the edge of Companaraya, after the Wine Co-op (11.3km, offering a glass of wine and pincho for €1), take the gravel path by the
picnic area through expansive vineyards to cross the highway and
a picnic area to the outskirts of Cacabelos.*

16.5 **Cacabelos**: A long typical camino town, Cacabelos once supported six pilgrim hospitals as a booming commercial center. In Roman times, it served as an administration center for gold mining. Today pilgrims can visit Iglesia de Santa María, with its 13th-century Virgen Mary on the concrete tympanum. At the bridge on the far side of town, an old mill and wooden olive press are displayed to the R. The town's unusual pilgrim albergue is located on the far side of the bridge alongside the Santuario de las Angustias, a hermitage with a most curious retablo featuring a young Jesus playing cards with San Antonio de Padua. *After Cacabelos, the route follows near the highway into the hamlet of Pieros.*

18.0 **Pieros**: La Iglesia de San Martín de Tours was commissioned in 1086 by Osmundo, the same bishop of Astorga who built the bridge of Ponferrada. The Templars ran a pilgrim hospital here as well as a leper hospice. ⚠ *Walk on the edge of the highway out of Pieros to an option to turn R off of the road or continue straight (18.6km). We prefer the R way via* **Valtuille de Arriba (20.0km)***, only 1km longer and through beautiful cherry orchards and fields mostly on a dirt path. [The road option is half highway and half dirt path. The two options come together just outside of Villafranca del Bierzo (22.9km).] The two most popular albergues are on the near side of town near the Iglesia de Santiago, farther from restaurants and stores. If you stay here, be sure to walk into the main part of town to see the wealth of historical buildings.*

18.1 **Pieros** Ⓐ Pop. 35
Ⓐ El Serbal y la Luna (priv, 🛏19, €5): 🍴 🅦 🖥,
c/El Pozo 15, 📞639-888924 📧 ⏰Mar-Nov

20.0 **Valtuille de Arriba** Ⓗ 🍴 🄴 Pop. 139
Ⓗ La Osa Mayor (dbl €40): 🅚 🅦 🖥 📶,
📞654-152305 📧

🍷 **Cacabelos**
Apr/May: Wine festival

Pilgrim statue in Villafranca

24.2 Villafranca del Bierzo A H ⛺🚲➕€⚙🚌🚉

Pop. 3,505, **ℹ** 🕐987-540028, Av. Diez Ovelar 10, 🕐10am-2pm, 4-7pm

1. **A Municipal** (🛏62, €6): 🔋🚻🅾️🚿🍴, 🕐987-542680, 🕐Mar-Nov, overflow of 100+ in summer
2. **A Ave Fenix** (assoc, 🛏80, €5): 🍴🚻🅾️🚿🍴, 🕐987-540229 📱, 🕐all year, communal meals, run by Jesús Jato, a classic camino character, reported dirty
3. **A Viña Femita** (priv, 🛏32, dm €8, dbl €35): 🍴🚻🅾️🚿🍴📶, c/Calvo Sotelo 2, 🕐987-542490 📱 🕐Feb 2-Dec 17, **burned down in 2012, scheduled to re-open in 2013**
4. **A H ⭐ De la Piedra** (priv, 🛏38, dm €8, dbl €24): 🔋🚻🅾️🚿📶🍴(free), c/Espíritu Santo 14, 🕐987-540260 📱, 🕐11:30, Mar-Nov, run by a delightful couple from Madrid
5. **H Hostal El Cruce** (sng €18, dbl €25, quad €40): 🍴📶, c/El Salvador 41, 🕐987-540185 📱
6. **H Hostel Burbia** (dbl €48): 🚿, c/Fuente Cubero, 🕐987-542667 📱
7. **H Casa Mendez** (dbl €49): c/Espíritu Santo 1, 🕐 87-540055 📱
8. **H San Francisco** (dbl €62): 🍴, Plaza Mayor 6, 🕐987-540465 📱
9. **H San Nicolás el Real** (dbl €55): 🍴, San Nicolás 4, 🕐987-540483, historic building
10. **H La Llave** (dbl €56): 🍴🚻📶, c/del Agua 7, 🕐648-030888 📱
11. **H La Puerta del Perdón** (dbl €45-100): 🍴, Plaza de Prim 4, 🕐987-540614 📱
12. **H Las Doñas del Portazgo** (dbl €78): 🍴, c/Ribadeo 2, 🕐987-540257 📱
13. **H Parador** (dbl €137): 🍴🚿, Av. Calvo Sotelo 28, 🕐987-540175 📱, pool and sauna, one of the least expensive Paradors

Puerta del Perdón of Iglesia de Santiago in Villafranca

24.2 Villafranca del Bierzo is one of the most beautiful towns on the camino, retaining much of its medieval and Renaissance character in spite of an increase of modern hotels and buildings. Several Roman *castrum* have been found in the area, with the strategic location at the confluence of the rivers Burbio and Valcarce and just below the mountain pass. This location later drew merchants from all over, giving the city its names (literally "city of the Franks" but more accurately, of the "foreigners.") Villafranca marks the end of the 10th stage in the *Codex Calixtinus* and was home to numerous pilgrim hospitals.

Life wasn't all that easy for the people of Villafranca, who suffered an outbreak of plague in 1589 and destruction by flood in 1715. In the Peninsular Wars of the early 19th century, French soldiers overtook the city only to be driven back by British soldiers who ravaged Villafranca, destroying the castle and stealing from churches.

Today it's a great place to rest up for the ascent toward O Cebreiro the following day and to wander the picturesque streets. On the way into town, pass the **Iglesia de Santiago** to the L, with its **Puerta del Perdón**, a doorway for pilgrims who were too sick to continue to Santiago. They could walk through the door in lieu of completing the pilgrimage and receive the same indulgences. **Iglesia de San Francisco**, according to legend, was founded by Saint Francis of Assisi himself on his pilgrimage to Santiago. Don't miss the Mudéjar ceiling and excellent Renaissance *Retablo de la Inmaculada* in the chapel to the R of the entrance. The church has been restored after being used as a military barracks. The 17th-century **Iglesia de San Nicolás el Real** has an interesting Baroque façade; Domenico Laffi mentions receiving Mass here in 1673. The **Convento de la Anunciada** features one of the oldest cypress trees in Europe at over 400 years of age.

Be sure to stroll down *Calle del Agua* to see the 19th-century mansions replete with original coats of arms. The castle destroyed by the French has been restored, but is privately owned and cannot be entered. One of the modern albergues, the Ave Fenix, is run by the Jesús Jato, somewhat of a camino legend. The original albergue burnt to the ground and was replaced by an intermediate tent city until the current building was completed. The albergue sometimes puts on a *queimada* and offers healing rituals to pilgrims.

Villafranca's lush botanical garden

🏛 **Villafranca**
May 1: Spring festival
June: Poetry festival
Sept 14: Patron saint day

Queimada celebration in Villafranca

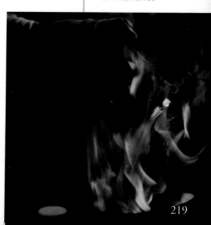

219

25

VILLAFRANCA TO LA FABA

23.7km
(14.7mi)

🕐 **6-8 Hours**
Difficulty: ▭▫◻️◻️
🅿 95%, 22.4km
Ⓤ 5%, 1.3km

A Albergues:
Pereje 5.6km
Trabadelo 10.0km
La Portela 14.1km
Ambasmestas 15.4km
Vega 16.9km
Ruitelán 19.1km
Herrerías 20.5km
La Faba 23.7km
Laguna 26.4km
O Cebreiro 28.7km

⚠️ **Alt. Route:**
Camino Duro,
+1.6km (p. 225)

Camino Duro Alt.
Triacastela to La Faba
🅿 57%, 14.3km
Ⓤ 43%, 11.0km

Mountain views from
the Camino Duro

Drink in captivating mountain and valley scenery on heather-lined earthen tracks, savor the shade of chestnut trees.

💡 While the trail doesn't officially enter Galicia until just before O Cebreiro, the culture, landscape and architecture today all reflect Galician characteristics. Leaving Villafranca, the routes split with the more challenging but beautiful route splitting to the R just before the bridge. While the flyover highway traffic can be distracting, the numerous Valcarce Valley villages provide quaint respite. Save energy for the final uphill to La Faba along sometimes muddy or slippery trails.

220

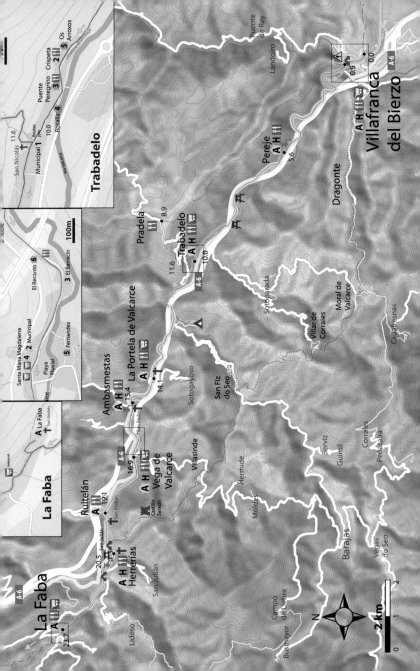

Villafranca del Bierzo

Pereje

Trabadelo

Pradela

La Portela de Valcarce

Ambasmestas

Vega de Valcarce

Herrerías

Ruitelán

La Faba

Trabadelo

Municipal **1**
Peregrino **3**
Crispeta **2**
Os Arroxos **5**
Rosalía **4**
San Nicolás 11.6
Puente
10.0

La Faba

A La Faba
San Andrés

La Portela de Valcarce

Santa María Magdalena
El Recanto **6**
Municipal **2**
El Sarracín **3**
Fernández **5**
Playa Fluvial

Landoiro
Puente de Rey
Dragonte
Sotoparada
Mora de Valcarce
Villar de Corrales
Castañasnas
San Fiz do Seo
Sotogayoso
Villasinde
Hermide
Moldes
Serviz
Guimil
Corrales
Peñafalla
Barjas
Vegas do Seo
Campo del Liebre
Busmayor

0.0
0.9
5.6
8.9
10.0
11.6
14.1
15.4
16.9
19.1
20.5
23.7

San Frdadel
San Julián
San Fiz do Seo
Castillo Sarracín
San Julián
Lidoso

2 Km
N
0   1   2

100m

⚠ Route Options:

Primary highway route, 23.7km; This shorter and more po
lar route is entirely paved and on the shoulder of a highway r
to a crash barrier all the way to Trabadelo.

Alternate high route "Camino Duro," 25.3km (p. 225);
While this route is 1.6km longer and climbs much more in e
evation than the highway route, the effort is rewarded with s
ning views and earthen paths. Rejoins alternate route in 10.7

Route Options:
Turn L for primary
route, R for high route

☀ The Camino Duro
route option reduces
the Triacasta to La Faba
stage from 95% paved
to 57%.

0.0 *Follow trail markings through Villafranca and across the river.* ⚠ *The split for route options (0.9km) is directly after the bridge and not well marked (see photo left).*

For the lower route, keep straight at the bridge leaving Villafranca. Much of the day's walking will be on a track parallel to the highway, with crash barriers providing protection from traffic. Because of the superhighway flyover passing above, the traffic on the old highway is fairly light. This primary route passes through Pereje, with its excellent municipal albergue, and rejoins the alternate route in Trabadelo.

5.6 Pereje A H▮ Pop. 39
A Municipal (muni, ⟲55, €5): 🔲W▯,
 c/Camino de Santiago, ☎987-540138, ◷all year,
 no bunk beds, beautiful new facility, green yard
H Las Coronas (dbl €42): c/Camino de Santiago,
 ☎987-540138

5.6 Pereje was the site of a pilgrim hospital, donated by Doña Urraca to the O Cebreiro monastery in 1118. The hospital was in commission until land reforms in 1835. *Continue along the road to Trabadelo.*

10.0 Trabadelo A H▮🖾✚ Pop. 456
1. **A Municipal** (⟲36, €6): 🔲▯W▯▯,
 c/Camino de Santiago, ☎647-635831, ◷Mar-Nov
2. **A H Crispeta** (priv, ⟲20, dm €6, sng €25,
 dbl €44): 🔲W▯▯🛜, c/Camino de Santiago,
 ☎620-329386, ◷all year
3. **H El Puente Peregrino** (dbl €30): ▮▮,
 c/Camino de Santiago 153, ☎987-566500
4. **H Rosalia** (dbl €45): ▮▮W,
 c/Camino de Santiago, ☎987-566498 ▢
5. **H Os Arroxos** (dbl €50): ▬,
 c/Camino de Santiago, ☎987-566529 ▢, jacuzzi

10.0 Trabadelo: Little remains of the historic buildings of Trabadelo, which included two chapels, a pilgrim hospital and castle, whose owners exacted pilgrims tolls until banned by the king. Iglesia de San Nicolás survives with its Romanesque virgin. The entrance to town features immense chestnut trees, and the modern lumber industry is evident with piles of fresh-cut logs. *The route continues on the main road out of Trabadelo to La Portela.*

14.1 Portela de Valcarce

After passing through a parking lot across from the Hotel Valcarce complex, (🛒 local products and fruit small shop), the path enters this wayside village. *Continue along the road to Ambasmestas.*

15.4 Ambasmestas

The name comes from the confluence here of the Balboa and Valcarce rivers. There is an 18th-century stone Iglesia de San Pedro. *Continue on the same road to Vega de Valcarce.*

16.9 Vega de Valcarce

The largest town of the day, Vega de Valcarce is located on a wider section of valley well-suited to agriculture, with many gardens. Emperor Carlos V is said to have spent the night in Vega in 1520 and records indicate the presence of a Jewish quarter. From here, 🏛 **Castillo de Sarracín**, a 9th-century castle reconstructed in the 14th-15th centuries, is visible below the village to the L. If you stay in Vega, save energy for a hike up to the ruins (30 min. each way). *Continue on the same road as it goes up to Ruitelán.*

14.1 Portela de Valcarce A H 🍴🛒🚌

Pop. 37, 🏛 Spanish: "gate of the Valcarce [river]"

A H El Peregrino (priv, 🛏28, dm €8, sng €25, dbl €35): 🍴🗲🖥🛜, c/Camino de Santiago 5, ☎987-543197 ✉, ⏲Mar-Nov

H Hotel Valcarce (sng €33, dbl €62): 🍴🛒, Autovia A-6, ☎987-543180

15.4 Ambasmestas A H🍴🛒

Pop. 46, 🏛 Spanish: "waters mixing"

A Das Animas (priv, 🛏18, €5): 🖥🖨🖥, c/Campo Bajo 3, ☎619-048626 ✉, ⏲Apr-Oct, across the creek in bright green building

H Residencia Los Sauces (dbl €52): Antigua Nacional VI, ☎987-233768

16.9 Vega de Valcarce A H🍴🛒➕🖥🚌

Pop. 703, 🏛 Spanish: "meadow on the Valcarce [river]," 🛜 in bakery/café

1. **A El Robel** (priv, 🛏18, €5): 🍴🖥🅳, CN 6 km 426, ☎603-290270 ✉, ⏲May-October
2. **A Municipal** (🛏72, €5): 🍴🗲🖥🅳, c/Pandelo, ☎987-543006, basic
3. **A Sarracín** (priv, 🛏13, €10): 🄺🖥🅳🛜, N-VI #32, ☎987-543275 ✉, ⏲Feb-Nov
4. **A Santa María Magdalena** (priv, 🛏13, €10): 🖥🖥, N-VI, ☎646-128423 ✉, ⏲all year
5. **H Pensión Fernández** (dbl €30) ☎987-543027
6. **H El Recanto** (dbl €44): c/Camino de Santiago 38, ☎987-543202 ✉

19.1 Ruitelán A🍴🛒 Pop. 23

A Pequeño Potala (priv, 🛏34, €5): 🍴🗲🖥🖥, Crta A Coruña 22, ☎987-561322 ✉, ⏲all year, Buddhist vibe, shiatsu massage €30, veg. dinner

19.1 Ruitelán

has the Iglesia de San Juan Bautista, which belongs to the far-off diocese of León. On the L at the end of town is the chapel of San Froilán, who lived as a cave hermit

☀️ Vega de Valcarce is the last "full-service" town until Triacastela, so consider if you need to top off on cash, pharmacy items or snacks.

Pilgrim shells for sale in Vega del Valcarce

here before becoming bishop of León. *The trail finally leaves the highway on a side road to the L through the hamlet of San Julián. Cross a 15th-century bridge to enter Herrerías. This is the last you'll see of highway walking until Palas de Rei—enjoy!*

20.5 Herrerías: As the name suggests, Herrerías was an iron-working town with the iron forge visible across the river. Domenico Laffi described the town in the 17th century as "situated on the riverbank. Here they excavate iron from the hills and bring it to the village, where there is a furnace for smelting it. They have a large iron hammer which is driven by waterpower, as well as forging tongs and bellows. All these tools are of immense size. The village is small and nearly all its huts are roofed with straw." Today a picnic area along the creek welcomes visitors. The fountain in town is known anecdotally as *La Fuente de Don Quiñones*, of jousting fame in Hospital de Órbigo. A 12th-century English pilgrim hospital was once located on the far side of town.

The trail begins climbing a quiet paved road, but splits to the L soon onto a steep rocky path through a lush chestnut forest on a delightful dirt path. The trail emerges into the tiny village of La Faba, a good place to rest and fortify for more uphill hiking tomorrow.

20.5 Herrerías A 🏠🍴🚌
Pop. 44, 🗺 Spanish: "the blacksmiths"
A Albergue Herrerías (priv, 🛏17, €5): 🍴🚿,
  📞654-353940 📱, 🕐Apr 15-Oct, vegetarian
H Casa Polín (dbl €30): 🍴, c/Camino de Santiago,
  📞987-543039 📱
H Paraíso del Bierzo (dbl €59): 📞987-684137 📱
H Capricho de Josana (dbl €65 w/🛁): 🍴📶,
  c/Camino de Santiago, 📞987-119300 📱

23.7 La Faba A 🍴🛒
Pop. 27, 🗺 Spanish: "the bean"
A ⭐ Albergue de la Faba (assoc, 🛏60, €5 w/🛁):
  🔑🚿🅿, 📞630-836865 📱, 🕐2pm, Mar 15-Oct,
  evening ecumenical service, German Association

23.7 La Faba's church, **Iglesia de San Andrés**, is the last of the diocese of Astorga, offering an evening pilgrim mass. A German confraternity operates the albergue next door. The Refugio Vegetariano, a decidedly eastern establishment, offers vegetarian meals, massage and some mattresses on the floor. A small, adequate shop could provide dinner fare, and the town bar offers a *menú*.

Pilgrim statue outside of La Faba albergue

⚠ Alternate: Camino Duro, +1.6km

The alternate Camino Duro route turns to the R just before the bridge leaving Villafranca (see photo on p. 222 where pilgrims are walking) and climbs a mountain, while the primary route stays in the valley.

*From the split, the path becomes a dirt path, which is initially very steep with nice views back to Villafranca. The track flattens out with lovely views and joins a paved road to the edge of **Pradela** 🍴 (8.9km). At the T turn L to continue on the trail or R to enter the Pradela. The path descends steeply on and off the paved road to **Trabadelo (11.6km)** (walk the road for a more gradual but longer descent), where the two routes join.*

Mountain scenery and earthen paths on the alternate route via Pradela

A typical green
Galician forest scene

In Galicia, **Xunta albergues** (municipal) have a standard fee (€5 as of 2013) that includes disposable sheet and pillow case. Available year-round, you may need to call for the key in winter. Xunta albergues tend to have two small oddities: 1) kitchens without cookware; 2) bathroom facilities that are not very private (such as showers without curtains or doors).

Highlights include flowing rivers, glorious mountain views, Celtic architecture and culture, timeless rural villages, and arriving to the grand cathedral!

Galicia is the last of the autonomous regions on the camino and home to the much-anticipated Santiago de Compostela. The official languages of Galicia are Spanish and Galician *(Gallego)*, spoken by a whopping 90% of inhabitants (compared to only about 30% of Basques who speak Basque).

Excavations have shown evidence of megalithic prehistoric cultures in Galicia, including a proliferation of dolmens, or megalithic burial chambers. Later the area was settled by a Celtic tribe who became known as Galicians, and many symbols of Celtic culture remain right down to the traditional bagpipe music. These inhabitants built fortified villages, or *castrum*, some of which were inhabited until the 8th century and some ruins can still be seen today.

Galicians, as the Celts they are, were known for being fiercely independent (think Braveheart) and resistant to foreign rule. Foreign occupations of the Iberian peninsula tended to peter out before conquering Galicia, as the Roman, Suevi and Muslim conquests all fell short of overcoming them. The region had a reputation for witchcraft and pagan beliefs. Even today, pilgrims can sometimes participate in the *queimada* tradition of preparing a drink from alcohol and setting it on fire to ward off evil spirits.

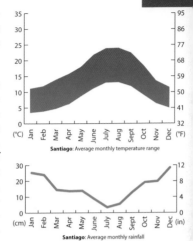

Santiago: Average monthly temperature range

Santiago: Average monthly rainfall

Galicia is known as *o país dos mil ríos*, "the country of a thousand rivers" for its free-flowing water, including the largest river, the Miño, which the camino crosses over at Portomarín. Its wet reputation extends to the weather, with high average rainfall, so be sure to have your rain jackets and pack covers handy! The forested and rainy ecology is quite a far cry from what is usually thought of as Spanish climate and you may feel like you have stepped into Ireland!

For local cuisine, seafood rules the roost, including the superlative *Pulpa a Gallego* (boiled octopus) as well as squid, razor clams and goose barnacles. Fishing is the largest industry in the region, which depends on its Atlantic coastline and the many rivers and fjords. *Caldo Gallego* (Galician stew) is also frequently on offer, a mixture of white beans, potatoes, turnips, ham, pork, chorizo and collard greens.

Many forests have been planted with invasive eucalyptus trees, used for papermaking and edging out the traditional rural occupation of raising cattle. Some original oak and chestnut forests remain, including ancient beauties before Ponferrada. Native species include the hearty Galician Pony, and woodlands provide an ideal habitat for rabbits, wild boar and deer.

The Galician language is very similar to Portuguese and has much in common with Spanish. The letter X is much more prominent, pronounced as "sh" sound. For example *Igrexa* instead of *Iglesia* (church). Vowel sounds are often drawn out and dipthongized (*cruceiro* instead of the Spanish *crucero*, or wayside cross). Galician also drops the "l" from definite articles (*la, los/ las*) so "the house" would be *a casa* rather than the Spanish *la casa* (*el* becomes *o*).

26

LA FABA TO TRIACASTELA

25.7km
(16.0mi)

⏱ **6-8 Hours**
Difficulty: ⬛⬜⬜
🅿 16%, 4.1km
Ⓤ 84%, 21.6km

A ALBERGUES:
Laguna 2.7km
O Cebreiro 5.0km
Hospital 10.5km
Alto do Poio 13.4km
Fonfría 16.8km
Triacastela 25.7km
A Balsa 28.3km
Calvor 39.3km

Mountain views on the way to O Cebreiro

Enter the misty mountains of Galicia and enjoy stunning views. Observe traditional rural architecture as you pass through villages to the historic town of Triacastela.

☀ The challenging climb to O Cebreiro is well rewarded with breathtaking mountain views. Traditional Galician villages provide frequent amenities and whimsical country scenery. Be prepared for cold, wet or foggy weather. The descent to Triacastela is quite steep and can be muddy and slippery.

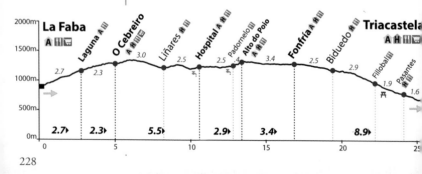

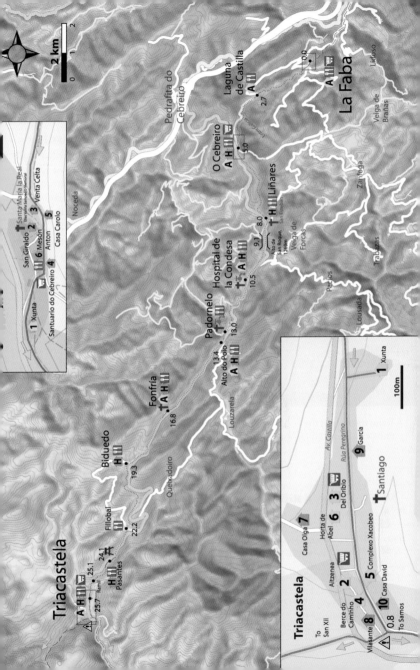

2.7 Laguna de Castilla A 🏠
Pop. 27, 📖 Spanish: "Lagoon of Castile"
A 🏠 **Albergue a Escuela** (Priv, 🛏18, dm €9, sng €25, dbl €40): 🏠🌐💻🚿, c/Camino de Santiago, ☎987-684786 ☗, 🕐12pm Easter-Oct

0.0 *Leave La Faba along a pleasant tree-lined lane. Stay to the R upon emerging from the trees to walk uphill with beautiful views to reach Laguna.*

2.7 Laguna de Castilla

is officially the last town in Castilla, modeling many typical Galician features such as *pallozas* (p. 231) and *hórreos* (one of the largest on the route, p. 199). About 1km after Laguna, a colorful cement *stele* will mark your official **entrance into Galicia**, the final region on the camino, where Santiago de Compostela is located. Cement markers count down the kilometers from here (inaccurate due to rerouting) and often helpfully note the name of hamlets so small they may not have street names or even be on the map. *Continue straight through the scrubby gorse and heather to meet the road into O Cebreiro.*

A stone stele marks the entrance into Galicia.

5.0 O Cebreiro is the camino's first official Galician town, a welcoming mountaintop village that retains its historic character. The albergue is the first of many run by the Xunta, the governing body of Galicia. They are mostly purpose-built modern buildings or renovated schoolhouses with good facilities but a somewhat sterile atmosphere (p. 227). O Cebreiro bears evidence of occupation since ancient times, including a Roman way station that guarded the road to the Galician mines. The town grew to greater prominence with the pilgrim road.

5.0 O Cebreiro A 🏠🏨🍴♿🅿 Pop. 1,228
1. **A** Albergue do Cebreiro (Xunta, 🛏104, €5): 🍳💻💧, ☎660-396809, 🕐1pm, all year, no cookware, credenciales available
2. 🏠 San Giraldo de Aurillac (dbl €55): c/Cebreiro ☎982-367125, next to church
3. 🏠 Venta Celta (dbl €37): ☎982-367137
4. 🏠 Santuario do Cebreiro (dbl €50): ☎982-367125
5. 🏠 Casa Carolo (dbl €35-48): ☎982-367168
6. 🏠 Mesón Anton (dbl €43): 🍴, ☎982-151336

The **Iglesia de Santa María la Real** is a reconstruction of the medieval church that was destroyed in the early 19th century. In the reconstruction, traces of a pre-Romanesque church were found. The baptismal font, virgin and chalice reliquary are from the medieval church.

Local tradition says that the **Holy Grail** (the chalice from which Jesus drank wine at the Last Supper) was hidden away in O Cebreiro. In the year 1300, a faithful parishioner trudged through a snowstorm to receive communion at the O Cebreiro church. The priest mocked the man for going to such trouble for just a bit of bread and wine. At that moment, the elements miraculously transformed into real flesh and blood. The virgin, still on display in the church, was said to have moved her head to have a better look. The event was later declared an official miracle by Pope Innocent VIII. When Queen Isabel passed through 200 years later she donated an ornate reliquary for the remains. The Galician coat of arms incorporates the chalice and host as central symbols. The church offers daily Mass at ☉7pm.

Iglesia de Santa María in O Cebreiro

Visit a 🏛 museum of local artifacts housed in a **palloza**, (free, ☉11am-12pm, 3-7pm) a traditional building type found all over the Celtic world. Pallozas are oval stone buildings with thatched roofs, well suited for the tough environment of Galicia, often divided with space for animals and for humans, as well as a lofted sleeping area. They have no chimneys, and smoke escapes through the thatch. These structures are visible in various stages of construction or decay along the pilgrimage road in Galicia. Pallozas were inhabited into the 1960s.

O Cebreiro is known for being the birthplace of **Father Elías Valiña Sampedro** (p. 20), a local priest who was instrumental in the 20th-century revival of the Camino de Santiago. He is said to have come up with the yellow arrow symbol and is also responsible for the cement markers in Galicia. A bust of his head to the R of the church commemorates his life and contributions.

Elías Valiña Sampedro bust in O Cebreiro

🏠 **O Cebreiro**
Sept 8-9: Santa María and Santo Milagro
March: Cheese festival
Late Sept: Cattle fair

After the Xunta albergue, either follow the arrows down to the paved road or the dirt path from behind the albergue; both lead to Liñares.

8.0 **Liñares** Pop. 69, Spanish: "linens"
- **Casa Jaime** (dbl €30): , c/Liñares 2, ☎982-367166, all of hamlet's services here

10.5 **Hospital de la Condesa** Pop. 17, Spanish: "the Countess' Hospital"
- **Xunta** (⏚20, €5): , ☎660-396810, ⏰1pm, all year, no cookware
- **Mesón O Tear** (dbl €25- €36): , Hospital da Condesa 14, ☎982-367183

13.4 **Alto do Poio**
- **Albergue del Puerto** (priv, ⏚16, €6): , Ctra LU-633, ☎982-367172, poor reports
- **Santa María do Poio** (dbl €35): Alto do Poio, ☎982-367167

Pilgrim statue at Alto San Roque

8.0 **Liñares** grew flax to make linen garments. The town is referenced in documents as far back as the 8th century and mentioned in the *Codex Calixtinus*. The stone Iglesia de San Esteban is originally from 1120 but has been restored. *After Liñares, the trail continues to the R on a smaller paved road, then a L onto a dirt path. Follow an incline up the Alto de San Roque.*

9.1 **Alto de San Roque** features a modern bronze statue of a windswept pilgrim. In spring and summer, the area is alive with wildflowers in every hue and is a good place to look for birds of prey circling above. *Continue on the dirt path across the street from the statue, joining a paved road into Hospital de la Condesa.*

10.5 **Hospital de la Condesa**: The name suggests there was once a pilgrim hospice here, but any sign of it has been lost. The rustic stone church at the far side of town was built in 1963. *Leave Hospital on the paved road and soon turn R onto a smaller paved road signposted Saburgos. In 300m, turn off L onto a dirt path and pass through **Padornelo** (13.0km), which once housed the priory of the Hospitalers of San Juan de Jerusalén and now has a late 19th-century church also dedicated to St. John. From here the trail climbs somewhat steeply up to Alto do Poio.*

13.4 **Alto do Poio** once housed a medieval hermitage and a church belonging to the Order of Saint John. Today it has a bit of a truck stop feel as the trail reconnects with the main road. *Continue to the R on a dirt track parallel to the paved road into Fonfría.*

16.8 **Fonfría** once housed the hospice of Santa Catalina, built in 1535, which was reported in 1789 to be in quite bad shape with the roof caving in. The lodging is recorded as providing heat, salt, water and a bed with two blankets to healthy pilgrims, and for ill pilgrims an extra 1/4lb of bread, eggs and butter. *Leave town on the dirt path parallel to the main road into the hamlet of Biduedo.*

19.3 **Biduedo** once had a pilgrim hospice and hermitage, but nothing remains. The modern stone church is said to be the smallest on the entire camino. *The trail continues on a wide rocky dirt path, descending steeply to cross the paved road into several small hamlets on the way into Triacastela:* **Fillobal (22.2km), As Pasantes (24.1km)** *and* **Ramil (25.1km),** *which contains several truly massive chestnut trees. The road is paved into town, with the Triacastela Xunta albergue on the L.*

16.8 **Fonfría** A H ▓
Pop. 41 ☖ Spanish: "cold fountain"
A H **A Reboleira** (priv, ⌂28+, dm €8, dbl €26): ▓▓▓▓▓, c/Camino de Santiago 15, ✆982-181271 ✉, ⏰1pm, Mar-Nov
H **Galego** (dbl €36): ✆982-161461
H **Núñez** (dbl €40): ✆982-161335

19.3 **Biduedo** H ▓ Pop. 31
H **Casa Quiroga** (dbl €30): ✆982-187299
H **Casa Xato**: ✆982-187301

Massive tree at the entrance to Triacastela

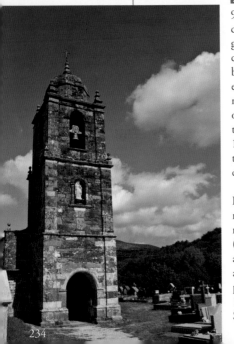

25.7 <u>**Triacastela**</u> was founded in the 9th century by Count Gatón, who was charged with repopulating the Bierzo region after the Reconquista. The three castles for which the town is named were built in the early 10th century and apparently destroyed in the same century with nothing remaining today, save the image on the coat of arms of Triacastela. The town held some political clout in the 13th century when Alfonxo IX spent time there and raised money for his successful bid to reconquer Sevilla.

In the *Codex Calixtinus*, Triacastela marked the end of stage 11 and signaled the end of the Galician mountains (though there are still a few smaller ups and downs to go before Santiago). The area is rich in limestone, and medieval pilgrims would often carry a large stone 100km to the limekiln in Castañeda near Santiago to be used in the making of the

cathedral. Imagine the many hands that helped to build! (And be grateful you don't need to add any rocks to your pack in this day and age.)

The **Iglesia de Santiago** is mostly from the 18th century—note the three castles on the coat of arms on the tower. Evening pilgrim Mass is offered here by a particularly passionate priest. Several cafés along the main street have pilgrim *menús*.

🛏 **Triacastela**
July 16: Virxe de Carme
Aug 17: San Mamede

Rounding the bend to Triacastela (above left)

Enjoying the rainbow at the Xunta albergue in Triacastela (above right)

Iglesia Santiago in Triacastela (left)

25.7 Triacastela A H ⓘⅡ🛏➕€🖥
Pop. 772, 🏛 Latin: "three castles"

1. **A Albergue de Triacastela** (Xunta, 🛏56, €5): 🚻🅦🅓, ©982-548087, ⏰1pm all year, one of the nicer Xunta albergues (rooms of 4 and green lawn)

2. **A Aitzenea** (priv, 🛏38, €8): 🅺🅦🅓🖥, Plaza Vista Alegre 1, ©982-548076, ⏰Apr-Oct

3. **A Del Oribio** (priv, 🛏27, €9): 🅺🅦🅓🖥, c/Castilla 20, , ©982-548085 🖼, ⏰all year

4. **A Berce do Caminho** (priv, 🛏27, €8): 🅺🅦🅓🖥🛜, c/Camilo José Cela 11, ©982-548127, ⏰all year

5. **A H Complexo Xacobeo** (priv, 🛏36, dm €9, dbl €40): 🅺Ⅱ🅦🅓🖥🛜, c/Leoncio Cadórnigo 12, ©982-548037🖼, good menú, ⏰all year

6. **A H Horta de Abel** (priv, 🛏14, dm €9, dbl €40): 🅺🅦🅓🖥, c/Peregrino 5, ©608-080556, ⏰Apr-Oct 15

7. **H Casa Olga** (from €16 per person): 🅺🅦🅓, Rúa do Castro, ©982-548134 🖼

8. **H Vilasante** (dbl €35): Camilo José Cela 7, ©982-548116

9. **H García** (dbl €40): c/Peregrino 8, ©982-548024

10. **H Casa David** (dbl €50): Ⅱ🖥, Travesía Baltasar 2, ©982-548144 🖼

235

TRIACASTELA TO BARBADELO

23.0km
(14.3mi)

☉ **5-6 HOURS**
DIFFICULTY: ▭▭☐☐
SAN XIL ROUTE:
P 42%, 9.8km
U 58%, 13.2km

A ALBERGUES:
A Balsa 2.6km
Calvor 13.6km
San Mamed 14.9km
Sarria 18.7km
Vilei 22.3km
Barbadelo 23.0km
Morgade 30.7km
Ferreiros 32.0km

⚠ **ALT. STAGE 27A:**
Samos Route,
29.5km (p. 242 **A**)

SAMOS ROUTE:
P 39%, 11.4km
U 61%, 18.1km

Picturesque chapel
in Calvor

Visit the Benedictine monastery of Samos. Feel the excitement of new pilgrims joining the path in Sarria.

☼ Two options lead to Sarria/Barbadelo; both follow a mix of paved and unpaved path and have pleasing rural scenery. The most direct primary route via San Xil is 6.5km shorter (23.0km), passing through small hamlets. The longer route (29.5km) passes the Samos monastery, a fascinating historical site that includes a pilgrim albergue. The Samos route includes some beautiful countryside, but the overall route has slightly more distance on pavement than the San Xil route (though a lower overall %). Both routes are lovely!

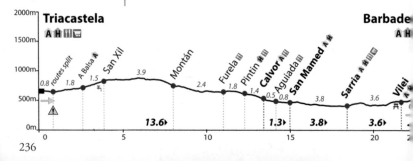

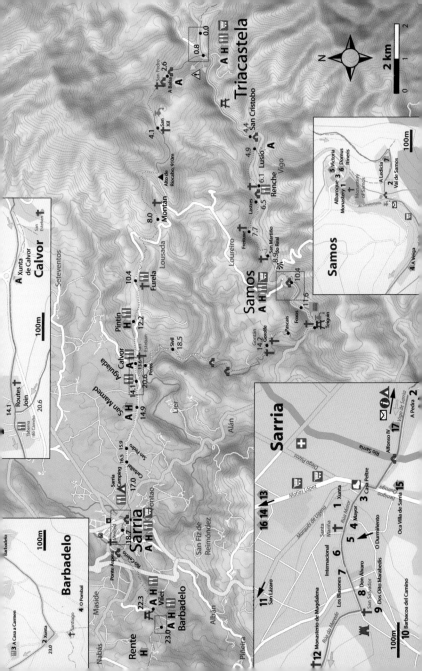

2.6 **A Balsa** **A**

A El Beso (priv, 🛏12, €8): 🏧🍴, 📞633-550558, 🕐all year, communal dinner by donation with vegetables from the garden

0.0 *Leave Triacastela via the main road.* ⚠ *At the far edge of town, the trail splits (0.8km), with the primary San Xil route to the R, and the alternate Samos route (p. 242) to the L. For the* **San Xil Route***, turn R and cross the main road (0.8km). Continue straight at the sign for San Xil on a minor paved roads through delightful forest. Turn off to the R and walk over a bridge over a creek. Walk through the hamlet of* **A Balsa (2.6km)** *and pass a small ermita, then pass over another small bridge. Pass a large pool of water with a huge seashell. Continue steeply uphill through oak and chestnut forest to the hamlet of San Xil.*

4.1 **San Xil** has a church that features a 15th-century chalice. Continue uphill to Alto de Riocabo and turn R on dirt footpath with nice views. *Keep walking to* **Montán (8.0km)***, whose Iglesia de Santa María has a Romanesque nave. The trail continues through hamlets including* **Furela (10.4km)***, with its Capilla de San Roque featuring a retablo. Continue through the hamlet of* **Pintín** 🏠 **(12.2km)***,* [🏠 **Casa Cines**: dbl €36, Lugar Pintín 5, 📞982-167939 📧]*; turn off the road to the R to follow a dirt path to Calvor.*

Shell fountain before San Xil

13.6 **Calvor** was once the site of a pre-Roman castro known as Astorica. While its Iglesia de San Esteban was founded in the 8th century, most of what remains today is from the 19th century.

14.1 **Aguiada**: The trail reconnects with the alternate route at a convenient café for an afternoon pick-me-up. *Follow the paved road on a parallel dirt track past Albergue Paloma y Leña in* **San Mamed del Camino (14.9km)** *and then*

CAMINO FINISTERRE

The original roots of the Finisterre pilgrimage are not decisively known, though many speculate that it may have been a pre-Christian pilgrimage route to the *Ara Solis* at Cabo Finisterre (p. 296). Before Columbus stumbled upon the new world, the western coast of Spain was literally thought of as the "end of the world" (📖 Latin: *finis* end, *terrae* earth).

Today the route to Finisterre is marked with yellow arrows as well as concrete milestones that indicate the distance to the coast. The waymarks from Santiago to Finisterre and from Hospital to Muxía are marked only in one direction (east to west), while the route from Finisterre to Muxía is marked in both directions. It is possible to walk Santiago-Muxía-Finisterre OR Santiago-Finisterre-Muxía. We recommend the latter, principally because of a delightful stretch of uninterrupted countryside between Hospital and Finisterre, though this book gives information for both itineraries. The trail can be walked any time of year, but May through September offer the longest daylight hours for covering the long distances. As in the rest of Galicia, rain is a constant possibility.

Pilgrim statue on the way to the Finisterre lighthouse

This additional trail serves as a kind of "epilogue" to the camino experience. The act of walking literally until the trail meets the sea can be helpful to shift gears and process the experience. In summer, hundreds of pilgrims gather at the lighthouse of Finisterre to watch the sun sink below the horizon, and some follow a tradition of burning an item of clothing there to signify the end of the journey (p. 298). Both the towns of Finisterre and Muxía are pleasant seaside towns with affordable accommodation options if you choose to stay a few days. While the sea is often too wild here for swimming, the Galician food and culture make for interesting exploring.

SANTIAGO COMPOSTELA TO NEGREIRA

21.9km
(13.6mi)

⏱ **5-6 HOURS**
DIFFICULTY: ▭▢▢
🅿 69%, 15.8km
Ⓤ 31%, 6.1km

A ALBERGUES:
Castelo 10.4km
Negreira 21.9km
Vilaserío 34.2km

Pilgrims enter
Sarela on the
Camino Finisterre

Walk through eucalyptus forests, picturesque traditional hamlets and over a legendary bridge.

☀ This shortest of Finisterre stages has been rerouted in recent years to eliminate road walking to be about 1/3 on natural paths. Waymarking is generally good, but pay some extra attention compared to the Francés route. The climb after Aguapesada is steep and tiring! There are several cafés en route but few accommodations. The Xunta albergue fills early, but luckily several new private albergues have opened. Continue on to Vilaserío (+12.3km) for a more challenging day.

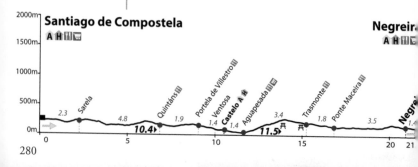

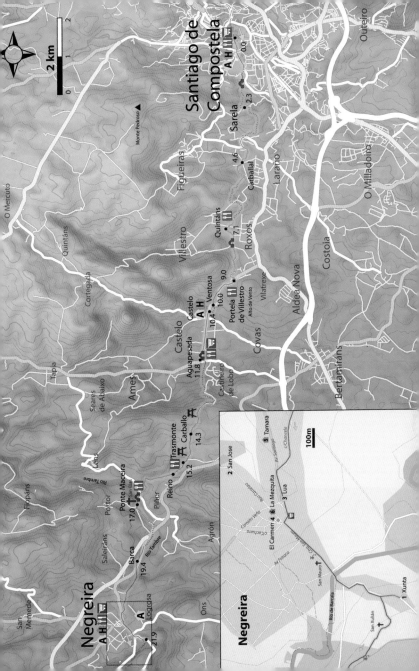

Santiago de Compostela
A H ▦ 0.0

Sarela ● 2.3

Carballa ● 4.6

Roxos ● 7.1
Quintáns ▦

Portela ▦ 9.0
de Villestro 10.0
Alto de Vento
Covas

Ventosa 10.4
Castelo A H
Aguapesada 11.8 ▦

Castiñeiro
de Lobo

Carballo 14.3 ⊼

Trasmonte 15.2 ▦

Reino ▦

Ponte Maceira ♆ 17.0 ▦
San Blas

Barca 19.4

Logrosa 27.9

Negreira
A H ▦
A

Monte Pedroso ▲

Outeiro

O Milladoiro

Larano

Vilatrexe

Aldea Nova

Costola

Bertamiráns

Covas

Villestro

Figueiras

Cortegada

Quintáns

O Mercato

Tapia

Ames

Seares de Abaixo

Cens

Río Tambre

Piñor

Agrón

Ons

Saleiráns

Pottor

San Mamede

Flipáns

2 km
0 1 2

Negreira

100m

2 San José

5 Tamara

3 Lúa
4 La Mezquita
El Carmen

San Mauro ✝

1 Xunta

San Xiillán ✝

Río de Barcala

Stone crucero

0.0 *To leave Santiago (map p. 268), go to the cathedral and walk downhill with the Parador to the R and police station* 🏢 *to the L. Cross at Rúa do Pombol to Rúa de Poza de Bar. Turn R through green park Carballeira San Lorenzo with huge oak trees and the 1216 **Convento de San Lorenzo (1.0km)**. Cross a small stone bridge onto a dirt path. When the path comes to a T with a paved road, turn L into **Sarela (2.3km)**. Be sure to take a look back at Santiago from this last vantage point. Turn R onto a gravel uphill path partway through town. Join a paved road that goes through **Carballal (4.6km)**. Turn R just after town onto a small paved road, turning to dirt. Rejoin the paved road through **Quintáns (7.1km)** past a rest area near a bridge. Return to dirt trail for a bit until passing **Portela de Villestro** 🍴 **(9.0km)**. Follow the paved road over Alto de Vento through **Ventosa (10.0km)**. Pass **Castelo** 🍴 **(10.4km)** with an albergue 200m to the R. Cross a bridge into Aguapesada.*

10.4 Castelo Ⓐ 🏠 🍴
Ⓐ 🏠 **Casa Ríamonte** (🛏6, dm €15 w/🚿, dbl €50 w/🚿): 🍴🛜🌐☎c/Castelo, ☎981-890356 📱

11.8 Aguapesada 🍴🛒 offers a pleasant halfway stop. *Now the trail begins to climb steeply on a dirt path through eucalyptus often accompanied by song birds. Meet a paved road and continue on it through the town of **Carballo (14.3km)**, through agricultural fields past a picnic area up to **Trasmonte** 🍴 **(15.2km)**. Continue on the paved road downhill through the hamlet of **Reino (15.7km)** to arrive to historic Ponte Maceira.*

Crossing Ponte Maceira over the Río Tambre

17.0 Ponte Maceira 🍴 (📖 Galician: "Bridge of the Apple"), true to its name, features an attractive 13th-century bridge across the Río Tambre (restored in the 18th century). According to legend, St. James and his followers were fleeing from the Roman army. The saint's crew ran across a bridge at this spot, but the bridge was divinely destroyed after them, leaving the Roman soldiers stranded on the other side. The image of the broken bridge is featured on the coat of arms of the local council. Maceira was also the site of a 13th-century battle between the troops of Diego Xelmérez, archbishop of Compostela, and the fighters of Pedro Froilaz de Trava and his sons Fernando and Bermudo. Today the town is beautiful preserved with traditional mansions lining the street displaying family coats of arms. The cool waters offer an ideal spot to soak weary feet. At the far end of the bridge is the 18th-century Capilla de San Blas with a stone roadside cross.

Negreira wedding

☀ Make sure you have enough supplies to make it to Cee in stage 34, the next full-service town.

*Turn L on a 1-lane road after town, which passes under an overpass and continues through agricultural fields to meet and cross the highway through **Barca (19.4km)**. Cross back over the highway and continue on the road into Negreira, with the turnoff (20.4km) for **Logrosa albergue** to the L.*

21.9 **Negreira** is a modern town with a full array of services, including some good seafood restaurants and the last full-size supermarket until Cee. The medieval *Pazo del Cotón* is an interesting historical marker with part of the original defensive wall, which adjoins the 18th-century Capilla de San Mauro. A modern sculpture depicts a man emigrating away from Galicia, a very common story in this region with high unemployment. On the far side of town, after the Xunta albergue, is the 18th-century Neoclassic Iglesia de San Xulián with a stone rollo.

+0.7 **Logrosa** A H ⓘ Pop. 54
A H **Logrosa Albergue** (priv, 🛏20, dm €17, sng €30, dbl €40 w/⬛): ⓘ W D ⬛ 🛜 ⬛(free), c/Logrosa 6, ☎981-885820 ✉, ⊙12pm, all year

21.9 **Negreira** A H ⓘ 🛒 ✚ ⊖ ⬛ Pop. 7,077
1. A **Xunta** (🛏20, €5): ⬛, c/Patrocinio, ☎664-081498, ⊙1pm all year, fills early
2. A **San Jose** (priv, 🛏50, €12): ⬛ ⓘ W D ⬛, c/de Castelao 20, ☎881-976934 ✉, ⊙11:30am Mar-Oct, linens & towels, excellent new facilities
3. A **Albergue Lua** (priv, 🛏40, €10): ⬛ W D 🛜, Av. de Santiago 22, ☎629-926802 ✉, ⊙10:30pm all year
4. A **Albergue El Carmen** (priv, 🛏36, €10): ⓘ W D ⬛ 🛜, c/Carmen 2, ☎636-129691 ✉, ⊙11am all year, same building and management as Hostal La Mezquita
5. H **Hotel Tamara** (sng €36, dbl €50): ⓘ, Av. de Santiago, ☎981-885201 ✉
6. H **La Mezquita** (sng €25, dbl €40): c/del Carmen 2, ☎636-129691 ✉

33

NEGREIRA TO OLVEIROA

33.3km
(20.7mi)

⏱ **8-10 Hours**
Difficulty: ▭▭□□
🅿 68%, 22.8km
Ⓤ 32%, 10.5km

A Albergues:
Vilaserío 12.3km
S. Mariña 20.9km
P. Olveira 31.5km
Olveiroa 33.3km

Colorful garden after
Negreira

Traverse tiny villages and beautiful gardens with decorated stone hórreos. Sleep in a traditional Galician building.

☀ This is the longest stage of the Finisterre route and over two-thirds of the day is on paved roads. Stock up on needed food in Negreira as there are no shops, with only a few cafés and drinking sources en route. For a shorter day, consider staying in intermediary albergues in Vilaserío or Santa Mariña.

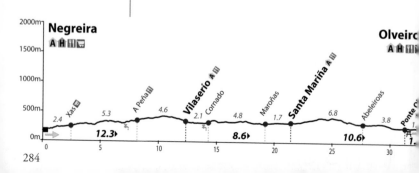

2 km

Negreira 0.0

Xas 2.4

Rapote 6.3

Plaxe 8.4
A Peña 7.7
Portocamiño

Vilaserío 12.3
Cornado 14.4

Maroñas 19.2
Santa Mariña 20.9

Bon
Xesús
Guelma

Xastro 23.8

Lago
Abeleiroas 27.7
Poteliñas 27.3

Corzón 30.0

Mallón 31.5
Ponte Olveira
Olveiroa 33.3

San Cristovo de Corzón

Río Xallas

Embalse de Fervenza

Río Xallas

A Picota

Serra de Outes

Outes

Asenso

Camiño Real

Pedralonga

Arzón

Pontevedra

Nantón

San Vicente

A Carballeira

A Campelo

A Pereira

Río Xallas

Os Currais

Os Vaos

Pazos

Ribadeza

Antes

Fontecada

Parada

Corneira

Paraxó

Arzón

Barcala

Tuñas

Meiro

Pesadoira

Pesadoira de Abajo

Colúns

Olveiroa

Xunta 2
Hórreo/Casa Loncho 1
As Pías 3
Santiago

50m

Graveyard and stone crucero

0.0 *From the Xunta albergue in Negreira, backtrack to turn up to the church and continue on a paved road to the forest, where it turns into a pleasant forest dirt path with pleasing views of the surrounding valleys. Meet a 2-lane road, turn R onto a narrow paved road at the mini market and continue through **Xas*** 🛒 *(2.4km), where evidently there was a dog wandering about on the wet cement! Leave Xas on a dirt road through field and forest. Skirt the town of Camiño Real and pass through **Rapote (6.3km)**.*

*Continue on dirt paths to **A Peña** 🍴 *(7.7km)* and **Piaxe** *(7.9km), joining a paved road. Soon windmills come into view ahead. Continue through **Portocamiño (8.4km)** before veering R onto a dirt path. Rejoin the 2-lane paved road until a dirt path to the L leads into Vilaserío.*

12.3 Vilaserío A🍴 Pop. 72
1. **A O Rueiro** (priv, 🛏30, €12): 🍴 W O 🛜,
   ☏981-893561 ✉, ☉all year
2. **A La Escuela** (muni, 10 mats, don): basic, mats on floor, far side of town, hospitalera comes from house #39 to request donation

---

20.9 Santa Mariña A🍴
A **Santa Mariña/Antelo** (priv, 🛏10, €10):
🍴 W O 🛜, ☏981-852897, ☉12pm all year
A H **Casa Pepa** (priv, 🛏16, dm €12, dbl €40):
🍴 W O 🛜, ☏981-852881, ☉all year

31.5 Ponte Olveira A🍴
A **O Refuxio da Ponte** (priv, 🛏10, €10): 🍴 W O 🛜
☏981-741706 ✉

12.3 Vilaserío offers a possible early stopping point or rest stop. *Pass the private Vilaserío albergue and continue to **Cornado (14.4km)**, where the trail turns to an earthen track to **Maroñas (19.2km)**. Return to pavement and pass the Iglesia de Santa Mariña before crossing AC-403 at Santa Mariña.*

20.9 Santa Mariña has a café and two albergues along the highway. *Stay along the highway and turn R to **Bon Xesús (22.8km)**, **Gueima (23.1km)** and **Xastro (23.8km)**. Return to dirt paths to **Lago (26.8)**, and follow pavement through **Poteliñas (27.3km)** to **Abeleiros (27.7km)** and turn R at the bus stop. The paved path arrives at a Y in **Corzón (30.0km)** with its Igrexa de San Cristóbal. Take the L fork and continue over a bridge to meet the main road. Turn R on*

Galician hórreo

the main road, with a special green lane for walkers. Pass through **Mallón (31.0km)** and over the Ponte Olveira bridge over the Río Xallas.

31.5 **Ponte Olveira** has a café and albergue with a green lawn. *Continue on the main road until the signposted L turn into Olveiroa. The Xunta albergue is a short detour R.*

33.3 **Olveiroa** is a charming traditional village said to have more *hórreos* than people. Observe magnificent examples of stone *hórreos*, some of which are beautifully illuminated at night. There is a small Igrexa Santiago as well as a stone *rollo*. There was no shop here at time of research, though Albergue Hórreo sells basic supplies. The Xunta albergue is spread over several sensitively restored historic buildings. A nearby café offers pilgrim *menús*.

33.3 **Olveiroa** A H 🍽 Pop. 129
1. A H **Albergue Hórreo/Casa Loncha** (priv, 🛏30, dm €12, dbl €30-40): 🛏🚿🍴📶🖥(free), 📞981-741673 📧, 🕐Mar-Nov, small shop
2. A **Xunta** (🛏34, €5): 🛏, 📞658-045242, 🕐1:30pm, all year
3. H **As Pias** (sng €40, dbl €50-60): 🖥📶, 📞981-741520 📧

Detail of Galician hórreo

34

OLVEIROA TO FINISTERRE

31.4km
+3.2km to
lighthouse
(19.5mi +2.0mi
to lighthouse)

🕑 **7.5-9 HOURS**
DIFFICULTY: ▭▭☐
🅿 42%, 13.3km
Ⓤ 58%, 18.1km

A ALBERGUES:
Logoso 3.6km
Cee 19.6km
Corcubión 20.0km
San Roque 22.0km
<u>Finisterre 31.4km</u>

View of Finisterre

Relish a long stretch of earthen path on the wild Galician countryside. Catch your first glimpse of the sea and walk along the beach to arrive at the "end of the earth."

☀ Another long stage, but there are more accommodations options starting in Cee. The day includes beautiful isolated walking through the high Galician countryside leading to stunning sea views. The route splits after Hospital, with the L path going to Finisterre and the R to Muxía (stage 34A). The path to Finisterre meanders along the beach to enter the city. From the Finisterre albergue, the walk to the lighthouse is an additional 3.2km. Pilgrims gather at the lighthouse for sunset.

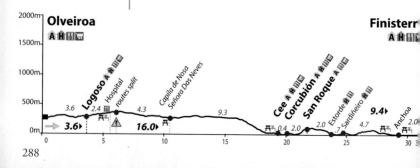

N

2 km

0 1 2

A Rebouta

A Rebouta

Paradela

Luncin

Colúns

Olveiroa

Logoso

A H

3.6

5.5

Hospital

6.0

O Castelño Café
(last supplies until
Cee 13.6km)

Vilarcovo

O Enxilde

Arcos

Xinzo

Figueiroa

Stone cross

Folgosa

Busteto

10.3

Nossa Señora
Das Nieves

Buxantes

Busto

A Figueira

Yestosa

O Ezaro

O Pindo

Vilar de
Paraíso

Best sea view

13.8

Vilanova

San Pedro
Mártir

Cavado

16.1

Raso

A Pontella

Canelinas

Berpún

San Xosé

A Catbaliza

Lagartería

Sembra

steep.

Cee

A H

19.6

Arnada

20.0

Vilar

map p.292

Redonda

Procar

Corcubión

A H

21.5

22.0

A

San Roque

Tedin

24.0

Estorde

H

Amarela

Uires

24.7

Sardiñeiro

H

A Canosa

Castrexe

Vigo

Castroniñán

Duio

Anchoa

29.4

Praia de Langosteira

Finisterre

A H

map
p.297

map
p.295

31.4

pilgrim statue

+3.2

Cabo Fisterra, 0.0km

lighthouse

0.0 *Leave Olveiroa on the main paved road, then turn L over a small bridge onto a dirt path. The trail climbs a beautiful windswept trail with low-lying brush, pine trees and views of windmills. Cross over a cement bridge to quiet Logoso.*

3.6 **Logoso** has a café, albergue and small shop all in the same building. The town of Hospital is opposite the road on the R, where a pilgrim hospital was once located. *Meet the main road that leads past* ***O Casteliño café*** 🍴 *(5.5km), the last service until Cee. Take the smaller paved road to the R after the café, which crosses the main road and brings you to a large roundabout where the path splits (6.0km).* ⚠ *Continue L for Finisterre past a monstrous carbide factory. In 500m, turn R onto a dirt path for 12km of heavenly walking in nature.*

Marker for the split: Finisterre or Muxía

A family hikes to Finisterre together

10.3 **Capela**: The path passes a stone *rollo* with a *Pietá* image (engraved CR for *camino real*) and the 18th-century Capela da Nossa Señora das Neves ("Our Lady of the Snow Chapel") with a peaceful sheltered picnic area. The water flowing here is said to be particularly beneficial to nursing mothers. A local pilgrimage to this spot takes place in September. *Continue uphill for a first glimpse of the ocean! Pass the nondescript* **Sanctuario de San Pedro Mártir (13.8km)**, *which also has a tradition of healing waters, said to cure arthritis in joints when submerged.*

A 100m detour is marked to the **Cruceiro do Armada (16.1km)**, *a recreation of an ancient stone cross. The view down to the bay is fantastic.* ⚠ *Exercise caution on the steep, loose track down to Cee. The trail through town is not very well marked. Toward the water the path emerges along the waterfront. New albergues make Cee an attractive overnight option.*

3.6 **Logoso** A H 🏠
A H **O Logoso** (priv, 🛏22, dm €12, dbl €30):
🅺🍴🚿🅆ⓦ📶🅓, ☎981-727602, ⊙all year

Tile on Capela da Nossa
Señora das Neves

Descending to Cee

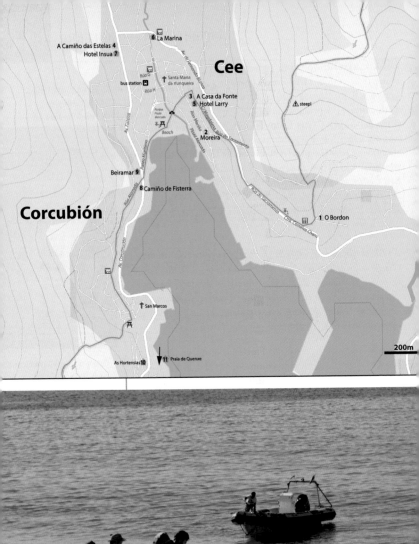

6 La Marina

A Camiño das Estelas 4
Hotel Insua 7

Cee

bus station

Santa María
da Xunqueira

Rúa G
Rúa H

3 A Casa da Fonte
5 Hotel Larry

⚠ steepl

Beach

2 Moreira

Corcubión

Beiramar 9

8 Camiño de Fisterra

1 O Bordon

San Marcos

As Hortensias 10   11 Praia de Quenxe

200m

6 Cee A H 🅷🚰🚿➕🄴🄿 Pop. 7,898

O Bordón (priv, 🛏24, €12): 🚿🆆🄾🛜🖥(free), Camiños Chans, ☎981-746574/655-903932 📱, 🕐12pm, all year, towel and sheets included

Moreira (priv, dm €12, dbl €30): 🚿🆆🄾, c/Rosalía 75, ☎981-746282, 🕐10am, Mar-Dec 15

A Casa da Fonte (priv, 🛏42, €10): 🆆🄾🖥🛜, Rúa de Arriba 36, ☎699-242711 📱, 🕐11am, Mar-Dec 15, spacious

O Camiño das Estrela (priv, 🛏30, €10): H🆆🄾, Av. Finisterre 78, ☎981-747575 📱, 🕐1pm, all year, part of Hotel Insua

Larry (dbl €50): H, c/Magdalena 8, ☎981-746441 📱

La Marina (dbl €50): H, Av Fernando Blanco 26, ☎981-747381 📱

Hotel Insua (dbl €70): H🛜, Av Finisterre 82, ☎981-747575 📱

0 Corcubión A H🚰➕🄴🄾🄿🄱

1,767, 🏰 Celtic: "circular bay," free 🛜 in library, 🛈 c/Explanada do Porto 17, ☎ 981-706163

Camiño de Fisterra (priv, 🛏14, €10): 🚿🆆🄾, c/Cruceiro de Valdomar 11, ☎981-745040/629-114122, 🕐all year

Pensión Beiramar (dbl €40): Av. Finisterre 220, ☎981-745040 📱

As Hortensias (sng €35, dbl €50): H🛜, Lg Praia de Quenxe, ☎981-747584 📱

Praia de Quenxe (sng €45, dbl €50): H🛜, Lg Praia de Quenxe 43, ☎981-706457 📱

Cee, the largest town along the Finisterre route, is a charming [fishin]g village turned lively seaside commercial center with a wide [rang]e of services. The historic port is still used for fishing and was [histo]rically used for whale hunting. Much of the town was destroyed [by N]apoleon's troops, but the Igrexa da Santa Maria da Xunqueira was [buil]t in late Gothic style with traces of its original vault. *Continue [along] the water and up Rúa Alameda to Corcubión.*

Corcubión, sister town to Cee, is just up the road with ad-[dition]al accommodations and beaches. The Gothic Igrexa de San [Marc]os was built in the 14th century with later additions after being [sack]ed by Napolean's troops. It contains a 15th-century image of the [patro]n saint. Beautiful manor houses display historic coats of arms.

[At th]e church, turn R up the steps and continue to the Campo de Rollo [plaza.] Cross the plaza past a children's play area and look for a large yellow [arrow] pointing up a dirt lane with high walls on either side. Follow this [way o]ut of Corcubión, which joins a paved road and leads through the [distric]t of **Vilar (21.5km)** to **San Roque (22.0km)**. Return to the road [and c]ontinue onto an earthen path. Pass through **Amarela (22.7km)** [and c]ontinue on a 2-lane paved road through Estorde and Sardiñiero.

🏛 **Cee**
Spring: Galician literature festival
Summer: Street theatre festival
Sunday is market day.

🏛 **Corcubión**
April 25: San Marcos, celebration of patron saint

Barefoot pilgrims enjoying the sandy beach

22.0 San Roque A

A **San Roque** (assoc, 🛏16, don): 🚻🛏,
📞679-460942, communal meals, 🕐all year,
strictly closed until 4pm, nice green park

24.0 Estorde 🚻🛏▲

H **Playa de Estorde** (dbl €72): 🛏📶,
📞981-745585, sea views

▲ **Ruta Finisterre Camping**: 🛏📶🚌,
📞981-746302 ✍

24.7 Sardiñeiro 🚻🛏🚌

H **Hostal Nicola**: 🛏, Sardiñeiro de Abajo,
📞981-743741 ✍

Picturesque fishing
port of Finisterre

24.0 Estorde and
24.7 Sardiñeiro are both along
the beach with restaurant and hotel
options. *Leave town on a dirt footpath
with elevated views of the sea, which
rejoins the main road and then departs
again to pass along the shore. The rest of
the way into Finisterre can be walked
on the sidewalk or by taking your shoes
off and walking along the sandy beach.
The beach* **Praia a Langosteira** 🛏🚻
*stretches about 2km prior to the en-
trance to Finisterre, passing the town of*
Anchoa (29.4km). *The Finisterre
Xunta albergue is located in the center
near the harbor and next to the bus station.*

31.4 **Finisterre** has drawn mystics and seekers to its rocky shores for thousands of years. The Romans named it *finis terrae*, "the end of the earth" and, staring out into the expanse of wild ocean from the lighthouse on Monte Facho, it's easy to see how it may have felt that way. Celtic pagans built an altar to the sun (*Ara Solis*) at Finisterre, and later Christians developed their own rituals around this place. From the town to the lighthouse is 3.2km, and numerous footpaths crisscross the peninsula's hilltop leading to interesting natural and religious sites.

This fishing village has grown as a tourist destination with many accommodations as well as seafood restaurants, mostly located near the vibrant historic port. The charming historic center has twisting streets perfect for exploring. Visit the 🏰 **Castelo de San Carlos**, which has been transformed

---

31.4 **Finisterre** A H 🏨 🛒 ➕ € 🅘 🅿

Pop. 4,983, Latin: *Finis Terrae* "the end of the world," (also Fisterra, Finisterra)

1. **A Xunta** (🛏36, €5): 🚿 W D 🧺, c/Real 2, 📞981-740781 ✉, 🕐1pm all year, kitchen locked in the morning- don't leave anything you want, administers the Finisterre completion certificate
2. **A O Encontro** (priv, 🛏5, €15): 🚿 W 🧺, c/del Campo, 📞696-503363, 🕐all year
3. **A H Da Sol y da Lua** (priv, 🛏18, dm €10, dbl €30): 🚿 W D 🧺, Rúa Atalaya 7, 📞981-740655
4. **A Finistellae** (priv, 🛏20, €12): 🚿 W D 🧺 🛜, c/Manuel Lago Pais 7, 📞637-821296 ✉, 🕐all year, can stay multiple nights and reserve for groups, sheets included
5. **A De Paz** (priv, 🛏30, €10): 🚿 W D 🧺, c/Víctor Cardalda 11, 📞981-740332, 🕐11am, all year
6. **A Cabo da Vila** (priv, 🛏28, €12): 🚿 W D 🧺 🛜, Av. de A Coruña 13, 📞981-740454, 🕐all year
7. **A Por Fin** (priv, 🛏11, €10): 🚿 W D 🧺 🛜, c/ Federico Avila 19, 📞636-764726, 🕐Apr-Nov
8. **H Pension Fin da Terra** (dbl €25 shared bath): 🚿W(free), c/Atalaia 30, 📞981-712030
9. **H Ancora Hotel** (dbl €25): 🍴, c/Alcalde Fernández, 📞981-740791 ✉
10. **H Rivas** (dbl €35): Alcalde Fernández 53, 📞981-740027
11. **H Mariquito** (dbl €42): 🍴 Rúa de Santa Catalina 44, 📞981-740044 ✉
12. **H Hotel Finesterre** (dbl €42): 🍴 🛜, c/Federico Ávila 8, 📞981-740000 ✉
13. **H Hospedaje Lopez** (dbl €50): Rúa Carrasqueira 4, 📞981-740449, sea views
14. **H Insula Finesterrae** (dbl €80): ▬, A Insua 76, 📞981-712211 ✉
15. **H O Semafora Hospedaje** (dbl €110): Finisterre lighthouse, 📞981-725869 ✉, sea views **295**

Wild Praia do Mar de Fora east of Finisterre

🏠 **Finisterre**
July 25: Festa da Praia (beach festival)
Aug 20: Fin do Camino
Sept 8: Virxe do Carme

Balancing on *Piedras Santas* on Cabo Finisterre

into a museum of local fishing culture. The 18th-century **Capela do Nosa Señora do Bo Suceso**, featuring a Baroque retable, is located in *Ara Solis Plaza*. On the way to the cape you'll pass the **Igrexa de Santa Maria das Areas**, originally built in the 12th century with funds from Doña Urraca, containing an image known as "Christ of the Golden Beard." According to legend, the image was sculpted by Nicodemus and was on a ship coming from England when a huge storm began. The sailors threw the statue into the ocean to ballast weight and the storm instantly stopped, apparently because the image wanted to make its home in Finisterre.

Cabo Finisterre

Take an extra day to explore Monte Facho further, which has marvelous views, wild beaches and interesting historical sites.

On the west side of Monte Facho, a series of massive rocks stand on stone outcroppings, known as the **Piedras Santas** ("Holy Rocks"). Two of these are known as the *Abalar* stones, which can both easily be moved back and forth if pushed on in the right manner. This was the site of a pagan ritual where the moving rocks judged if a woman was apt to be a priestess. A Christian legend says Mary appeared to Santiago at this place to encourage him on his missionary journey. According to legend, the Celtic witch Orcavella lived in a stone tomb in this area and would lure hapless shepherds in and use them as a mattress.

In the 11th century, **San Guillermo** (St. William of Penacorada) built a hermitage on Monte Facho. Its ruins remain, and a particular rock is believed by tradition to enhance fertility, and it is said that couples hoping to conceive come at night to copulate on it.

Fertility rock at Ermita San Guillerme

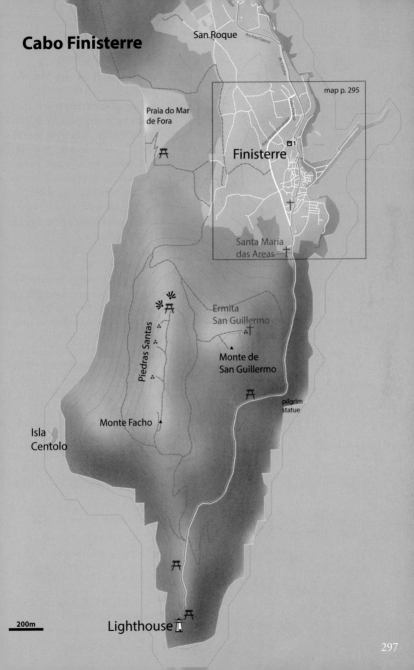

Cabo Finisterre

San Roque

Praia do Mar
de Fora

map p. 295

Finisterre

Santa María
das Areas

Piedras Santas

Ermita
San Guillermo

Monte de
San Guillermo

pilgrim
statue

Isla
Centolo

Monte Facho

200m

Lighthouse

0.0 ⚑ Lighthouse at the End of the World

On arrival in Finisterre, you may wish to check into an accommodation before embarking on the 6.4km round-trip journey to the lighthouse, where many gather to watch the sun sink below the endless watery horizon. One pilgrim ritual is to burn shoes or clothing to symbolize the end of the pilgrimage.

The end of the road at kilometer 0.00 before the Finisterre lighthouse

The setting sun at Finisterre serves as an appropriate symbol of the ending of the journey and an atmospheric setting to ponder the return trip and transition to whatever is next. Rest assured that millions before you, and likely millions after, have pondered the same questions and perhaps felt the same bittersweet emotions upon reflecting on the pilgrimage. Revel in the satisfaction of completing such an expedition. Give thanks for the people you have met along the way. Grieve the ending of this journey and welcome the dawn of the next.

🚌 There is frequent bus service from the Finisterre town center back to Santiago (leaves near the abergue), or you can continue one day further to Muxía (see stage 35).

Pilgrims contemplate the sea

Finisterre lighthouse (above right)

Sunset from Finisterre lighthouse (below right)

To process your camino experience for a few days, author Tracy Saunders offers her house near Muxía, called *A Casa Do Raposito* (House of the Little Fox), as a post-camino retreat on a donation basis. Arrange in advance: ☎981-730842 ✉

34A

OLVEIROA TO MUXÍA

31.6km
(19.6mi)

⏰ 7-9 HOURS
DIFFICULTY: ▭▭◻
🅿 50%, 15.8km
🆄 50%, 15.8km

A ALBERGUES:
Logoso 3.6km
Dumbría 9.7km
Muxía 31.6km

Rooftop crosses at
Iglesia San Martiño

Walk through rolling countryside, delight in magnificent sea views and visit the holy rocks on Muxía peninsula.

☀ This route is only marked thoroughly in one direction, from Olveiroa to Muxía, so if returning from Muxía this way be extra aware of reversed arrows and surroundings. This route is less popular than the route to Finisterre (stage 34) and feels more remote and wild. Dumbría has an impressive new albergue that gets very little use. Walk out to the Muxía church at sunset for a fulfilling end to the day.

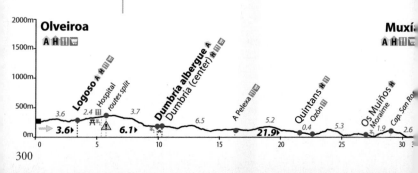

Ubiquitous eucalyptus forest before Muxía

0.0 *For the description from Olveiroa to the **trail junction (6.0km)**, see p. 290. ⚠ From the split after **Hospital**, take the R option along the road then turn off to the L onto a dirt path. Follow this path through **As Carizas (8.8km)** to Dumbría.*

9.7 Dumbría A H ⚄⚄⚄⊕€
Pop. 1,000, 🏰 Celtic: "fortified town"
1. **A A Conca** (Xunta, 🛏26, €5): ⚄⚄⚄, next to municipal pool to L of camino, ☏981-744001, 🕐1pm all year, ⚄⚄ at pool
2. **H Argentino** (dbl €30-40): 🍴, ☏981-744051 ✉
3. **H Casa Curiña** (dbl €48-60): c/Estiman, ☏981-744024 ✉

9.7 Dumbría has a well-designed albergue, funded by the owner of the Zara clothing store chain. *Walk past the albergue into town passing the 17th-century Iglesia de Santa Eulalia. Continue on the main paved road, which crosses over a small bridge and the highway after which it becomes a dirt track up through **Trasufe (13.6km)**, with its Capela a Virxe do Espino. There is a spring with purported healing power behind the bus stop. Local people tie pieces of cloth to the tree as a prayer ritual. Continue east on a paved road over the bridge crossing the Río Castro and go R at the Y on minor road into **A Pelexa** 🍴⚄ **(16.2km)**. Turn L in town past mini market Agrodosio through the hamlet of **A Grixa (17.1km)** with its roadside crucero and Igrexe de San Cibran. Turn L after Grixa, then R on a dirt path to Quintáns.*

21.4 **Quintáns** houses the modest Capilla de San Isideo. *Turn L and leave town on a dirt road. Pass by a massive hórreo with 22 stone supports! Pass* **Ozón (21.8km)** *to the Iglesia de San Martiño with a Romanesque apse and ruins of a Benedictine Monastery. After town, take a hard L turn through* **Vilar de Sobramonte (23.5km)** *on the road and turn R on a footpath. Come to a paved road close to the sea; turn L into Os Muiños.*

21.4 **Quintáns** **H** **ii** Pop. 240
H **Hospedaje Plaza** (dbl €35): Quintáns-Muxia, ⓒ981-750452 🖃

27.1 **Os Muiños**: pass through the village that has a panadería for provisions. *Leave town on the paved road, then straight on a grassy trail crossing the highway through* **Moraime (28.1km)**, *the site of the Iglesia de San Xiao de Moraime, an influential medieval monastery. Turn R after town and cross the highway onto an small dirt road to pass the* **Capela de San Roque (29.0km)** *with a stone crucero in the forest. Continue on the dirt path through* **Chorente (29.5km)**. *The path will emerge on a boardwalk along the sea. Follow the shore into* **Muxía (31.6km)**, *p. 307.*

27.1 **Os Muiños** **H**
🖃 Galician: "the mills," panadería
H **Pension Paris**: Os Muiños 41, ⓒ981-750616

Huge hórreo after Quintáns

FINISTERRE TO MUXÍA

28.0km
(17.4mi)

⏲ **7-8 Hours**
Difficulty: ▭▮▯
🅿 54%, 15.2km
🆄 46%, 12.8km

A **Albergues:**
Muxía 28.0km

Iglesia de Nosa Señora
da Barca in Muxía

Roam the wild coastal moors and idyllic countryside on this less-traveled route. Marvel at the seaside church of Muxía and mysterious rock formations.

☀ This is a pleasant and isolated stage, the path winding through forest and village with the sea often in sight. Several cafés provide refreshment. To stay in the Xunta albergue in Muxía and receive a certificate of completion (Muxiana, p. 309), remember to **get a stamp in As Lires**. The path is less traveled than Finisterre and has a sense of wild sea and idyllic countryside.

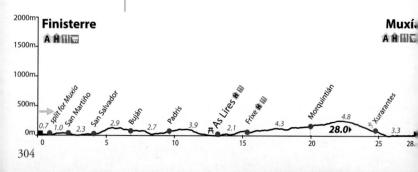

Finisterre — Muxía

map
p. 309

Muxía
A H 🍴 🛒

28.0

26.1 • Praia de
Lourido

24.7 • Lourido
• Xurarantes

Os Muíños

Quintáns

Ozón

Suxo

A Casiña

Cebráns

Castelo

Boallo

Serantes

Martineto
Vilela

O Vilariño

Añobres

Vilarmide

Sendande

Santa
Maria † • Morquintián
19.9

Viseo

Prado

Couceiro

Boallo

Campos

Touriñán

Cabo
Touriñán

Guisamonde • 18.1

Bardullas

Río Do Castro

Bustelo

Dumbría
A H 🍴 🛒

Folgosa

Loalo

Castro

Praia de
Nemiña

Frixe
† H 🍴
15.6

14.2

A Ponte
Nova

Ría de
Tires

Vaosilveiro •

Río Do Castro

San Xosé

13.5
As Lires •
Get a stamp!
† H 🍴
11.7 • Canosa

Procar

Bernum

Vilanova

9.6
• Padrís

Tedín

A Carbaliza

Cavado

Lagartería

Vilar de
Paraíso

Buxantes

Busto

A Filgueira

Xestosa

7.9
• Suarriba

Buján • 6.9

Sembra

Cee
A H 🍴 🛒

Praia de
Rostro

Castromiñán

4.0 • San Salvador
Vigo

3.7
Hermedesuxo •

Escaselas

Corcubión

Raso

A Pontella

Redonda

2.9 • Amboa

San Martiño
1.7 •

Praia de
Langosteira

Hotel
Arenal • 1.1

Praia de
Mar do Fora

0.0

map
p. 295

Finisterre
A H 🍴 🛒

map
p. 297

⚓ Cabo Finisterre

Caneliñas

O Ézaro

O Enxibre

Arco

O Pindo

N

2 km

0   1   2

Finisterre or Muxía?
The choice is yours

0.0 *From the Finisterre Xunta albergue, walk up Rúa Catalina past the Concello and post office (maps p. 295 and p. 297). Continue along the main road and turn L on Aldea San Marín de Abajo at a bus shelter after the sign for Hotel Arenal (a camino marker reads San Martiño, the next town, 1.1km). Stay straight through lower* **San Martiño (1.7km)** *past a housing development and then through upper San Martiño. Pass cornfields until going through* **Escaselas (2.9km)**; *turn L at a crossroads. Continue straight through* **Hermedesuxo (3.7km)**, *which has a stone crucero. At the crossroads, take the diagonal R into* **San Salvador (4.0km)**, *past Hotel Dugium. At the far end of town, the road turns to dirt and continues straight past an hórreo. Wind through a eucalyptus forest before passing through Rapadoiro and back onto an earthen track to* **Buján (6.9km)**. *After town, turn R on a paved road past a lumber factory into the forest. Continue on dirt through* **Suarriba (7.9km)**, *then turn L on a track with views of the sea. Meet the paved road to walk uphill, then turn L onto a dirt road with many yellow arrow markers at* **Padrís (9.6km)**. *The trail is paved through* **Canosa (11.7km)**, *then turns off to the L on dirt. Cross a small bridge to enter As Lires.*

13.5 As Lires 🛏🍴 - get a stamp!
Pop. 165, 📖 Galician: "the lyres"
🛏 **As Eiras** (dbl €50-70): 🍴, 📞981-748180, popular cafe
🛏 **Casa Jesus** (dbl €36): 🍴, 📞981-748158 📱
🛏 **Casa Raul** (€37 w/shared bath): 🅆, 📞981-748156 📱
🛏 **Casa Lourido** (dbl €49): 📞981-748348 📱
🛏 **Casa Luz** (dbl €58): 📞981-748924 📱

13.5 As Lires is such a small town that the accommodations have no street addresses—ask around if you have trouble finding one. ⚠ **Make sure you get a stamp from café As Eiras.** The Xunta albergue in Muxía requires this stamp to prove you didn't arrive by bus. There is a stone crucero and Igrexa San Esteban. *Walk through Lires on the main road, then turn off onto a smaller road that will turn into a dirt path. Cross over a new bridge—look to the L to see the stepping stones that until recently pilgrims used to ford the river.*

*Enter tiny **Vaosilveiro (14.2km)** and continue on the dirt path that meets with a paved road. Turn L and then a quick R to cross the highway and pass through the outskirts of Frixe,*

15.6 **Frixe** 🏠🍴

🏠 **Casa Ceferinos** (dbl €50): 🍴🖥📶, Frixe 11, ☎981-748965 ▣

*(15.6km), with Romanesque Iglesia de Santa Leocadia onto a dirt path. A sharp L downhill goes into **Guisamonde (18.1km)** on the paved road. Follow the paved road past a crucero and water fount (non-potable) into **Morquintián (19.9km)**, with its Romanesque Iglesia de Santa María. Continue on the paved road until it comes to a T. Turn R (ignoring the old cement maker), then turn off to the L on a dirt path. Continue through forest into **Xurarantes (24.7km)**. Turn L in town on a paved road curving around the forest. For the fastest way into Muxía, continue on the road. If you'd like to visit the attractive beach of **Praia de Lourido (26.1km)**, follow the markers straight on a dirt path that will turn to sand. There is not a clear path here so walk toward the water, and turn R to rejoin the main road.*

Enter Muxía via the sidewalk along the main road. To go directly to the albergue, turn R at the sign on Rúa Os Malatos and follow signs uphill through town to the albergue. To head to the church and seaside promenade, take the main road. The camino is not well marked through town (map on p. 309).

Muxía coast line on the eastern side

28.0 **Muxía** A H 🏠🍴➕€ℹ️🚌

Pop. 6,634, 📖 Archaic: "the monks"

1. **A** **Xunta** (🛏️32, €5): 🅚, c/Enfesto,
📞610-264325/620-112902, 🕐 1pm all year

2. **A** **Bela Muxía** (priv, 🛏️36, dm €12, dbl €40):
🏠🖥️🅞🅿️📶, Rúa da Encarnación 30,
📞687-798222, 🕐all year, opened 2012,
exibits about Galician writers and local shipwrecks

3. **H** **La Cruz** (dbl €30): Av. de López Abente 34,
📞981-742084 📇, with sea views

4. **H** **Pedra d'Abalar**: 🍴, c/La Marina 35,
📞981-742094 📇

5. **H** **Casa de Lorena** (dbl €60): c/Virxe da Barca 3,
📞981-742564 📇

6. **H** **Casa Anxelino**: 🅚🅦, c/Real 40,
📞670-523048 📇

7. **H** **A de Loló** (sng €70, dbl €80): 🍴📶,
Rúa Virxe da Barca 37, 📞981-742422 📇

View of Muxía from
Monte Corpiño

28.0 **Muxía** is a picturesque fishing town located on a small peninsula, known for its fish and hand-made lace, but best known as the home of **Nosa Señora da Barca** ("Our Lady of the Boat"), housed in a rustic church built over the rocky shore mere meters from the crashing waves. Legend has it that Mary appeared here in a stone ship to deliver a message to a discouraged Saint James. She informed him that he had been successful and should return to Jerusalem, his mission in Spain complete. She also gave him the image of herself displayed in the church. The second Sunday in September is 🎉 *La Festa de Nosa Señora da Barca*, one of the most important celebrations in Galicia. Thousands come from far and wide to visit the church, dance, sing, eat *caldareta* (fish stew) and parade the virgin through the streets.

The large rocks outside the church are said to be the remains of her boat—*Pedra dos Cadris* represents her sail, the kidney-shaped *Pedra do Timón* the rudder and *Pedra da Abalar* (a rocking stone similar to those in Finisterre) represents the hull. The rocking stone was used in pre-Christian times to determine the guilt of an accused party, and it continues rocking even after being broken during a storm in the 1970s. One legends says that when thieves were trying to rob the church, the stone rocked back and forth so loudly that the neighbors awoke and chased away the thieves. There is also the *Pedra dos Namorados* where couples come to declare their love.

Walk out to the sanctuary via a very pleasant promenade on the northeast side of the peninsula passing the 14th-century Marine-Gothic style **Iglesia de Santa María de Muxía**. Return by walking up the hill behind the church past the monument remembering the tragic Prestige oil spill of 2002. Walk up to the top of **Monte Copino** for an elevated view. This return path is known as the *Camiño da Pel* ("Way of the Skin") because pilgrims would wash themselves in a nearby fountain before entering the church.

Be sure to stop by the helpful ❶ **Tourist Information** 🏨🛜🖥 (📞981-742563, 🕐M-F 10am-2pm, 4-8pm; Sa/Su 11am-1pm, 3-5pm; summer M-F 9am-9pm, free internet) Present your credencial to receive the *Muxiana*, a decorative certificate of completion similar to the *Compostela*.

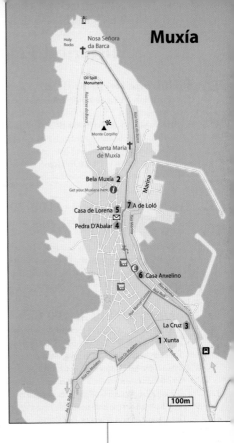

Muxía

Nosa Señora
da Barca
Holy
Rocks

Oil Spill
Monument

Monte Corpiño

Santa María
de Muxía

Bela Muxía **2**
Get your Muxiana here ❶

❼ A de Loló

Marina

Casa de Lorena **5**
Pedra D'Abalar **4**

❻ Casa Anxelino

La Cruz **3**
❶ Xunta

100m

🚌 **Transportation**
Muxía to Santiago:
Bus services at
🕐6:45am and 2:30pm
M-F, Sa 7:30am and
2:30pm, Su 7:30am and
6:45pm, confirm by
calling Hermanos Fer-
rín, 📞981-873643 📠.
For more options, take
a bus to Cee, which has
more buses per day to
Santiago.

309

Historical Timeline of Spain

Prehistoric (∞-1100 BCE)
- **1.2 million BCE- 400,000**: Some of oldest hominid remains in Europe were discovered at Atapuerca (p. 130), including a previously undiscovered species.
- **Paleolithic: 15,000-10,000 BCE:** Cro-Magnon entered the Iberian peninsula from the north and left behind sophisticated cave art, like the famous cave paintings at the Cave of Altamira along the Camino del Norte.
- **Neolithic 6000-1100 BCE**: Homo sapiens came from Mesopotamia and Egypt bringing farm implements and megalithic dolmens (can be seen in areas near Melide, p. 256).

Traders & Invaders (1100-200 BCE)
- **1100 BCE: Phoenicians and Greeks** arrived from Lebanon and Greece bring in new technology.
- **800 BCE Seafarers:** Celts brought Castro culture, still visible especially in Galicia.
- **250 BCE Carthaginians:** (Phoenicians from modern Tunisia) settled in the south, General Hannibal marched his famous elephants over the Alps to attack Rome, but was conquered by the Romans in Spain.

Romans (200 BCE-400 CE)
- The **Romans** brought a sophisticated network of roads, remnants of which can be seen after Cirauqui (p. 84) and near Calzadilla de los Hermanillos (p. 169).
- Romans also contributed aqueducts, temples and Christianity. The modern languages of Spain (except Basque) come from Latin.
- In 40 CE, Saint James is said to have preached in Iberia. Legend says his body was brought by ship to Galicia after his martyrdom in 44 CE.
- The Romans exploited the gold, silver, grain, wine and lumber of Iberia. Stability and prosperity endured under *Pax Romana* until German invasion.

German Visigoths (500-800 CE)
- **Germanic Invasion**: German tribes (Visigoths, Suevi, Vandals and Alans) gradually took control of Iberia, maintaining many Roman practices and institutions

Moors/Reconquista (771-1492 CE)
- **711: Muslim conquerors** took much of Iberia except for the "unruly northerners" forming the Muslim state of Al-Andalus. Christians streamed to the north and constant fighting between Christians and Muslims characterized the Middle Ages. Jewish philosophy thrived under Muslim tolerance in Iberia.
- **778: Battle of Roncesvalles** took place, in which the legend of Roland was born, later immortalized in *La Chanson de Roland* (p. 47).
- **813:** Legend has it that the **shepherd Pelayo** found the bones of St. James in the field where Santiago de Compostela cathedral is now located.
- **844: Battle of Clavijo**, where Santiago was said to arrive on a white horse and help the

Christian army in vanquishing the Moors, beginning the image of Santiago Matamoros.
- **1075-1128: The Cathedral of Santiago de Compostela** was constructed. The cathedrals of Burgos and León followed suit in the early 13th century.
- **1140:** The *Codex Calixtinus* (p. 16), the first guidebook to the Camino de Santiago, was written. Pilgrimage to Santiago reached its medieval peak in the 12th century.
- **Christian kingdoms** of Aragon, Castile and Navarra emerged in northern Spain. The kingdoms of Aragon and Castile gradually expanded south.

Golden Age (1492-1600)
- **1492: The "Reyes Catolicas" (Catholic monarchs)** Ferdinand and Isabella united the two most powerful kingdoms (Castilla and Aragon) of Spain and completed the Reconquista by conquering Granada. They sent Christopher Columbus to discover the "new world" and began the Inquisition, which cast out religious minorities or forced them to convert to Catholicism.
- **Peak of Spanish power,** most powerful state in Europe and largest empire in the world.
- **The arts flourished** and many famous works of art and literature were produced

Decline (1600-1900)
- Spain lost most of its foreign possessions and sank into widespread poverty characterized by internal wars.
- **Napoleon invaded in 1808** and was driven out by British forces who destroyed towns on their way out. The **Spanish War of Independence** raged from 1808-1814.
- **1833 to 1876: The Carlist Wars** were a series of conflicts between followers of Carlos V against the Spanish government, which they considered too liberal.

20th Century (1900-2000)
- **1936-1939: Spanish Civil War,** a coup in 1936 led by right-wing Nationalists dissolved into war led by General Francisco Franco, who defeated the left-wing Republicans.
- **1940-1975: Franco** ruled as dictator until his death in 1975, King Juan Carlos I returned to democracy.
- Religious freedom was established in the 1970s, but vast majority of Spain is Catholic. Spain moved toward democracy, joined the EU in 1986 and built a strong economy.
- **1985: Father Elias Valiña Sampedro** began coordinating resources for reinvigorating the camino. Albergues began to open and the trail begins to be marked with yellow arrows.
- **1992: Olympic Games** were held in Barcelona.

21st Century (2000-present)
- **2004: The Madrid bombings,** 191 were killed by Al Qaeda bombs on commuter trains.
- Spain was financially prosperous until the **market crash of 2008,** when unemployment went from 6% to 20%.
- **2010: The Holy Year** saw over 272,000 pilgrims receive the Compostela in Santiago.
- **2011: The Basque separatist group,** known as the ETA, announced a cessation of violence after decades of armed conflict.

Local Languages

The main language you'll hear on the camino is Spanish, though each region has at least one other official language, such as Basque (*Euskara*) in Basque country and Galician in Galicia. Many local people along the camino do not speak English. Learning some phrases in Spanish will greatly enhance your experience and reflects a respect for local culture and the humility of being a visitor that is often much-appreciated by local people. But don't let not speaking Spanish deter you from the camino—many walkers get by without speaking the language.

Question words

What - *qué*
When - *cuando*
Why - *por qué*
How - *cómo*
How many - *cuánto*
Where - *dónde*

Greetings and Small Talk

Hello - *hola*
Goodbye/see you later - *adiós/hasta luego*
Good morning - *buenos días*
Good afternoon/evening - *buenas tardes*
Good night - *buenas noches*
Yes/no/maybe - *sí/no/quizás*
Please - *por favor*
How are you? - *¿Cómo estás?*
I am fine. - *Estoy bien.*
Where are you from? - *¿De dónde eres?*
I'm from... - *Soy de...*
The USA - *Los Estados Unidos*
Canada - *Canadá*
England - *Inglaterra*
Ireland - *Irlanda*
Australia - *Australia*
South Africa - *Sudáfrica*
Thank you - *gracias*
You're welcome - *de nada*
Excuse me - *disculpa*
Welcome! - *Bienvenidos!*
Nice to meet you. - *Mucho gusto.*

I'm single, married. - *Estoy soltero/a, casado/a*
I (don't) have children. - *(No) tengo hijos.*
I (don't) understand/Do you understand? - *(No) Entiendo/¿Entiendes?*

Useful Phrases

Do you speak English? - *¿Habla Inglés?*
I don't speak Spanish/French/Italian. - *No hablo Español/Francés/Italiano.*
Please speak more slowly. - *Por favor, hable más despacio.*
One minute, please. - *Un momento, por favor.*
Walk well/happy trails - *Buen camino!*
What does … mean? - *Qué significa …?*
What time does it open/close? - *¿A qué hora abre/cierra?*
Where is the...? - *¿Donde está(n) …?*
bathroom - *los servicios* 🚻
hospital - *el hospital*
Where can I find water? - *¿Dónde puedo encontrar agua?*
Do you have wifi? 📶 - *¿Tiene wifi?* (wee-fee)
Password - *contraseña, clave*

Hospitality

Thank you (very much). - *(Muchas) gracias.*
You are so kind. - *Es usted muy amable.*
I would love some. - *Me encantaría.*
No, thanks. - *No, gracias.*
I'm full. - *Estoy lleno/llena.*
Sorry, I'm in a hurry. - *Lo siento, tengo prisa.*

Problems - *problemas*

I'm lost. - *Estoy perdido.*
I'm hungry/thirsty. - *Tengo hambre/sed.*
Help! - *Ayúdame!/Socorro!/ Que alguien me ayude!*
Call the police! - *Llama a la policía!*
Call a doctor! - *Llama a un médico!*
I need a doctor/dentist. - *Necesito un doctor/un dentista*
Go away! - *Véte!*
Leave me alone! - *Déjame en paz!*

Pilgrimage Terms

Pilgrim - *peregrino/a*
Church - *iglesia* ✝
Chapel - *capilla* ✝
Monastery - *monasterio* ✝
Christian/Muslim/Jew - *Cristiano, Musulmán, Judío*

Cloister - *claustro*
Wayside cross - *crucero* ✝
Saint - *santo/a*
Altarpiece - *retablo*
Priest - *el cura/el sacerdote*
Monk/nun - *monje/monja*
Mass service - *la misa*
Shell - *la concha*
Passport stamp - *el sello*
Pilgrim's passport - *credencial*

Hiking Terms

Way/route/path - *camino/
  sendero/ruta/senda* ➡
Arrows (waymarks) - *flechas*
Pilgrim hostel -
  albergue de peregrinos Ⓐ
Is there/Are there? - *Hay?*
Right - *derecha*
Left - *izquierda*
Straight - *derecho, todo recto*
North - *norte*
South - *sur*
West - *oeste*
East - *este*
Here - *aquí*
There - *allí*
Up - *arriba*
Down - *abajo*
Come here - *ven* (informal)
Near - *cerca*
Far - *lejos*
Steep/Flat- *escarpado/plano*
Easy/Difficult- *fácil/difícil*
Can you show me where I
  am on the map? -
  *¿Me puede indicar dónde
  estoy en el mapa?*
How many kilometers to...?-
  *¿Cuántos kilómetros hay
  hasta...?*
Altitude/elevation -
  altura/elevación
Sign - *cartel/letreros*
Entrance - *entrada*
Exit - *salida*

No entry - *Prohibido el Paso*
Closed - *cerrado*
Open - *abierto*
Prohibited - *prohibido*
Toilets - *servicios* 🚻
Danger! - *peligro/peligroso!*
Military zone - *zona militar*
Maps - *mapa/plan*
Guide - *guía*
Border - *frontera/límite*
Bridge/footbridge - *puente/
  pasarela* 🌉
Lake/river - *lago/río*
Riverbank/shoreline - *orilla*
Stream - *arroyo/riachuelo*
Spring/fountain - *fuente* ⛲
Valley - *valle*
Hill/slope - *cerro/cuesta*
Mountain - *montaña*
Summit - *cumbre/pico* ▲
Pass - *col, collado, alto*)(
Farm - *granja*
Hut - *cabaña*
Shelter - *refugio*
Plateau - *meseta*
Park - *parque*
Garden - *jardín/huerta*
Cave - *cueva*
Waterfall - *cascada*
Woods/forest - *bosque*
Cliff - *acantilado*
Coast - *costa*
Lighthouse - *faro* 🗼
Viewpoint - *mirador* 🔭
Ruins - *ruinas* ⁙
Castle - *castillo* 🏰
Church/chapel/hermitage –
  iglesia/capilla/ermita ✝
Cathedral - *catedral* ✝
City/town - *ciudad/pueblo*
Village - *aldea*
Town center - *centro*
Old city - *casco antiguo*
Town square - *plaza*
Road/street - *calle, c/...*
Highway - *carretera*

Traffic light/signal - *semáforo*
Bank - *banco*
ATM - *cajero automático* 💶
Post office -
  oficina de correos ✉
Tourist information office -
  oficina de turismo ℹ
Water: drinkable/undrink-
  able water - *agua: potable* ⛲
  /agua no potable

Packing List

Clothing - *ropa*
Footwear - *calzado*
Boots - *botas*
Laces - *cordones de bota*
Socks - *calcetines*
Raincoat - *chubasquero*
Sunglasses - *gafas del sol*
Wool - *lana*
Synthetic - *sintético*
Cotton - *algodón*
Size - *talla*
Large - *grande*
Small - *pequeño*
Backpack - *mochila*
Tent - *tienda*
Sleeping bag - *saco de dormir*
Sleeping mat/pad -
  colchoneta aislante
Batteries - *pilas*
Cooking pot - *cazo*
Water bottle - *botella de agua*
Camp stove - *hornillo/
  camping gas*
Fuel canister - *cartucho
  de gas*
Pocket knife - *navaja*
Sunscreen -
  crema de protección solar
Flashlight- *linterna*
Walking poles -
  palos telescópicos

Spanish Phrasebook

313

Spanish Phrasebook

Accommodations - *alojamientos*

I'm looking for a ... for one night - *Busco a ... para una noche*

Hotel - *un hotel* **H**

Dorm - *un dormitorio* **A**

Room - *una habitación*

Private room - *una habitación privada*

Single room - *una habitación individual*

Double room - *una habitación doble*

...with private bathroom - *...con baño privado*

...with shared bathroom - *... con baño compartido*

Is a room available? - *¿Tiene una habitación disponible?*

Do you have a cheaper room? - *¿Tiene una habitación más barata?*

Bed - *cama* 🛏

Full (booked, no beds available) - *completo*

Swimming pool - *piscina*

Kitchen- *cocina*

Camping ▲

Is there a good place to camp near here? - *¿Hay un buen lugar para acampar cerca de aquí?*

Can I pitch my tent here? - *¿Puedo poner mi tienda aquí?*

Is it permitted? - *¿Está permitido?*

Campsite - *sitio de acampar, cámping* ▲

Shower - *ducha*

Food - *comida*

Breakfast - *desayuno* 🍳

Lunch - *almuerzo*

Dinner - *cena*

Restaurant/bar/café - *restaurante/bar/cafetería* 🍴

May I see the menu? - *¿Puedo ver a la carta?*

I would like …. please. - *Me gustaría... por favor.*

I'm a vegetarian/vegan. - *Soy vegetariano/a.*

Menu - *carta*

Menu of the day/set menu - *Menú del día*

Sandwich - *bocadillo*

Desert - *postre*

Hot/cold - *caliente/fría*

The check/bill - *la cuenta*

Bread - *pan*

Fruit - *fruta*

Apple - *manzana*

Banana - *plátanos*

Cherries - *cerezas*

Raspberries - *frambuesas*

Tomatoes - *tomates*

Vegetables - *verduras*

Lettuce - *lechuga*

Onion - *cebolla*

Green pepper - *pimiento verde*

Garlic - *ajo*

Carrot - *zanahoria*

Cucumber - *pepino*

Cheese - *queso*

Snack - *bocado/tentempie*

Egg - *huevo*

Salad - *ensalada*

Drink - *bebida*

Water - *agua*

Milk - *leche*

Coffee - *café*

Beer - *cerveza*

Tea - *té*

Red wine - *vino tinto*

White wine - *vino blanco*

Meat - *carne*

Ham - *jamón*

Pork - *cerdo*

Beef - *ternera*

Lamb - *cordero*

Chicken - *pollo*

Seafood - *marisco*

Fish - *pescado*

Octopus - *pulpo*

Squid - *calamares*

Tuna - *atún*

Shopping - *compras*

How much does it cost? - *¿Cuánto cuesta?*

Store - *tienda* 🛒

Supermarket - *supermercado* 🛒

Gear store - *tienda deportiva* 🎒

Bakery - *panadería*

Butcher - *carnecería*

I want to buy… - *Quiero comprar…*

Cash - *efectivo*

Credit/debit card - *tarjeta de crédito/débito*

Books (in English) - *libros (en Inglés)*

Shoe store - *zapatería*

Weather - *tiempo*

What is the weather like? - *¿Como está el tiempo?*

It's hot. - *Hace calor.*

It's cold/cool. - *Hace frío.*

It's raining. - *Está lloviendo.*

It's sunny. - *Hace sol.*

It's cloudy. - *Está nublado.*

Foggy/fog - *neblina/niebla*

Windy/wind - *ventoso/viento*

Snow- *nieve*

Stormy - *tempestuoso*

Clear - *despejado*

Temperature - *temperatura*

Sunrise/sunset - *salida del sol/ puesta del sol*

Spanish Phrasebook

Transportation - *transporte*
How do I get to...? -
¿Como puedo ir a(l)...?
Bus station -
la estación de autobuses 🚌
Train station -
la estación de tren 🚆
Airport - *el aeropuerto* ✈
Timetable/schedule - *horario*
Ticket - *billete*
When does the next/first/last
bus leave? - *¿Cuándo sale el*
próximo/el primero/el último
autobús?
I want a ticket... -
Quiero un billete...
One way - *de ida*
Round trip - *de ida y vuelta*
I want to go to... -
Quiero ir a...

First aid

Medicine - *medicamentos*
Pharmacy - *farmacia* ✚
Hospital - *hospital*
Medical center/clinic -
centro de salud
Blister - *ampolla*
Fracture/sprain - *fractura*
I'm sick. - *Estoy enfermo/a.*
I'm allergic to -
Tengo alergia a...
Penicillin - *la penicilina*
Bee sting - *picadura de abeja*
Beg bugs - *los chinches*
Pain - *dolor*
My ... hurts -
Tengo dolor de(l)...
Foot - *pie*
Ankle - *tobillo*
Leg - *la pierna*
Knee - *la rodilla*
Thigh - *muslo*
Shoulder - *hombro*
Back - *la espalda*
Head - *la cabeza*

Time - *tiempo* 🕐
Today - *hoy*
Yesterday - *ayer*
Tomorrow - *mañana*
Last night - *anoche*
Morning - *mañana*
Noon - *mediodía*
Evening - *tarde*
Night - *noche*
Year - *año*
Month - *mes*
Week - *semana*
Day - *día*
Hour - *hora*
Minute - *minuto*
What time is it? -
¿Qué hora es?
It is ... *Es la una. Son las*
dos, tres, cuatro, cinco....
0:15 - *...y cuarto*
0:30 - *...y media*
0:45 /quarter til -
... menos cuarto

Days/weeks/months -
días/semanas/meses
Sunday - *domingo*
Monday - *lunes*
Tuesday - *martes*
Wednesday - *miércoles*
Thursday - *jueves*
Friday - *viernes*
Saturday - *sábado*
January - *enero*
February - *febrero*
March - *marzo*
April - *abríl*
May - *mayo*
June - *junio*
July - *julio*
August - *agosto*
September - *septiembre*
October - *octubre*
November - *noviembre*
December - *diciembre*

Seasons - *estaciones*
Spring - *primavera*
Summer - *verano*
Fall - *otoño*
Winter - *invierno*

Numbers
0 - *cero*
1 - *uno*
2 - *dos*
3 - *tres*
4 - *cuatro*
5 - *cinco*
6 - *seis*
7 - *siete*
8 - *ocho*
9 - *nueve*
10 - *diez*
11 - *once*
12 - *doce*
13 - *trece*
14 - *catorce*
15 - *quince*
16 - *dieciséis*
17 - *diecisiete*
18 - *dieciocho*
19 - *diecinueve*
20 - *veinte*
21 - *veintiún*
22 - *veinte dos*
30 - *treinta*
40 - *cuarenta*
50 - *cincuenta*
60 - *sesenta*
70 - *setenta*
80 - *ochenta*
90 - *noventa*
100 - *cien/ciento*
200 - *doscientos*
1000 - *mil*
2013 - *dos mil trece*

Suggested Reading

There are literally dozens of books in English about the Camino de Santiago, ranging from academic to instructive to personal accounts. These are some of the best known books about the camino which we recommend for deeper exploration. Those available in e-book format are marked ⬚.

Camino History and Culture

- ⬚ *The Pilgrimage Road to Santiago: The Complete Cultural Handbook* by David Gitlitz and Linda Davidson, 2000. Thorough and well-researched guide to historical and cultural items of interest along the trail. Authors tell the history of each town with an emphasis on minority narratives.
- ⬚ *The Pilgrim's Guide to Santiago de Compostela* edited by William Melczer, 2008. Translation of 12th-c. *Codex Calixtinus* with scholarly commentary.
- *A Journey to the West: The Diary of a Seventeenth-Century Pilgrim from Bologna to Santiago de Compostela* by Domenico Laffi, translated by James A. Hall, 1998. Colorful 17th-c. pilgrim story of the journey from an Italian perspective.
- *The Pilgrimage and Path to St. James* translated by John Durant, 2003. Account of 15th-century German pilgrim Hermann Künig von Vach.

Camino Memoirs

- ⬚ *Off the Road: A Modern-Day Walk Down the Pilgrim's Route into Spain* by Jack Hitt, 2005. A few anecdotes from this book are used in the 2010 film *The Way*.
- ⬚ *I'm Off Then: Losing and Finding Myself on the Camino de Santiago* by Hape Kerkeling, 2009. By famous German comedian, translated to English.
- *The Way Is Made by Walking: A Pilgrimage Along the Camino de Santiago* by Arthur Boers, 2007. A Mennonite pastor and teacher reflects on his modern pilgrimage experience with spiritual insights.
- ⬚ *The Pilgrimage: A Contemporary Quest for Ancient Wisdom* by Paulo Coelho, 1997. A classic about the author's mystical journey on the camino on a quest for a sword. Includes whimsical exercises.

Pilgrimage

- ⬚ *The Art of Pilgrimage: The Seeker's Guide to Making Travel Sacred* by Phil Cousineau, 2012.
- ⬚ *The Sacred Journey: The Ancient Practices Series* by Charles Foster, 2010.

Film

- *The Way* directed by Emilio Estevez and starring Martin Sheen. Martin Sheen plays a father whose adventurous son dies while walking the camino. Sheen comes to recover his son's body and ends up walking the route in his place.

Web Index

Every guidebook is out of date by the time it goes to print. We have done our best to ensure that the information contained in this book is accurate. However, things change, so the most up-to-date information about this guidebook is on our website, **www.hikingthecamino.com**. There you can find:

- Any **updates** to this book, including changes in route, accommodations, contact information, availability, etc.
- **Relevant websites** (those marked ☐ in text)
- **GPS files** of every hike in this book, free to download to your personal device (GPS or smart phone) for foolproof navigation
- **Planning information:** Gear selection, fitness and training, biking and horses, blister prevention, foot care, bedbugs precautions, maps, navigation, GPS, Google Earth
- **Travel Information**: Visas and entry, transportation (flights, buses, trains, taxis), medical care and health insurance, tours and tour operators, luggage transfer
- **Advice:** Confraternities, alternate itineraries, budgeting, albergue etiquette, phone and internet providers, families with children, Leave No Trace principles, camping, dietary restrictions, winter walking
- **Inspiration:** Photos of each stage of the camino, descriptions of other pilgrimage trails around the world, blog entries

VILLAGE TO
VILLAGE PRESS

Village to Village Press specializes in publishing hiking travel guides with an emphasis on pilgrimage and community development in the Middle East and Mediterranean regions and the Camino de Santiago in Spain. We offer a range of services in the publishing process including writing, editing, layout and design, graphic design and web/social media integration.

We specialize in consulting services for trail, community and travel development.
- Trail development strategy and implementation
- Communications strategy
- Practical travel resource development for tourism services
- Tourism product branding and identity
- Public relations and marketing

www.villagetovillagepress.com

Acknowledgements

The work of producing a guidebook of this depth involves many more people than simply the authors. Our task has been greatly assisted by a wide variety of friends and supporters who have offered their time to enrich the end product.

We would like to thank Dan and Mary Ann Conrad, who hospitably opened their home in Flagstaff for us to use as a writing base. Thanks also to Bila and Koby Inon, who offered their Negev home to us for solitary writing and editing. Our colleagues with the Jesus Trail, Maoz and Shlomit Inon, have always been supportive and helpful. Thanks to Steve Kriss and Bill Brubaker, who accompanied David on his first walk to Finisterre in 2007. Thanks to Ohad Sharav and Danny Schapiro of Steinhart Katzir Publishers Ltd.

Thanks to our parents, who are always supportive of our work and willing to lend a quiet place to work. Thanks to Betsy Dintaman, Rosemary Landis and other friends and family for reading over the manuscript and offering advice and corrections. Thanks to Barcelona native Rebecca Moyano Gonzalez for proofreading the phrase book and offering valuable suggestions. We appreciate Stefan Szepesi and our colleagues at the Abraham Path Initiative who have encouraged our work and allowed us needed time off to write.

Thanks to all who have supported and enriched the pilgrim experience by contributing to the general body of camino research and reflection through confraternities, online forums and social networking. Thanks to the many pilgrim friends we have met along the Way, who have comforted, listened and supported. Thanks to the many hospitaleros who have volunteered their time to care for the wayfarers and strangers who happen upon their door. We think of the millions of pilgrims who walked the camino, risking their lives in medieval times, and risking stepping outside of the box in modern times. Your many footsteps, blisters, conversations and prayers have made the camino the experience that it is.

Our apologies to anyone we may have overlooked in this list of supporters and friends of the project. Any mistakes in the text are solely the fault of the authors. If you find errors in the book or have updated information, please contact us at **info@hikingthecamino.com**.

To all supporters and contributors: *eskerrik asko, grazas, gracias* and thank you!

About the Authors

Anna Dintaman has lived, worked and traveled in South America, the Middle East and Eastern Europe. She studied religion and anthropology, as well as NGO management, and has worked in nonprofit development and responsible tourism initiatives, especially with the development of the Jesus Trail and other routes in the Holy Land. Anna's trekking experience includes Torres del Paine in Patagonia and various trips on the Camino de Santiago, though her favorite outdoor adventure spot is still her home area in the Shenandoah Valley of Virginia.

David Landis's enthusiasm for pilgrimage journeys began with a study semester in the Middle East in 2002. Since then, he has led numerous pilgrimage experiences in the Mediterranean region, including the Saint Paul Trail in Turkey and the Camino de Santiago. In 2007, he designed and cofounded the Jesus Trail, a pilgrimage hiking route that connects sites from the life of Jesus. David currently works with the Abraham Path Initiative developing a long-distance walking trail across the Middle East.

David Landis and Anna Dintaman on the Camino de Santiago

The pair coauthored *Hiking the Jesus Trail*, an in-depth hiking guide to pilgrimage sites in the Galilee region of Israel. They also founded a publishing house, **Village to Village Press**, which specializes in adventure and pilgrimage travel that emphasizes responsible travel and encourages self-reflection. David and Anna take pride in doing all their own research, writing, photography, maps and layout and design. They have been married since 2010 and live in Jerusalem.

We welcome your ideas, feedback, comments and corrections.

Contact the authors at:
info@hikingthecamino.com

HIKING THE CAMINO DE SANTIAGO

Legend

Camino/Trails

—— Primary route (highlighted)
—— Alternate route (not highlighted)
—— **P** Paved trail
—— **U** Unpaved trail
⚠ Trail junction or "pay attention!"
➔ Direction of camino to Santiago.
Routes described are waymarked with
yellow arrows unless stated otherwise.

Map & Town Symbols

A Albergue (dorm beds available):
priv (private), par (parochial),
muni (municipal)
H Hotel (private rooms available)
A Camping
🎐 Water (potable)
🍴 Restaurant/café (water available)
🛒 Supermarket or small shop
† Church, chapel, hermitage, wayside cross
• Towns, route junctions
⌂ Bridge
≰ View point
▲ Peak, high point
)(Pass, high point
🅰 Picnic area
ℹ Tourist information
🚻 Public WC/toilets
🚌 Bus access (daily)
🚆 Train access
✈ Airport nearby
〰 Swimming area
🏧 ATM
🛍 Outdoor gear store
➕ Pharmacy
🏛 Museum
∴ Ruins
🏰 Castle or fortress
✉ Post office
🗼 Lighthouse
🌀 Windmill

Contour lines: minor 20m, major 100m
Towns on route, Towns off route

Accommodations, Sites

🛏 Breakfast included
🍴 Meals available for fee
A Camping
🛒 Small shop, provisions available
📶 Wifi
🖥 Internet terminal
🍳 Kitchen
🍲 Microwave only (no stove in kitchen)
▬ Swimming Pool
W Washer
D Dryer
✉ Website or email address
🛏 Number of dormitory beds
🕐 Open time/dates
⭐ Recommended
don: Payment by donation *(donativo)*

Elevation Tables

Bold places have albergues
6.8 Distances between points •
6.8▸ Distances between albergues

In the book

📛 Meaning of name
📞 Phone number
🕐 Open hours
✉ Expanded on **www.hikingthecamino.com**
🎉 Festival or cultural information
💡 Tip or advice
📖 E-book available
L/R/T/Y: left/right/"T" junction/"Y" option
+1.3km: distance off route
Town with accommodation/amenity box
c/: Street *(Calle de)*
Crta: Highway *(Carretera)*
Av.: Avenue *(Avenida)*

All prices and open hours in the book are
approximate, subject to change and may
vary by season.